942.422

CW01651209

This book is due for return on or before the last date shown below.

Don Gresswell Ltd., London, N21 Cat. No. 1207

DG 02242/71

THE HARVEY GRAMMAR SCHOOL

016700

# EAST KENT

## A CENTURY IN PHOTOGRAPHS

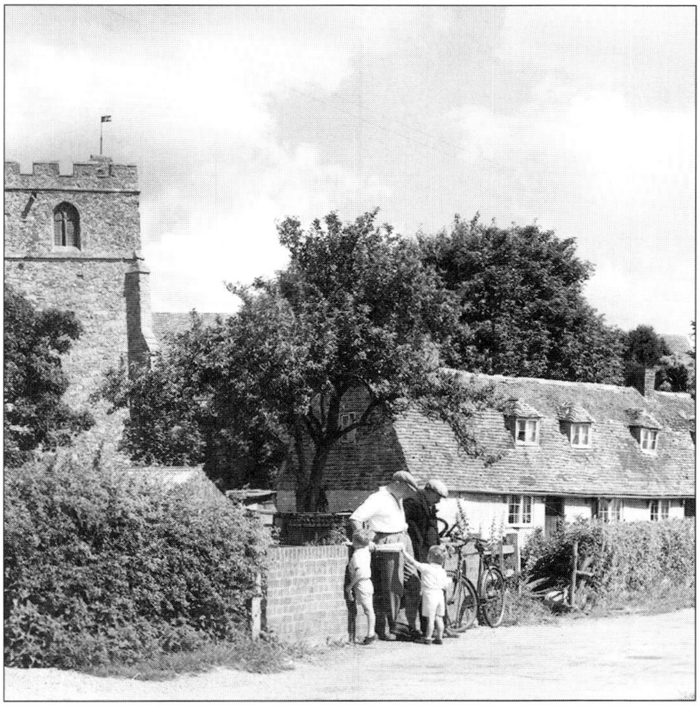

Published jointly by
East Kent Federation of Women's Institutes and
Countryside Books

First published 1997
© East Kent Federation of Women's Institutes 1997

All rights reserved.
No reproduction permitted without the prior permission of the publisher:

COUNTRYSIDE BOOKS
3 Catherine Road
Newbury, Berkshire

ISBN 1 85306 471 8

Front cover photograph of church cottages at Snargate in 1940
supplied by Mrs J. Fuller, Brenzett W.I.

Back cover photograph of the Wall's ice cream tricycle in 1936
supplied by Priscilla Harper, Egerton W.I.

Designed by Graham Whiteman

Produced through MRM Associates Ltd., Reading

Printed by Borcombe Printers plc, Romsey

# Contents

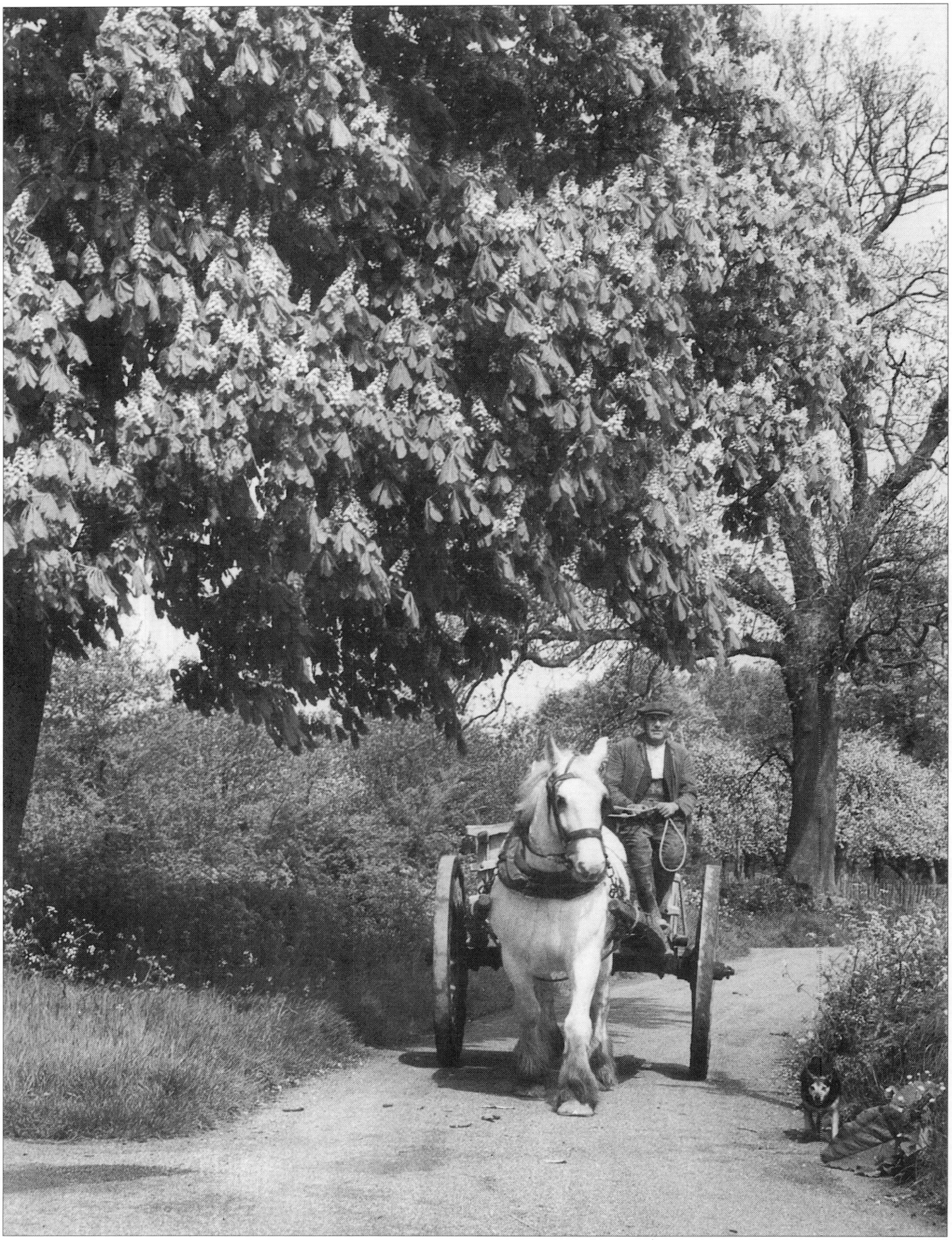

*Harry Marsh, the Waggoner, in the 1950s with Punch, the last of the heavy horses on Goff Hall farm where he was all his working life.* (Lillian Freeman – Preston, Elmstone and Stourmouth WI)

# Foreword

Geography has ordained that we in East Kent were never to be allowed to drop into sleepy oblivion. These pictures, taken from the start of the century and produced now from the homes of our members, show us in our quiet country village life but being involved in the big events of the times.

It was from our ports that the armies of both world wars set off to France and here we received back the pathetic wounded of the first war and survivors from Dunkirk in the next. We, as well as the Netherlands, suffered the floods of 1953 and then faced the 'hurricane' of 1987. We, too, had coal mines that endured the long strike of 1984/5 and the death of our mining villages that followed and, in the glare of the world's publicity, we welcomed the Pope to Canterbury and watched the building of the Channel Tunnel.

As the country progresses, so we progress with it. Ever more extensive means of crossing the Channel are developed, bringing tourists to our B & B ladies and trippers to our shops and Cathedral. The WI, in the forefront as ever, includes computer studies and science technology in its activities. Small farms are being bought up by bigger farms and ever larger tractors and combines join the traffic on our roads that increases with everyone else's.

Our pictures show some of this modernity as it happened but also, throughout the century, continue to show village scenes with village parishioners beating the bounds and picking apples for market in our orchards.

**_Pam Dobson_**
*County Chairman*


# Acknowledgements

It was the enthusiasm of so many of our members who entrusted to us their treasured photographs, who took endless trouble to establish facts and some of whom brought photographs personally to us while others received us into their homes, that made the task of co-ordinating so enjoyable. No less than one and a half thousand pictures were eventually delivered to Countryside Books who throughout were as co-operative and understanding as ever.

My most grateful thanks to them all. This book could not have happened without them and all the help from my husband.

**_Celia Armitage_**
*Project Co-ordinator*

# INTO THE 20TH CENTURY

## (1900 – 1919)

Queen Victoria's death in 1901 was widely mourned, but her passing marked the beginning of a new century and a new world. There was great celebration for the coronation of King Edward VII in every town and village in East Kent, as there was later for George V.

The horse still held sway both for transport and for work on the land, but the first cars, soon to be seen on the roads, were still the preserve of the wealthy and brought villagers to their doors to see them pass by. Roads were usually unmade, muddy in winter and dusty in summer. Then in 1904 an eight-seater steam-driven bus began a service between Hythe and Shornecliffe, followed two years later by the first local motor bus service between Canterbury and Herne Bay. Railways provided a good service, even in rural areas, and in 1905 the principal railway works were started at Ashford, to become a major source of employment in the area.

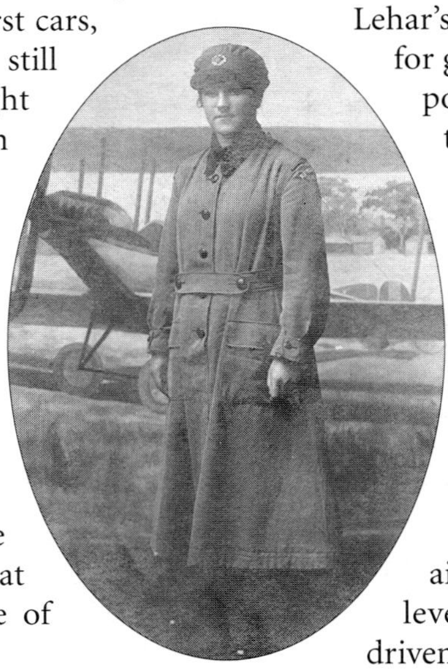

Win Allard, who worked in the officers' mess on several sites, in her Royal Flying Corps uniform at the age of 17 in 1918 (Mrs C. Murday – Wye WI)

The majority of men in East Kent worked on the land, though along the coast men found their living from the sea as they had for centuries. Oyster fishing was thriving in Whitstable and in 1912 over 19 million oysters were sent by waggon to Billingsgate Market. There were riches beneath the earth too, and in 1912 the first commercial quantities of coal were mined at Tilmanstone, the beginning of an industry that became a way of life for Kent's mining families. Most girls worked on the farms, or went into service, though usually only until they married.

It was a time of contrast between life in the big country houses and the small country cottages, but they shared a lack of indoor plumbing, electricity and all those other 'mod cons' that would become essentials of life. Many families still lived in the area their ancestors had inhabited for generations.

An awareness of the need to protect the environment was growing, and in 1907 Dungeness Bird Reserve became the first conservation area in the county.

Pleasures for most people were few and simple, and the popularity of light music such as Franz Lehar's *The Merry Widow* reflected a desire for gaiety that typified society. Sports were popular too, and followers of cricket saw the Kent team win the County Cricket Championship four times between 1906 and 1913, with Frank Woolley a prominent member of the side.

East Kent was a spectator when the first flights were being made – in 1909 Bleriot landed on top of Dover Cliffs after making the first cross-Channel flight, and a year later C.S. Rolls flew across the Channel and straight back again; sadly he died in an air crash just one month later. At sea level, the first cross-Channel turbine-driven steamer ran in November 1900.

The century had begun with Britain at war in South Africa, and in August 1914 East Kent saw the first troop movements of the First World War. This is a front-line county in a continental conflict and the troops left Dover and Folkestone in their hundreds of thousands for France. The Dover Patrol was started to protect the convoys. Of 125,000 vessels that crossed the Straights during the war, only 73 were lost.

Some dangers were closer to home. In 1914 HMS *Bulwark* exploded in the Medway, as did the *Princess Irene* a year later. In 1916 a munitions factory at Faversham blew up.

The war came to the people of East Kent. There were nearly 100 air raids over Ramsgate by Zeppelin and Gotha bombers, leading local people to develop

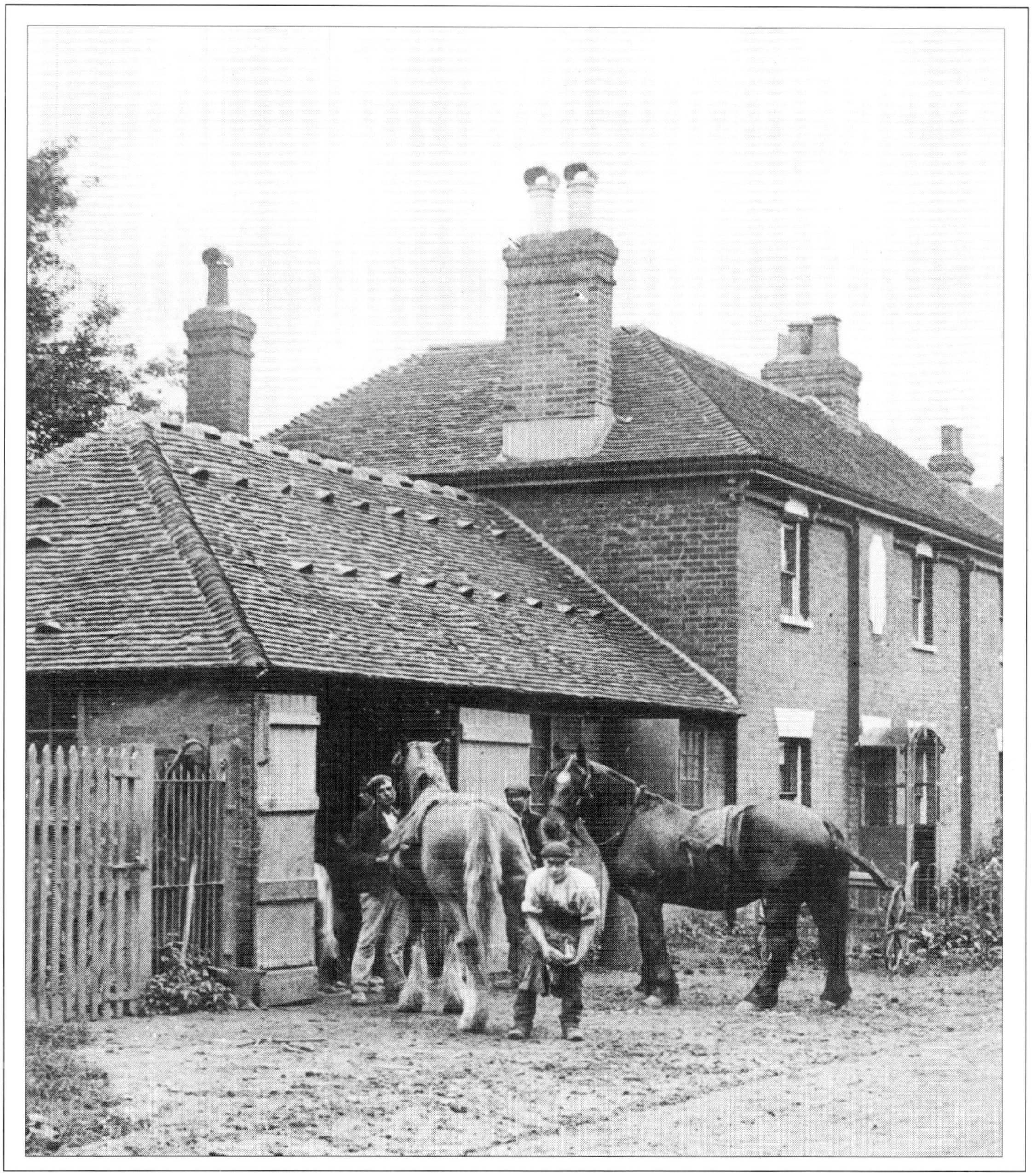



*Tom Thornby's forge at East Brabourne – two cart horses are being shod, probably ridden down by the farmer's men using only sacks on the horses' backs. The forge was later run by his nephew George Barrett, and closed in 1950.*
(Mrs A. Hammon – Stowting WI)

the railway tunnel to Margate into an elaborate air raid shelter. The Kent Fencibles were trained volunteers who undertook civil defence, while Voluntary Aid Detachments (VADs) staffed hospitals for wounded soldiers. On 22nd June 1918 the one millionth wounded man was landed at Dover.

Women's involvement in the war was an element in the creation of the Women's Institute movement, and in 1917 Institutes in Wye and Upper Hardres were the first in the county and among the first in the country. There was a massive voluntary effort all over the county. In Wye the villagers provided premises, labour and funds for a War Hospitals Supplies Depot; this sent urgently needed equipment to military hospitals. Wye also ran a 'Soldiers and Sailors Hut' for the men billeted on them and totally supported 20 Belgian refugees.

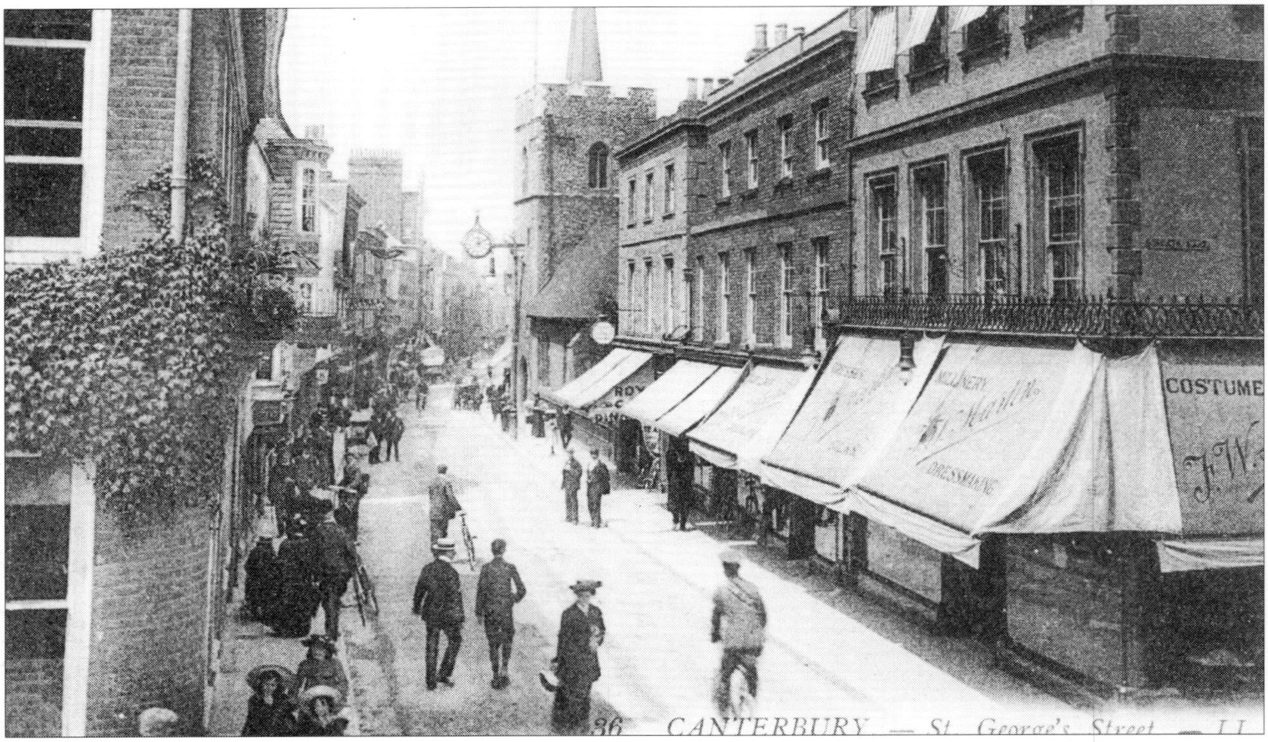


***Above*** *Looking along St George's Street, Canterbury. All these properties, with the exception of the church tower, would later be destroyed during the Second World War Blitz, on 1st June 1942.*
(Jean Jordan – South Street WI)

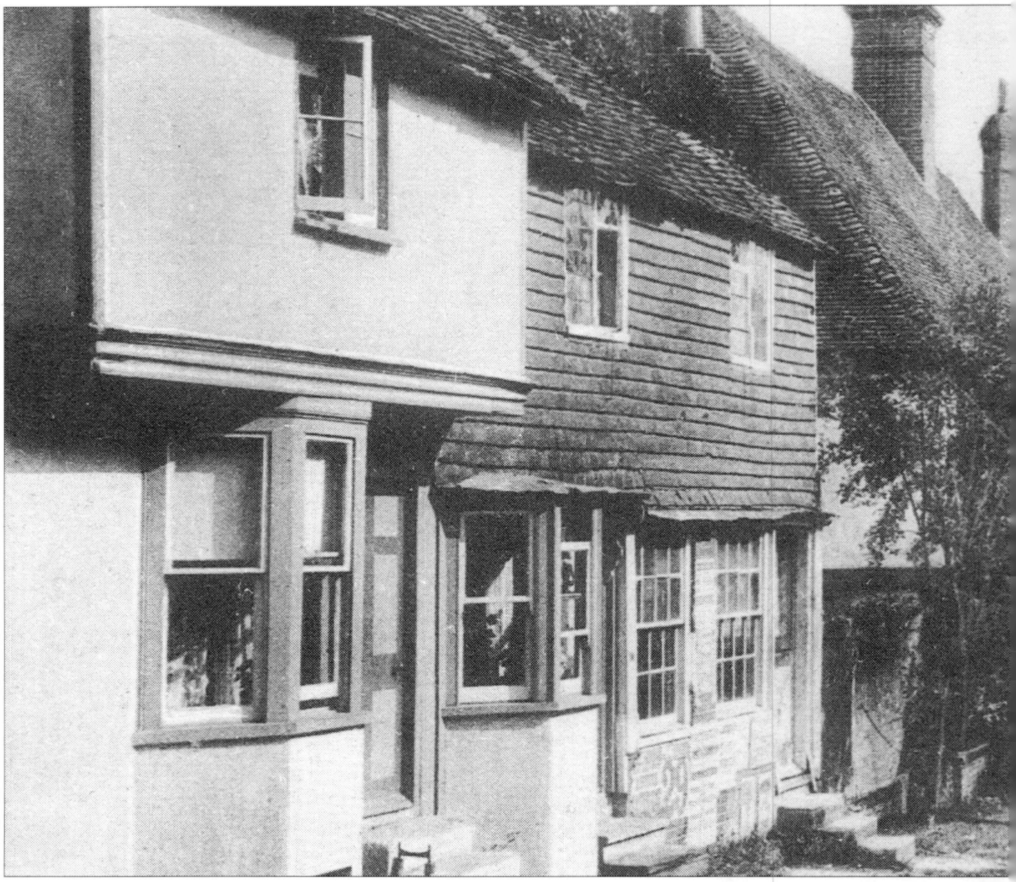

***Right*** *Chilham High Street in the early years of the century. Today the view has hardly altered, except to include the ever-present motor car.*
(Dorothy Martin – South Street WI)

*The construction of the Winter Gardens at Margate, 1911, carried out by Dove Bros. of Islington. All haulage work was done by horse and cart, and smoking on the site was strictly forbidden – it was instant dismissal if caught. East Kent Federation meetings are held here every year in March.*
(Rosalind Wildash – Doddington & District WI)

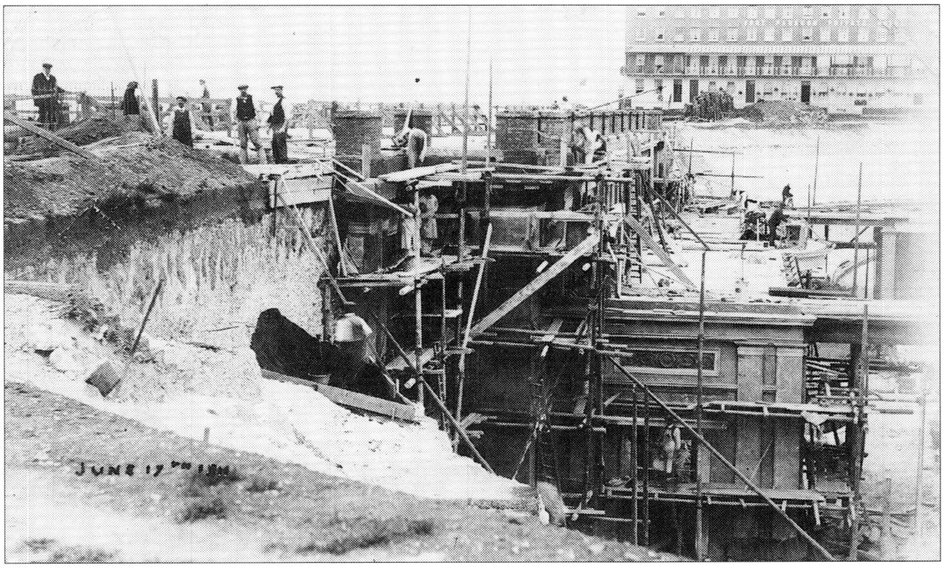

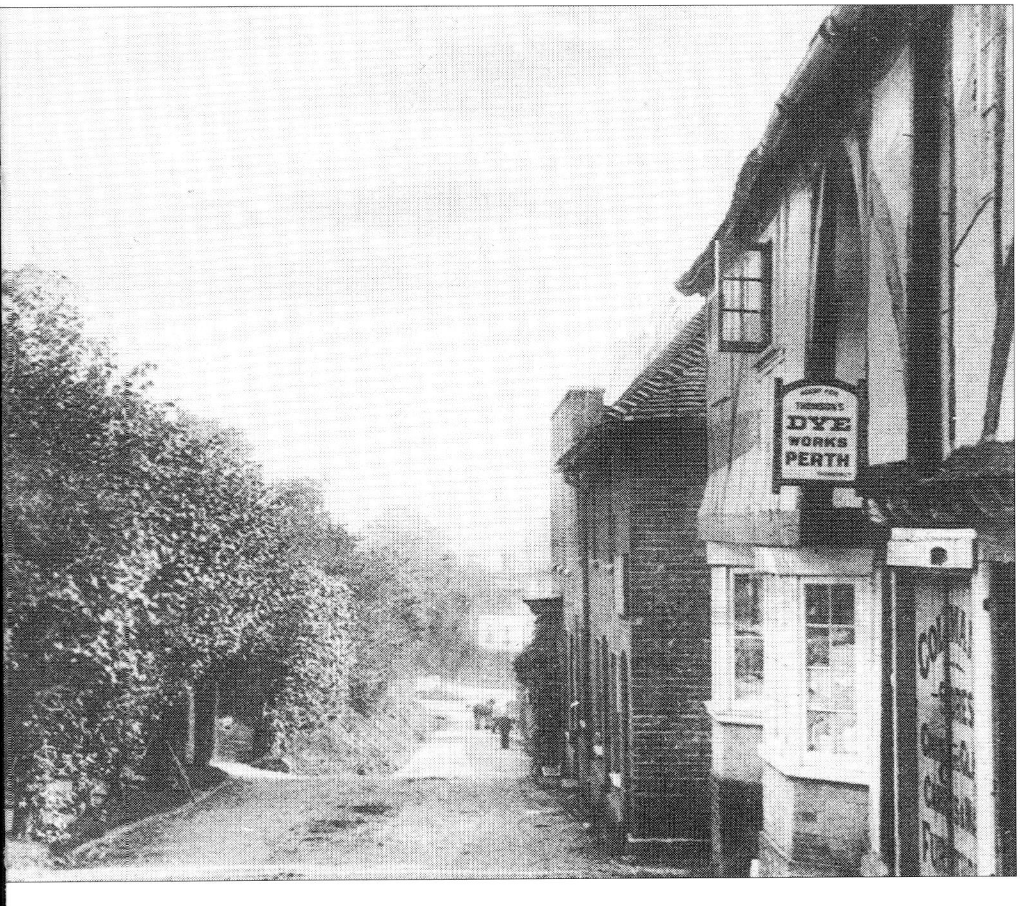

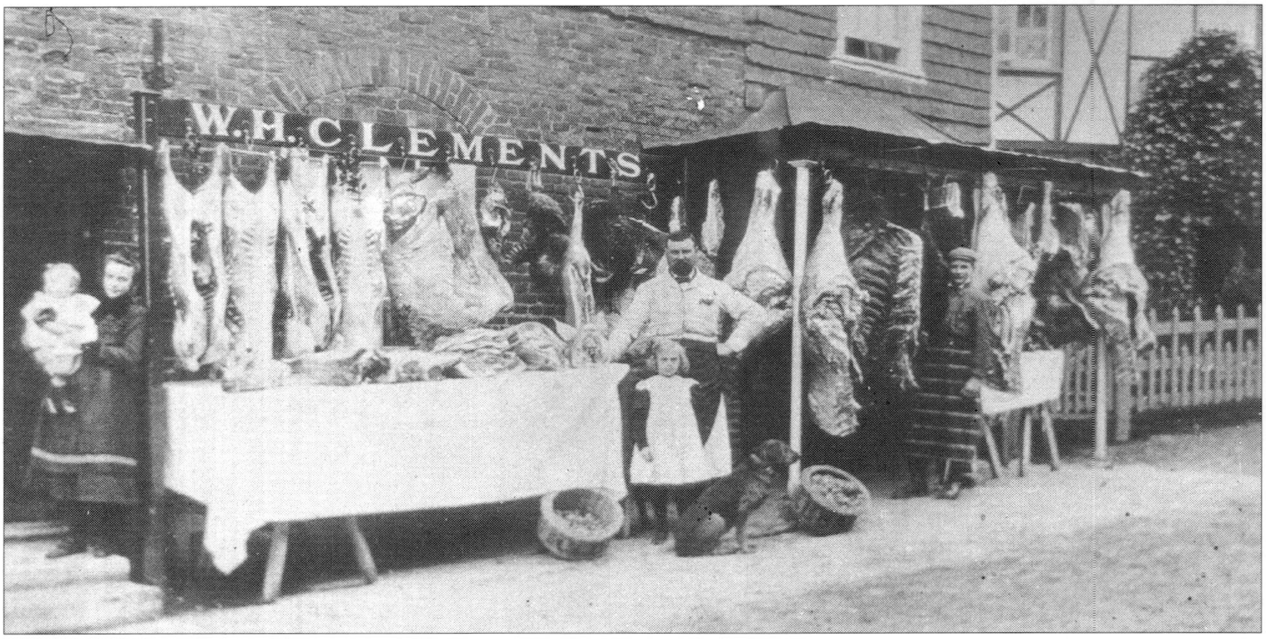


*Meat on open-air display at the butcher's shop at Chilham early in the 1900s, believed then to have been the oldest butcher's shop in the county. It continued trading until the 1980s.* (Joyce Jury – Chilham WI)

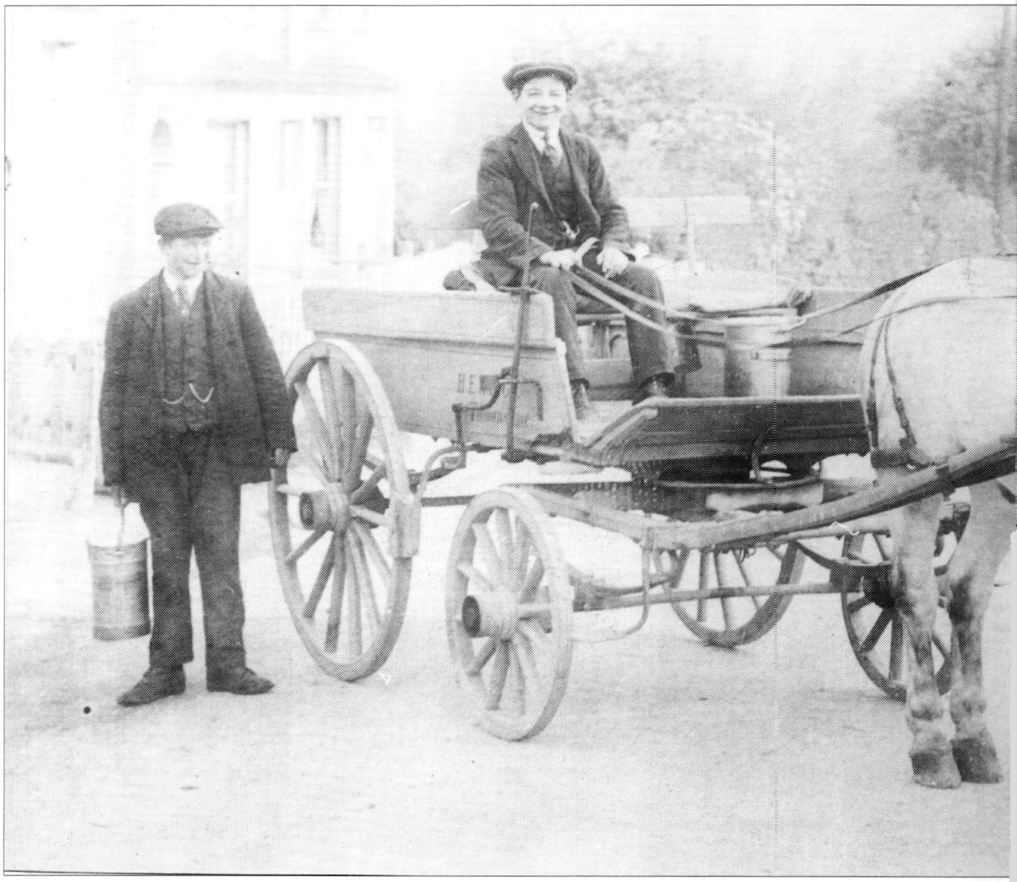

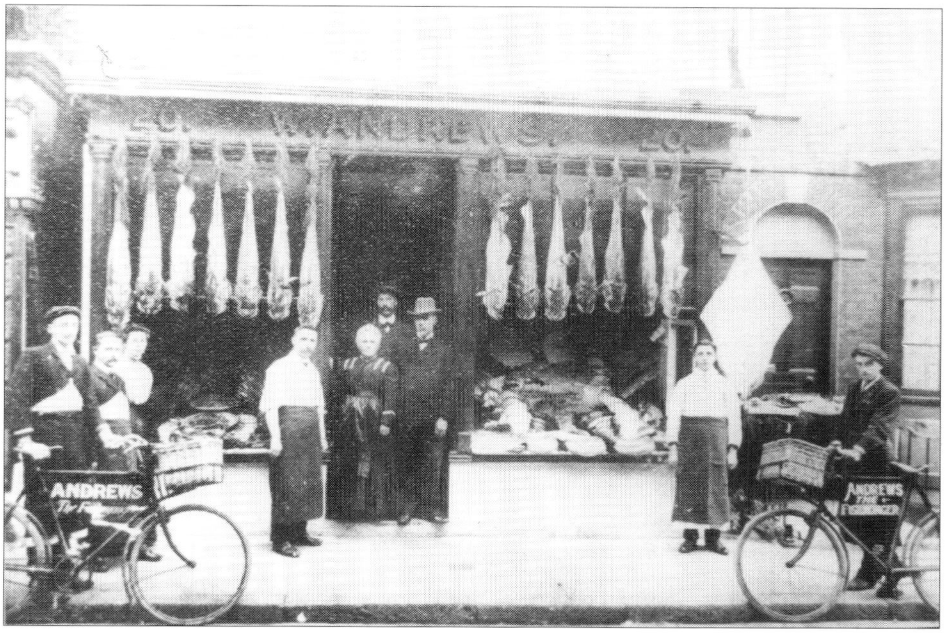


*Andrews' fishmonger's shop, Ramsgate, in 1909, when the window had been specially prepared for a competition.*
(Mrs D Belsey – Sandwich WI)

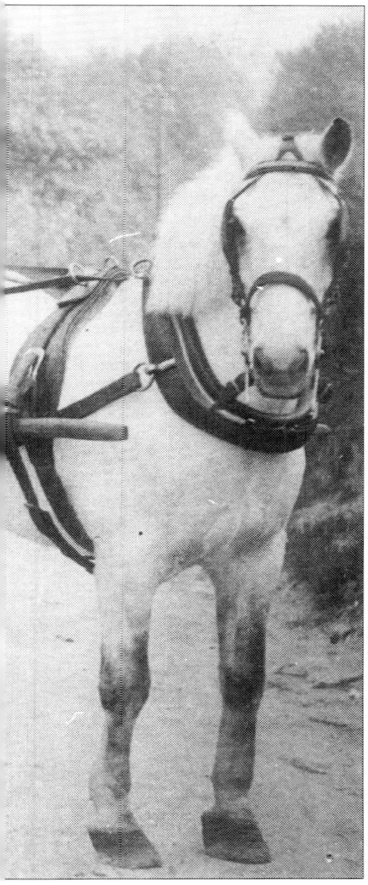

***Left*** *Wally Marsh and Arthur White delivering milk at Tilmanstone. The milk came straight from the farm each day, measured out from the churn into the householder's own jug.* (Hollingsbee Collection – Tilmanstone WI)

*The counter staff outside the International Stores, Margate. Service was personal and attentive, making shopping a pleasure.*
(Mrs A. Webb – Hernhill WI)

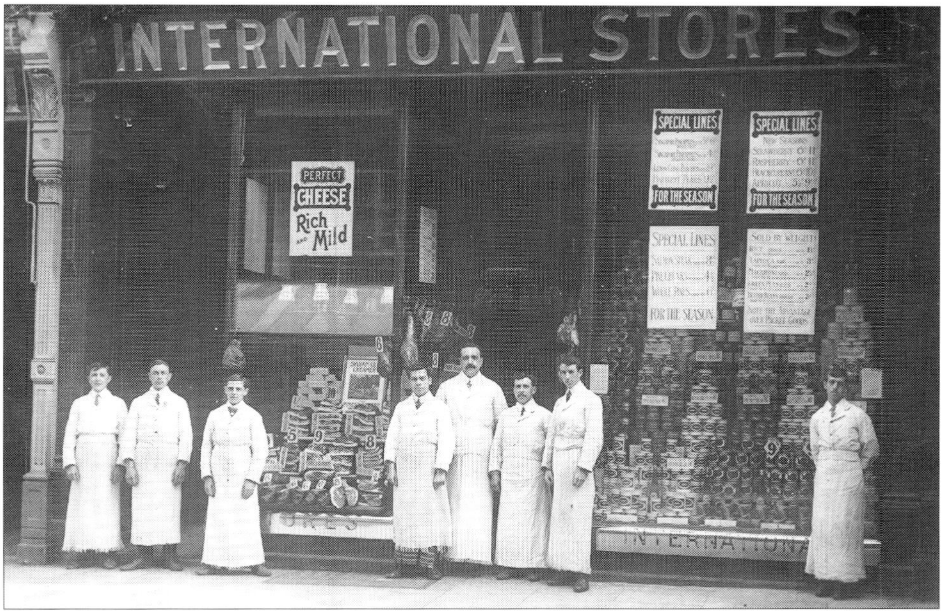

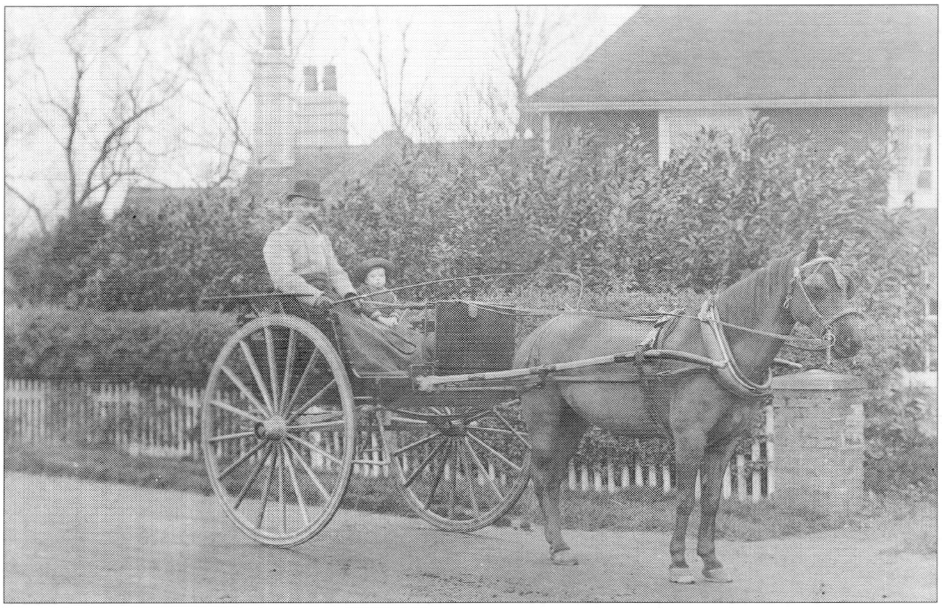

*The pony and trap remained a popular form of transport for some years, especially in country districts. Dr Toms of Ham Street is pictured on his rounds c1910.*
(Barbara Ware – Orlestone, Ham Street & Ruckinge WI)

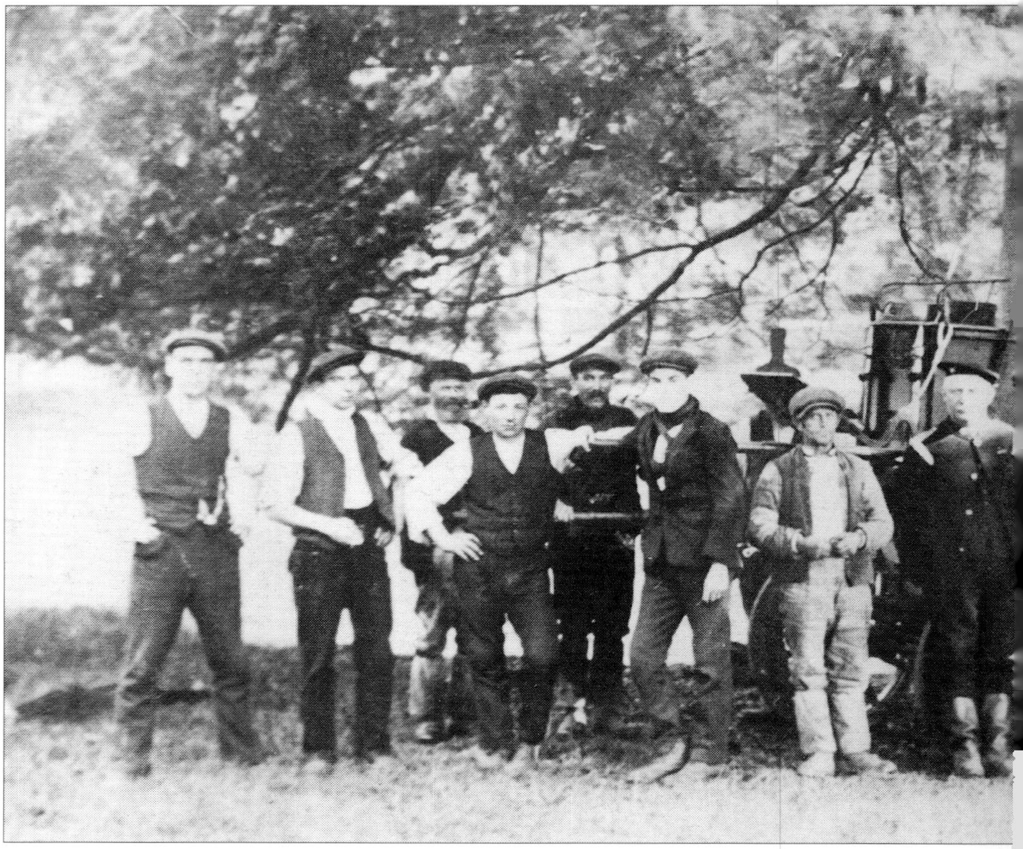

*The Sandwich fire engine was called out to a major fire at Waldershare Mansion in 1913, but is reputed to have 'got lost' in the fog and ended up in nearby Eythorne. Steam-powered, it had a crew of five, including the fire officer Mr Finnis of Sandwich – the other men were volunteers.*
(Hollingsbee Collection – Tilmanstone WI)

*The first car in Brabourne was owned by the village doctor, Dr Joseph Garman. This brand new 1909 Rover 6hp (the RAC identify it as the de luxe model because it has a windscreen and hood), is being shown off by the doctor's wife and his chauffeur/handyman Arthur Conley.*
(Mrs D. Willett – Brabourne WI)

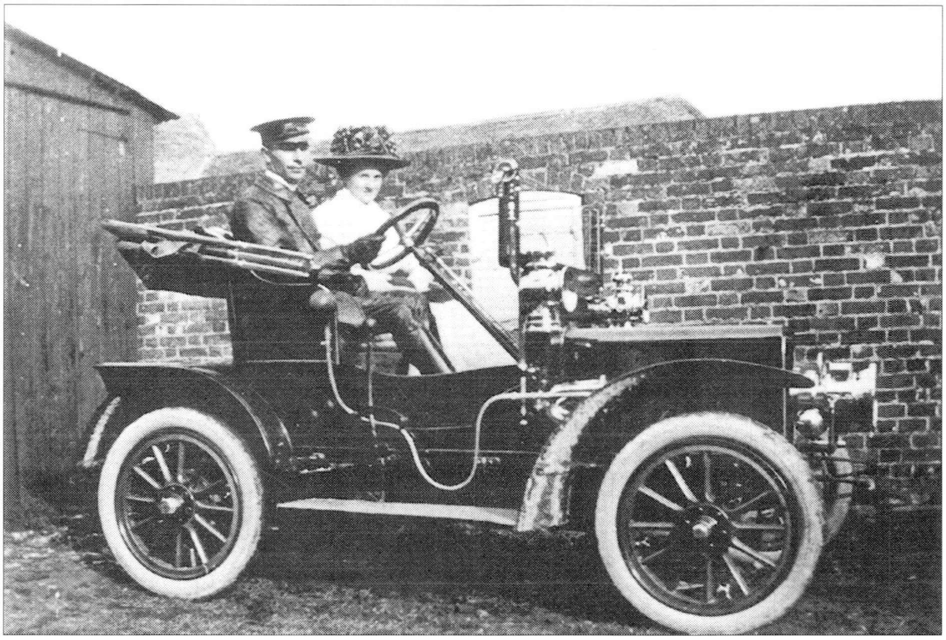

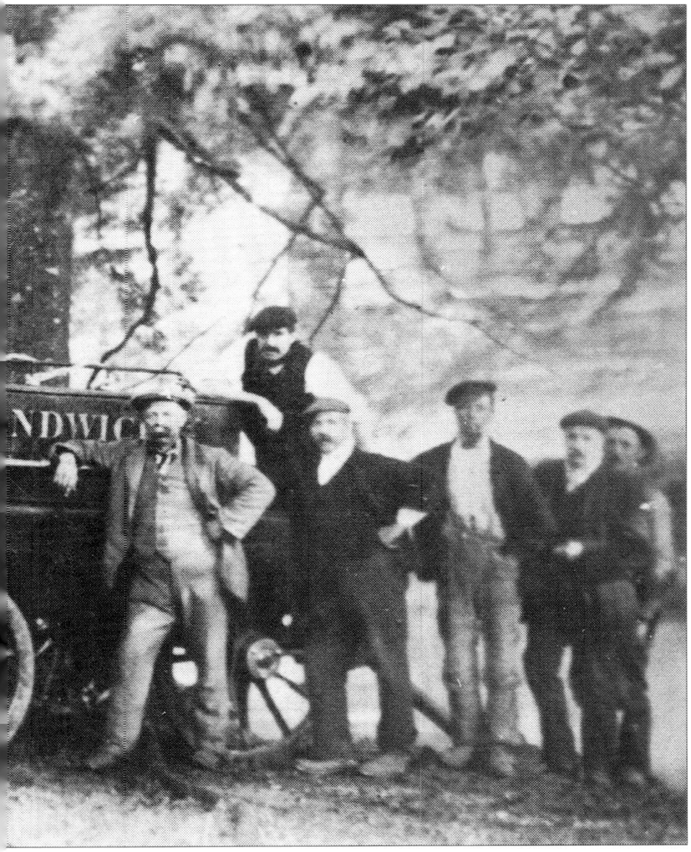

*A country kitchen in the early 1900s. Alice Rye, who worked in service in several country houses, probably had this photograph taken to send to her brother, serving in South Africa with the Royal East Kent Regiment (the Buffs).*
(Mrs M. Court – St Martins WI)

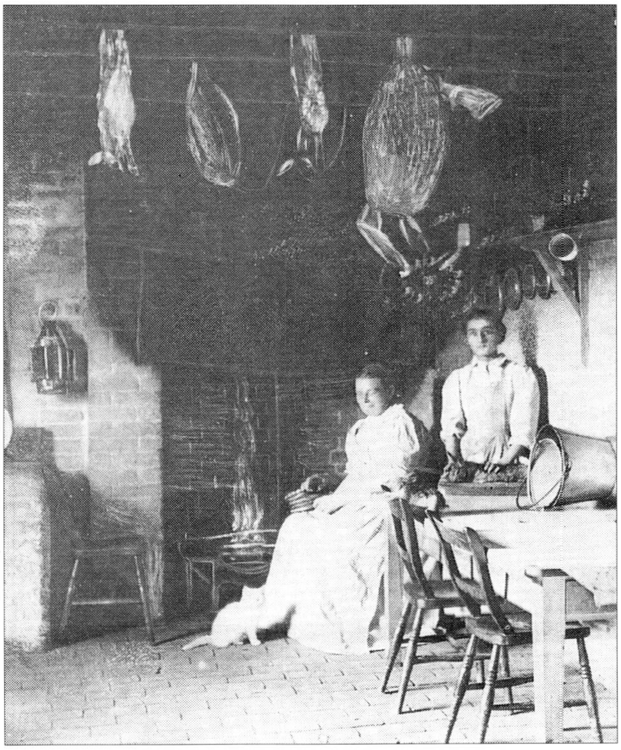

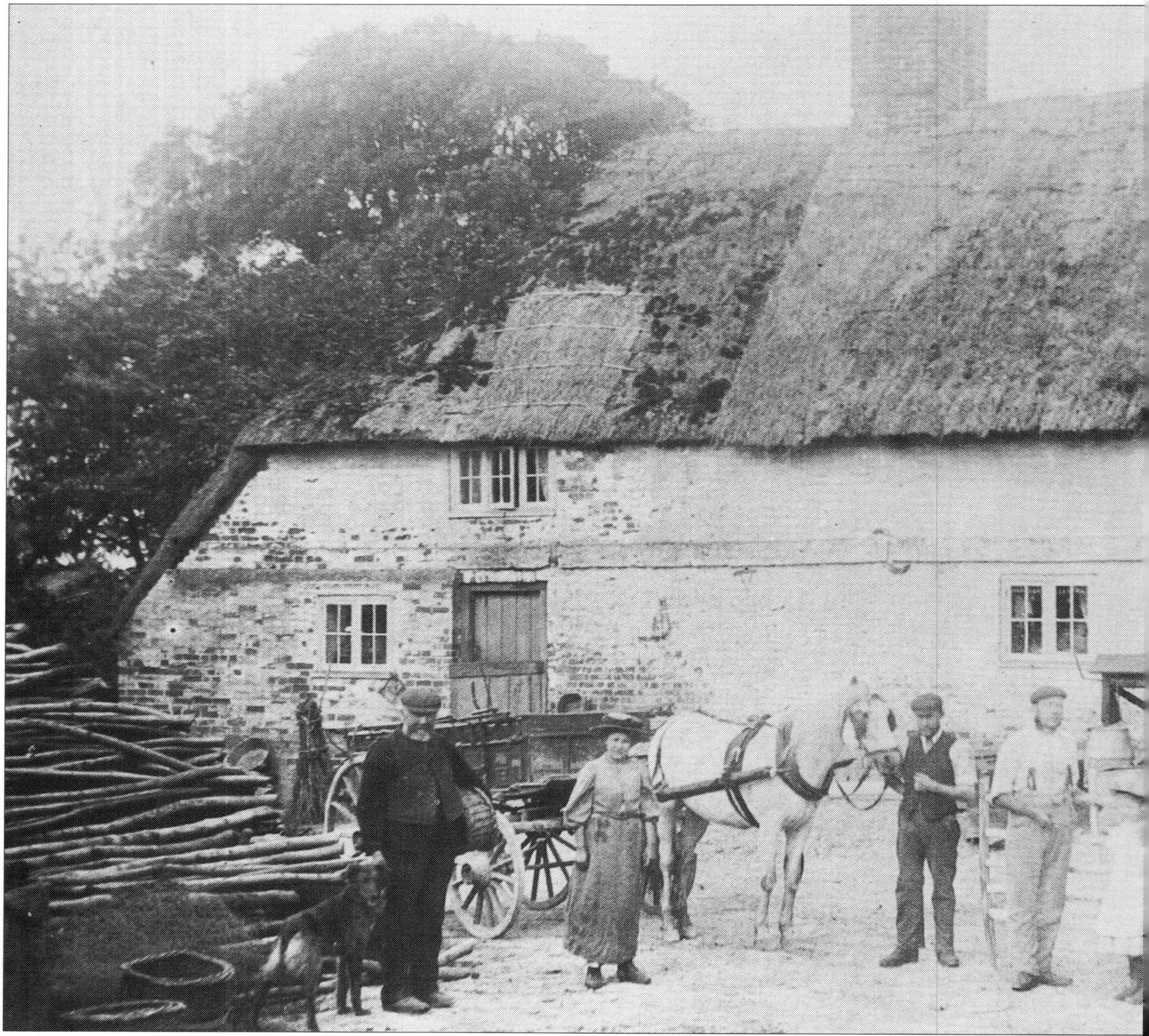

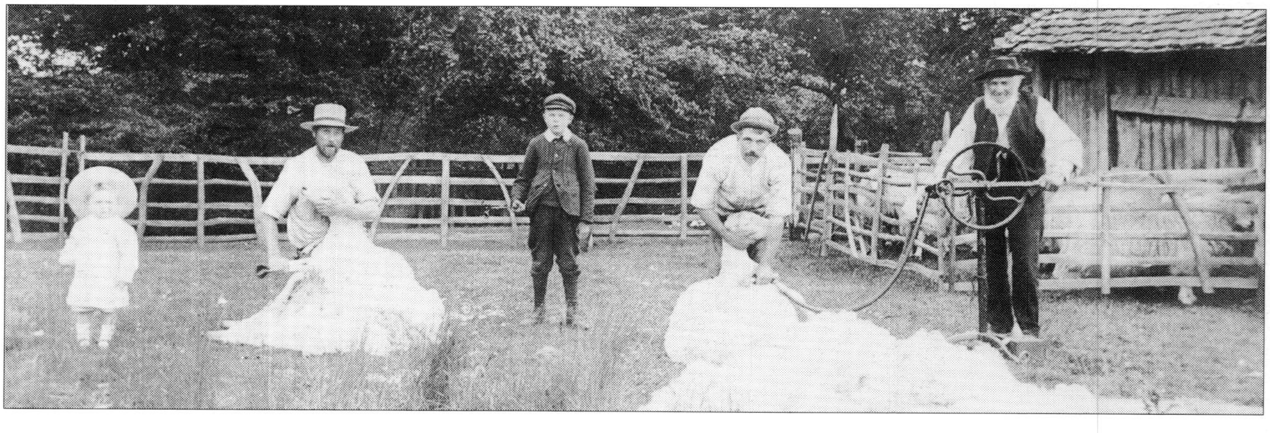

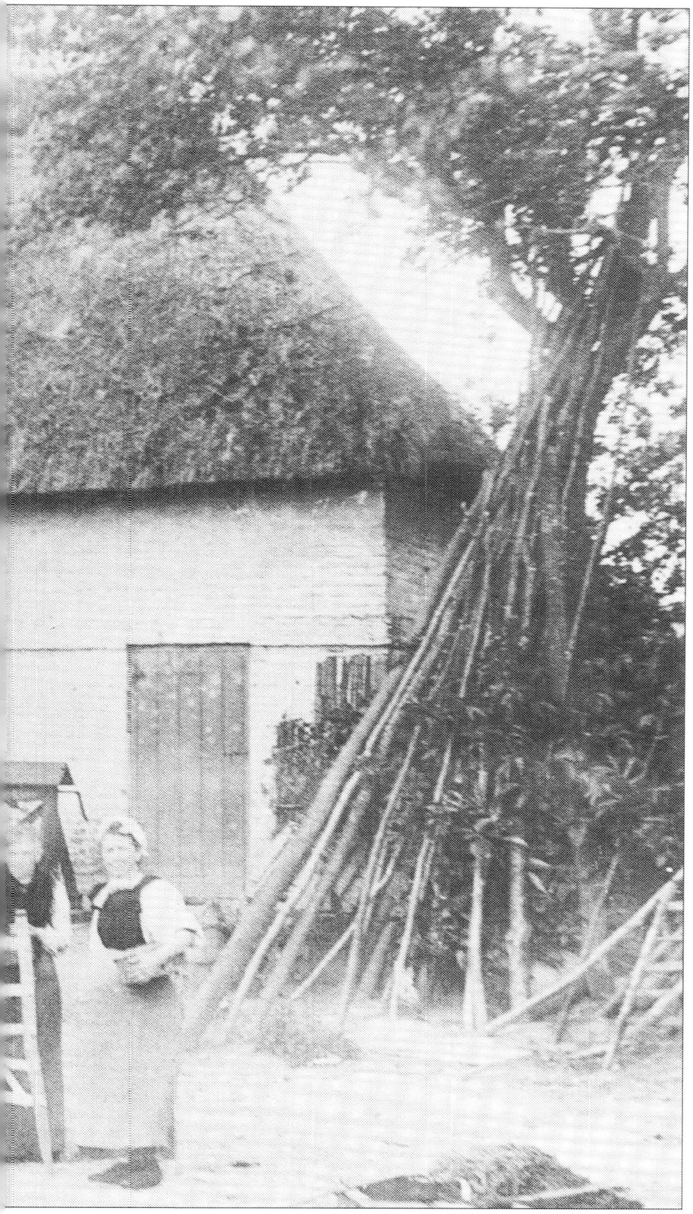

*Lower Venson farmhouse, c1907. The farmer was Samuel Coushion (left) and his wife Emma, his daughter and grand-daughter are on the right. Mrs Meers of Thornton Oast, Samuel's son in law George Andrews, and Mr Husk the hurdlemaker make up the group. The horse and cart were used to carry market produce to Dover shops.*
(Hollingsbee Collection – Tilmanstone WI)

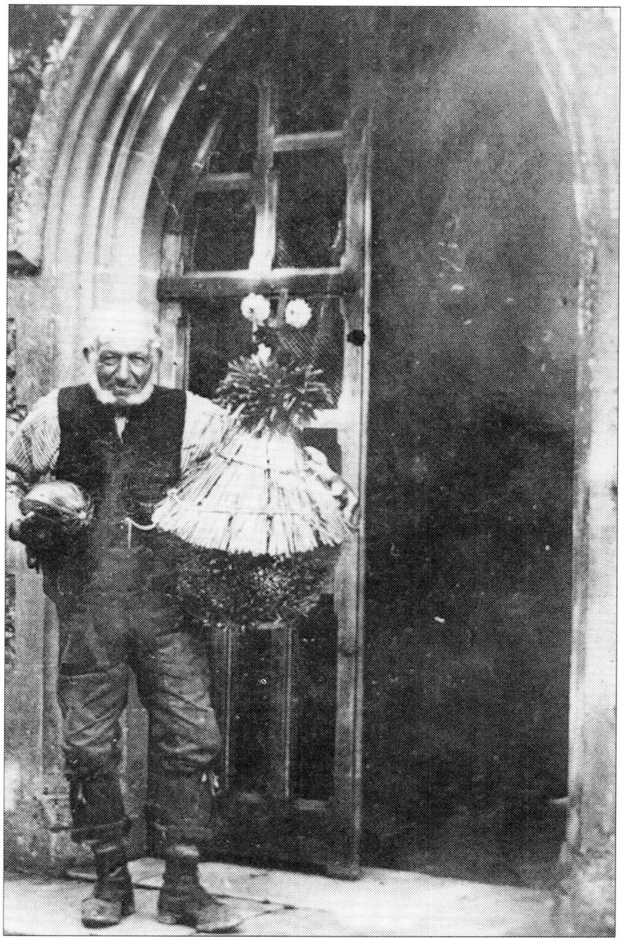

***Left*** *The Goldsack family sheep shearing at Waldershare in 1911. They are using both manual and mechanically powered shears.*
(Hollingsbee Collection – Tilmanstone WI)

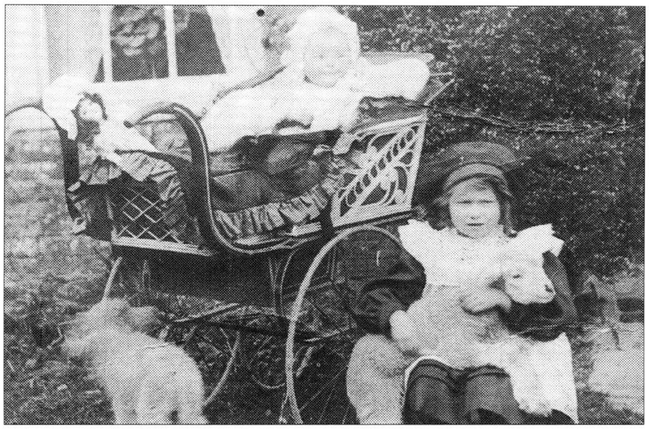

*Richard Goldsack taking his specially made celebration haystack, and a marrow, to Harvest Festival in Alkham church, October 1910.*
(Susan Lees – Alkham WI)

*Little Frances Kirby and sister Kate in her very sturdy pram (known as the 'mail cart') at Box Tree Cottage in 1907.*
(Susan Lees – Alkham WI)

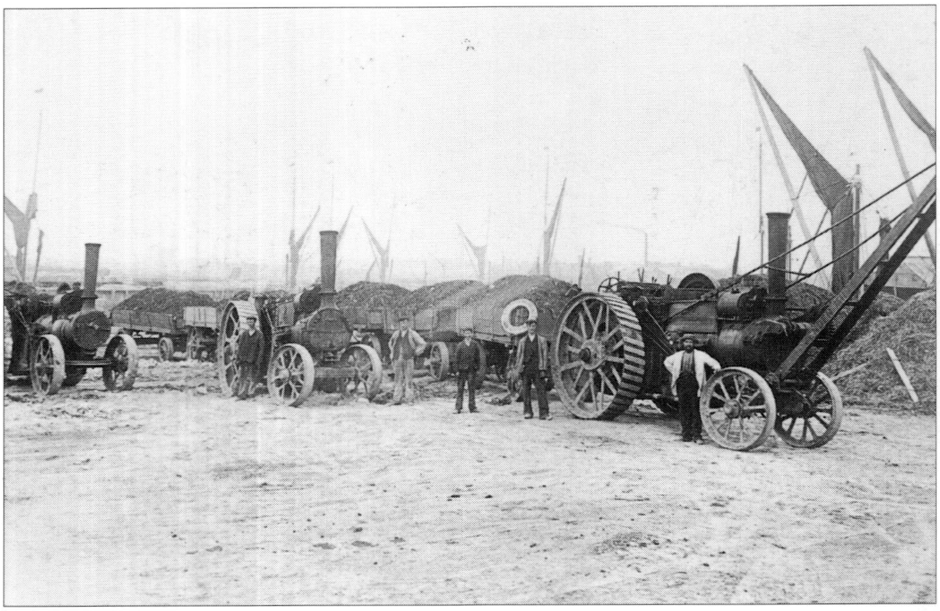

*Murrell's Wharf at Milton. Here barges arrived from London loaded with the city's household refuse, stable manure and stale fish from Billingsgate, called politely London Mixture. This was delivered by steam engine and trailer, by the family firm of Ovenden's, to local fruit farms for manure. 'Father used to come home stinking.'*
(Mrs D. Ovenden – Kennington WI)

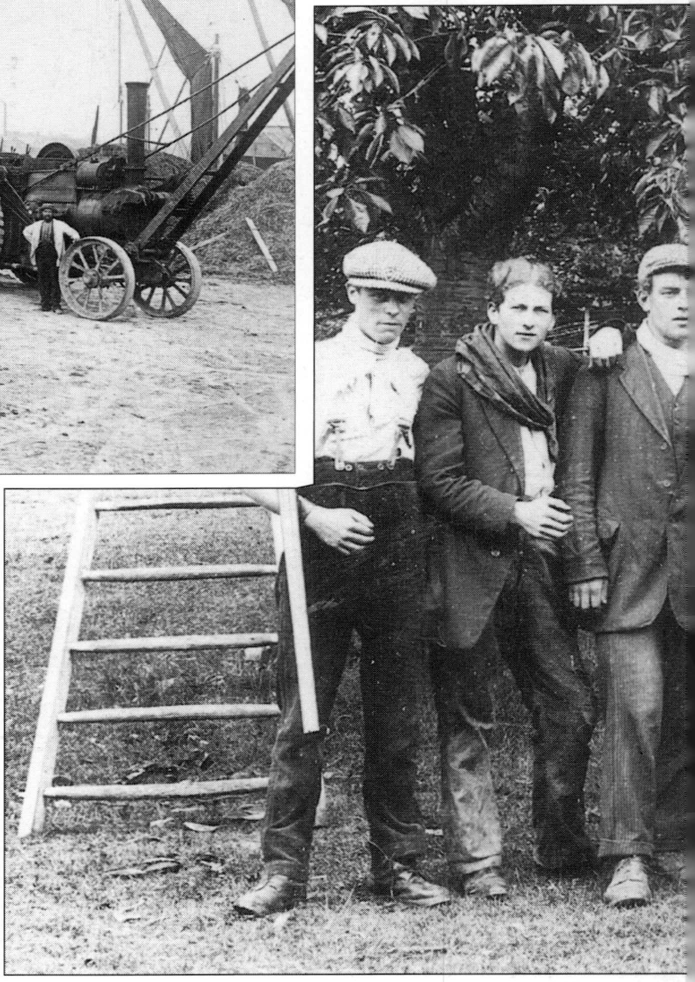

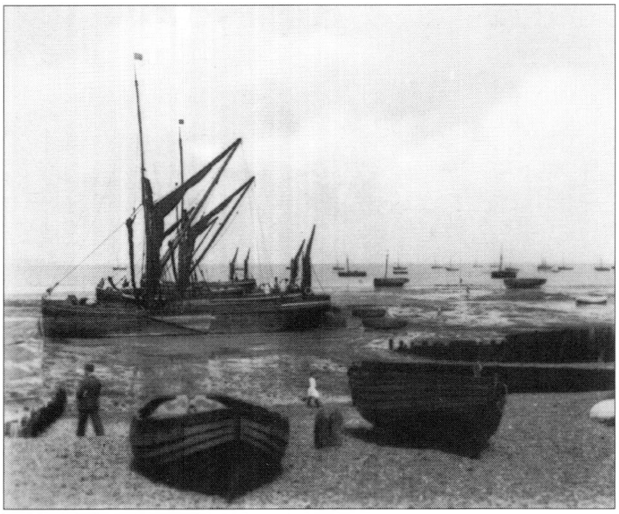

*The oyster fleet at Whitstable, where oysters have been fished for over 200 years. The Whitstable Oyster Fishery Company had beds of several thousand acres, all tended as carefully as flower beds, stretching out over six square miles of the Swale Estuary. Here, because of a peculiar mixture of sea and fresh water and the local algae, the oysters thrived. In 1912 over 19 million oysters were sold, mostly to Billingsgate market. The later introduction of the diesel engine and oil seeping into the oyster beds was blamed for the ruin of the company.*
(Mrs V. Charters – South Street WI & Mrs M. Williams – Kennington WI)

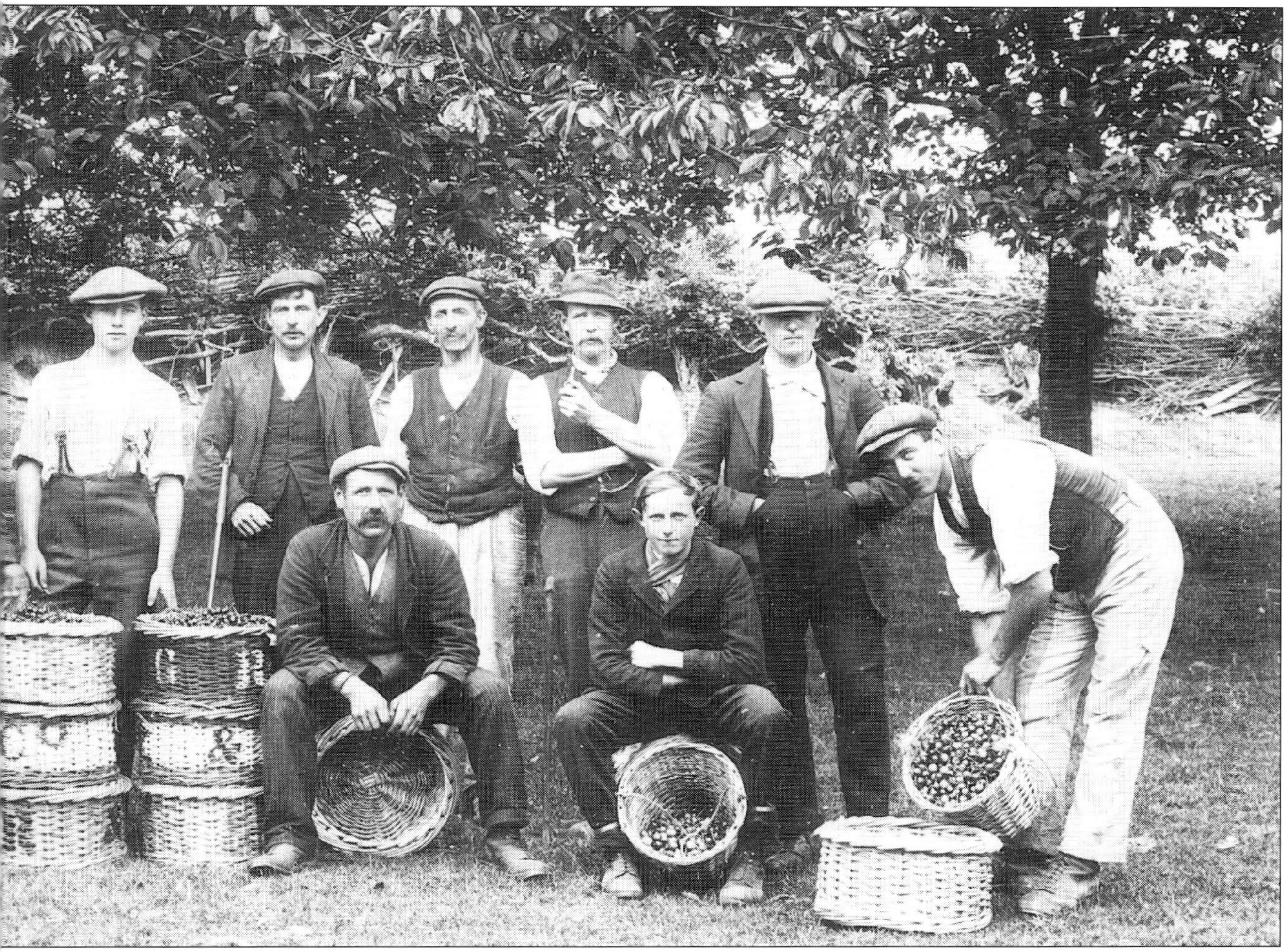

*Cherry pickers working for Mr Maylam at Home Farm, Ham Street in 1910. Firing a gun (see the man on the left) was one way to keep the birds away from the crop.*
(Barbara Ware – Orlestone, Ham Street & Ruckinge WI)

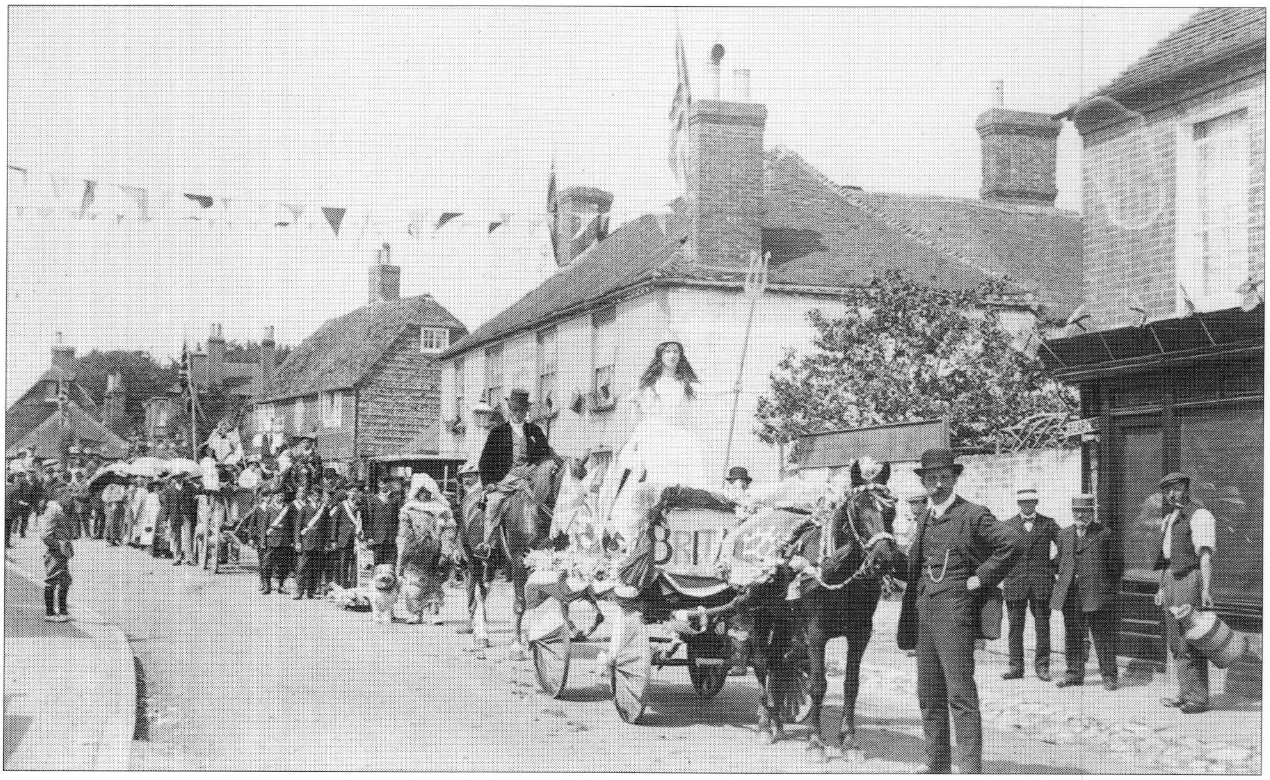

***Above*** *The Empire Day procession, headed by Britannia, forming in the High Street at Ham Street in 1907. The village celebrations included maypole dancing and a sit-down tea.*
(Barbara Ware – Orlestone, Ham Street & Ruckinge WI)

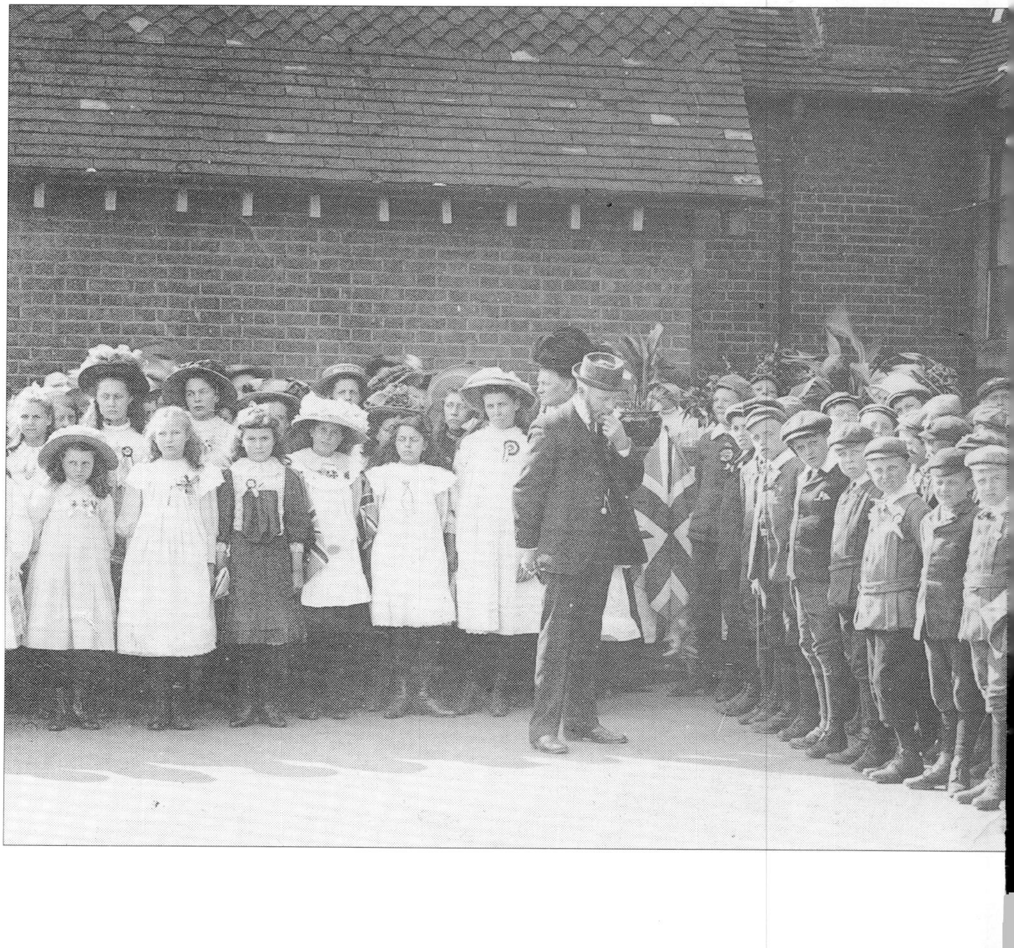

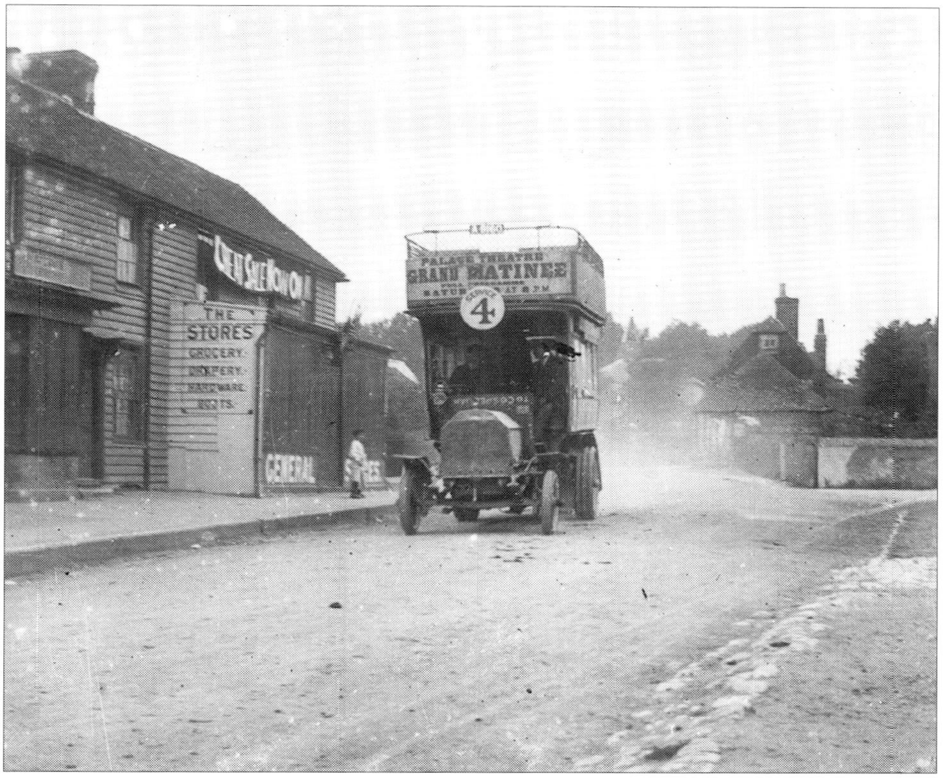


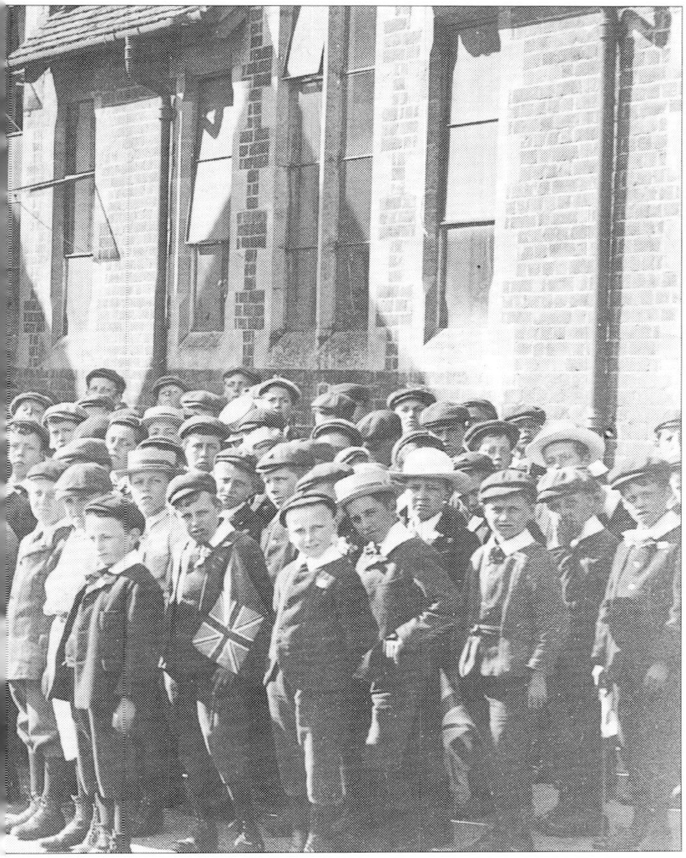

***Above*** *A visit to the theatre was a great treat – this early bus going down the high street at Ham Street is advertising a 'Grand Matinee' at the Palace Theatre.*
(Barbara Ware – Orlestone, Ham Street & Ruckinge WI)

*Lined up for Sandwich primary school Empire Day celebrations on 24th May 1908. Empire Day, celebrated on Queen Victoria's birthday, remained part of every schoolchild's year until eventually it was superseded by Commonwealth Day.*
(Audrey Lowley – Whitfield WI)

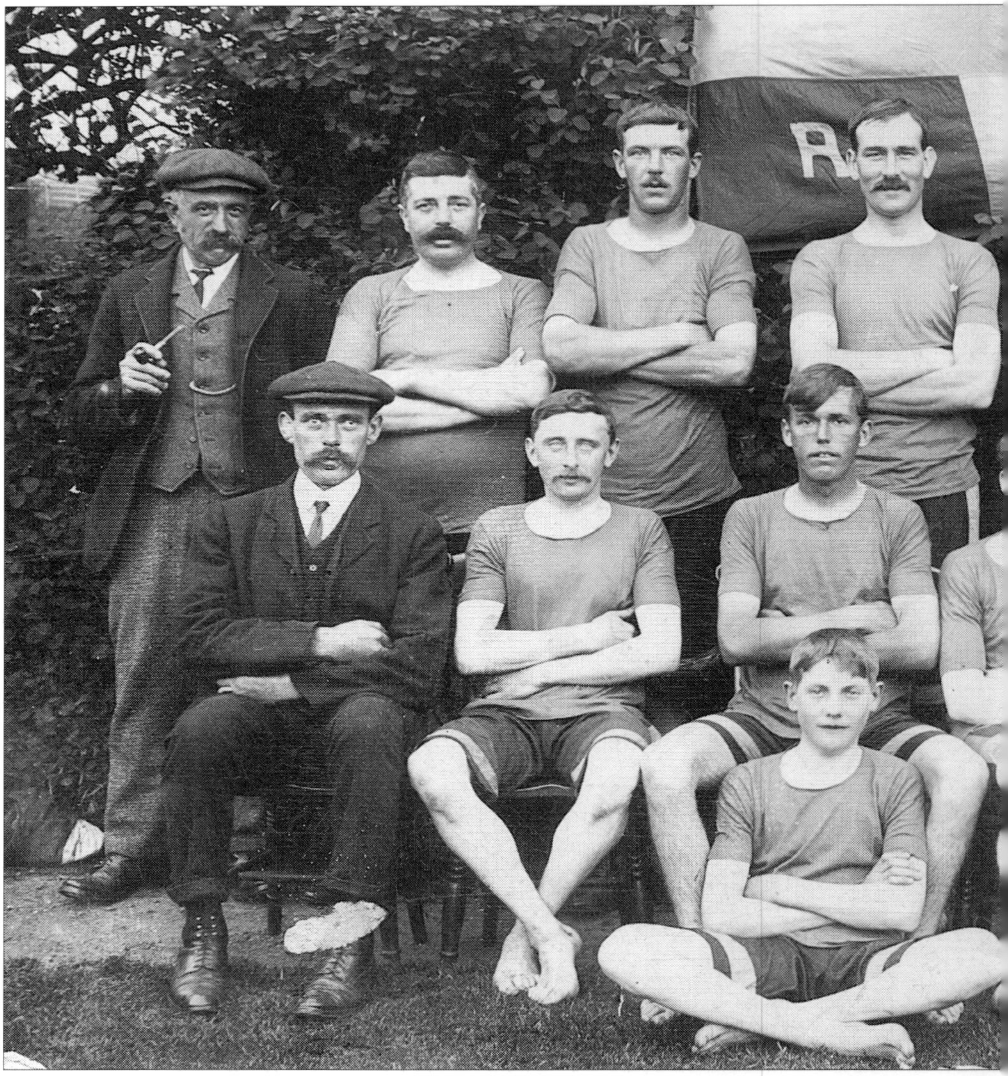

*Wye goal running team c1908. Goal running was widely played between village teams in Kent, on any available large, rectangular piece of grass. Each team attempted to reach its goal as often as possible but had to avoid being touched by a member of the other team, this touch being called a 'stroke'. The totals of goals and strokes decided the winners. 'The game was played in large open spaces, such as on the old racecourse near the Crown above Wye. It was not considered suitable for ladies to attend the games. Much beer was consumed.'*
(Mrs C. Murday – Wye WI)

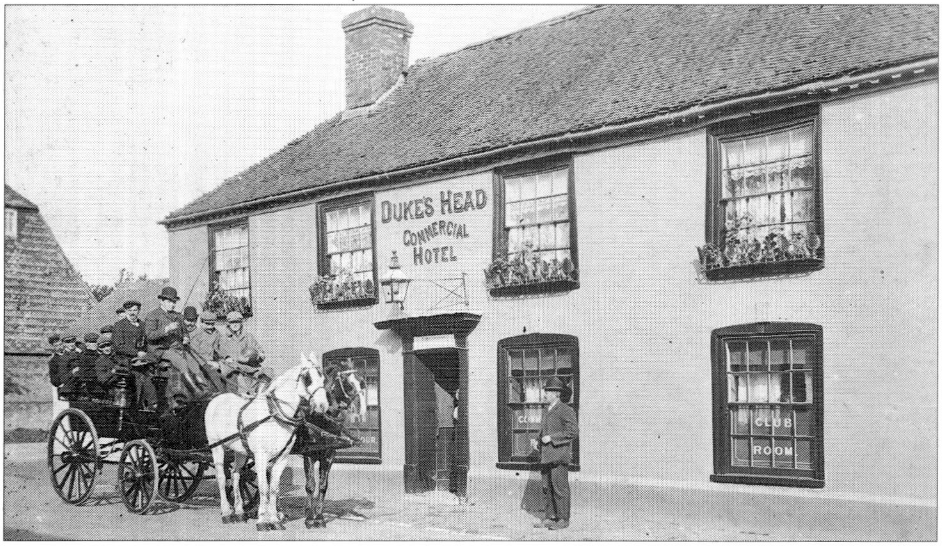


*The Ham Street goal running team setting off for a match from the Duke's Head in 1911.*
(Barbara Ware – Orlestone, Ham Street & Ruckinge WI)

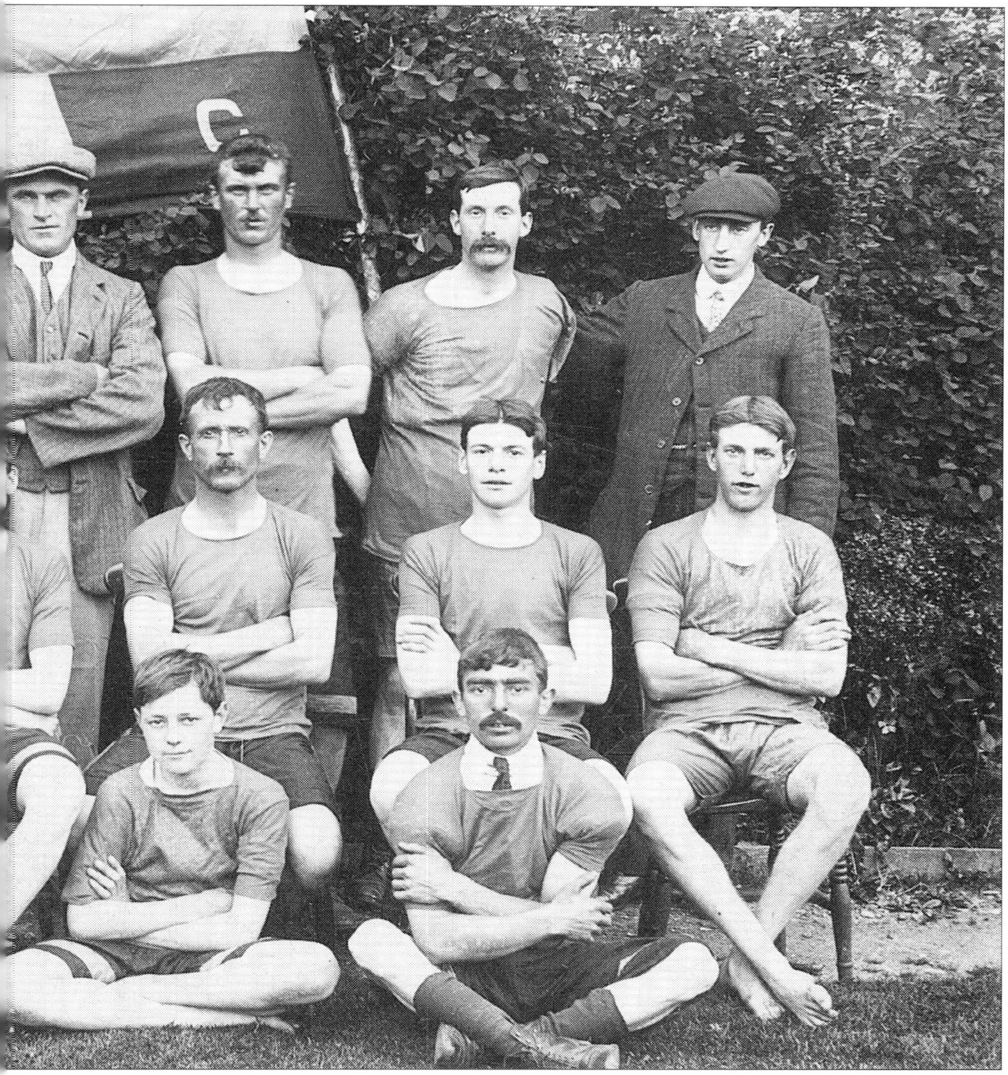

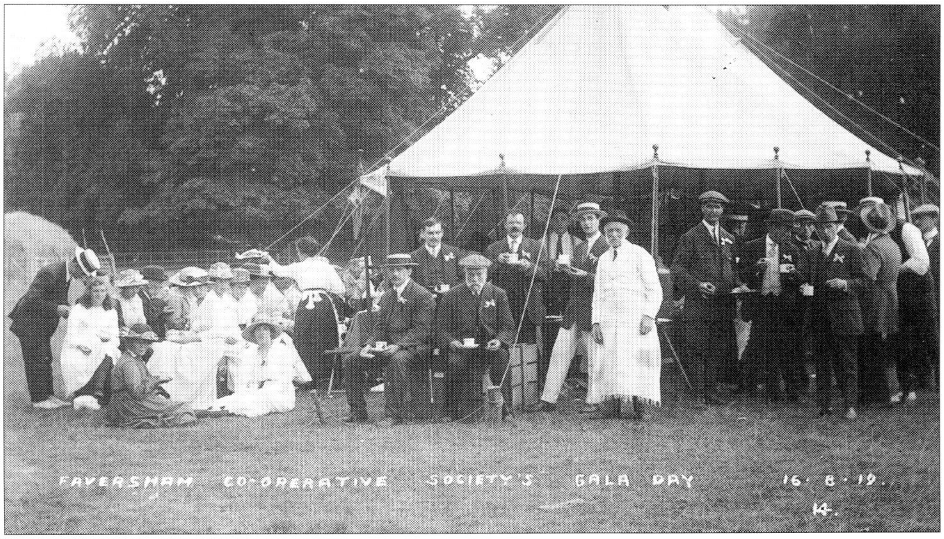


*A welcome cup of tea and a cake at Faversham Co-operative Society's Gala Day, August 1919.*
(Mrs A. Webb – Hernhill WI)

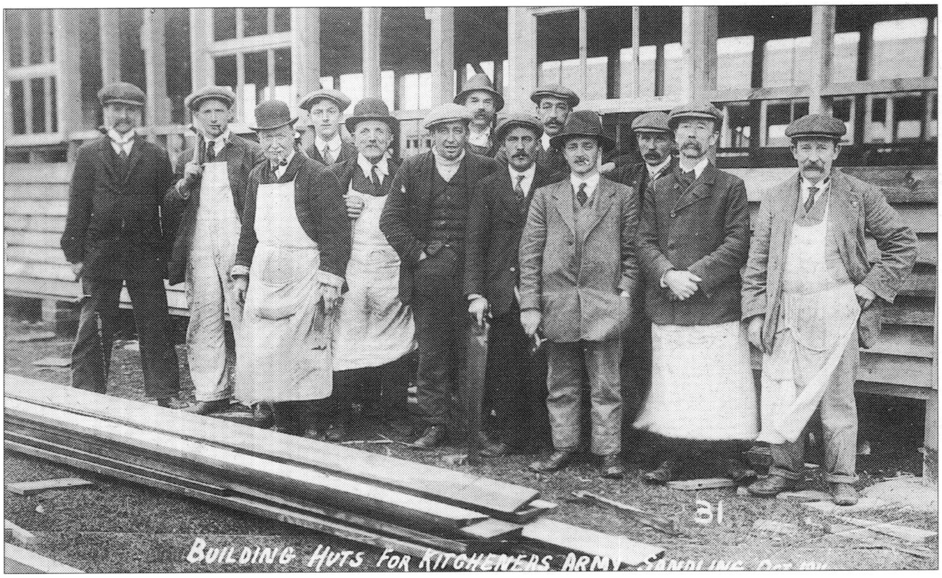


*In the early months of the First World War, builders were brought in to Sandling from Sandwich to build 'huts for Kitchener's Army'.* (Audrey Lowley – Whitfield WI)

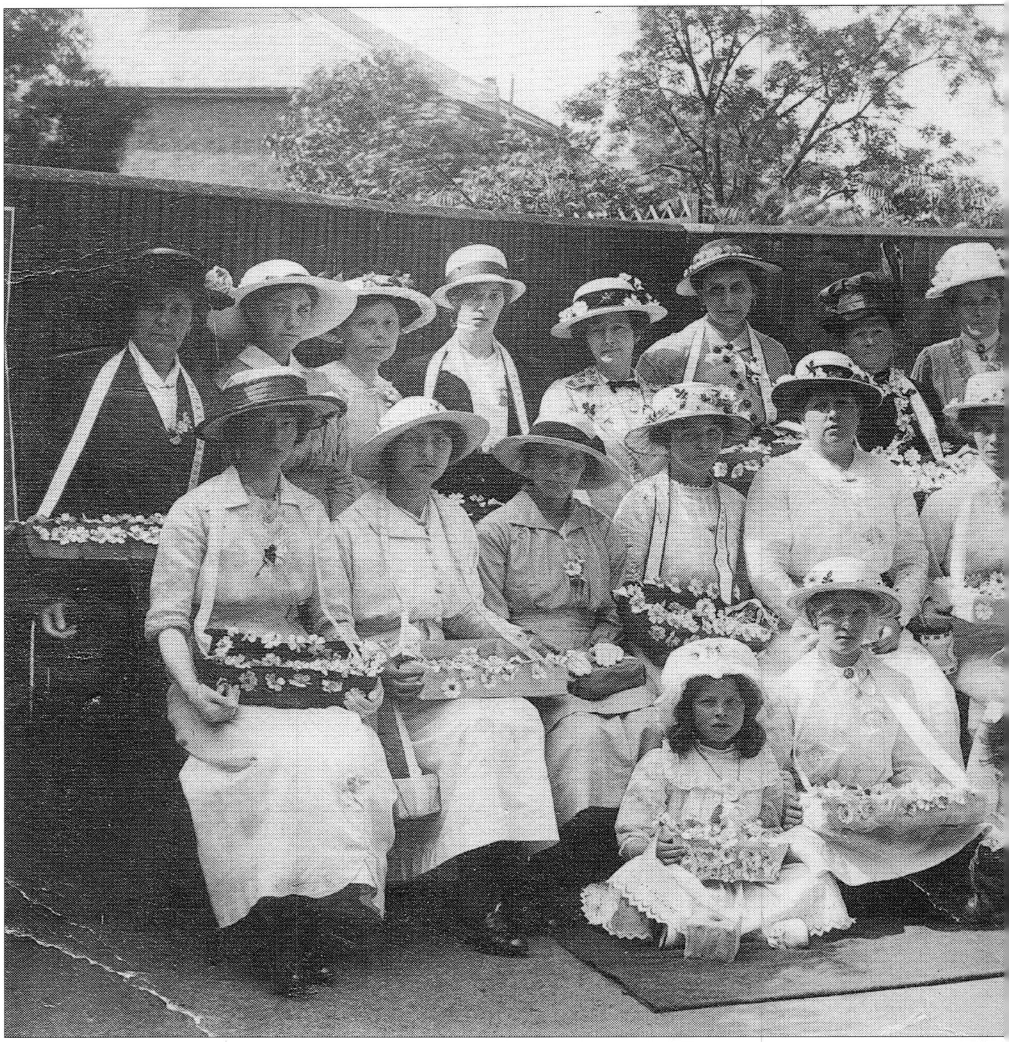

*Queen Alexandra Rose Day collectors in Ashford in 1912. Queen Alexandra had that year inaugurated a day specially to collect funds for the hospitals, which were then greatly dependent on charitable contributions.* (Grace Thompsett – Kennington WI)

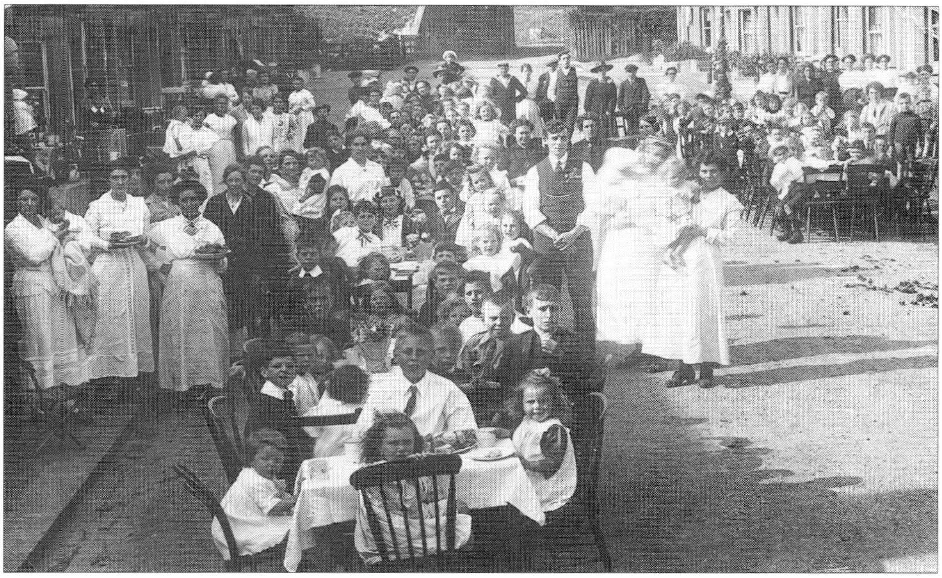

*The Peace Treat, a street party held in Glenfield Road, Dover in 1919 to celebrate the ending of the war. Celebrations were tempered by the loss of so many men from towns and villages all over East Kent.*
(Miss E. Davidson – Cheriton WI)

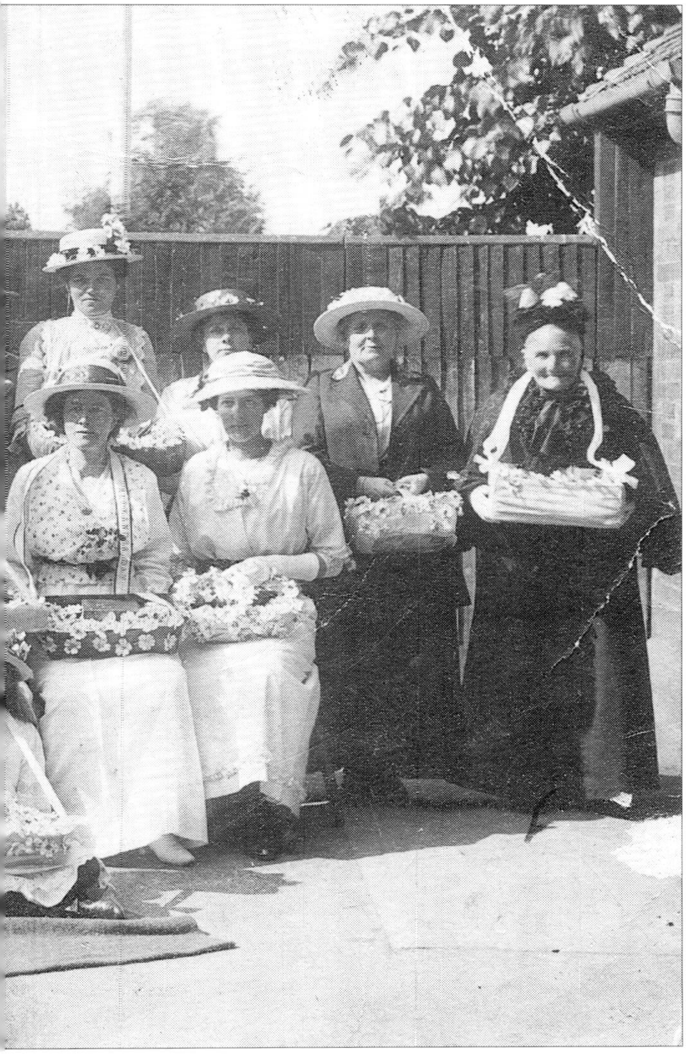

*The outbreak of war meant that Kent's men and women found themselves in places and situations they would never have thought possible just a short while before. Tom Tester was a chauffeur at Martin Hale, Rolvenden before the war, but soon he was driving a field ambulance.*
(Lena Burton – Bethersden WI)

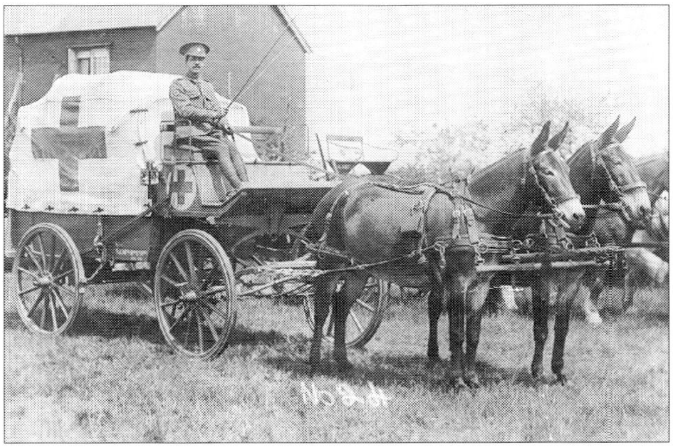

# THEN & NOW
# COAL MINING

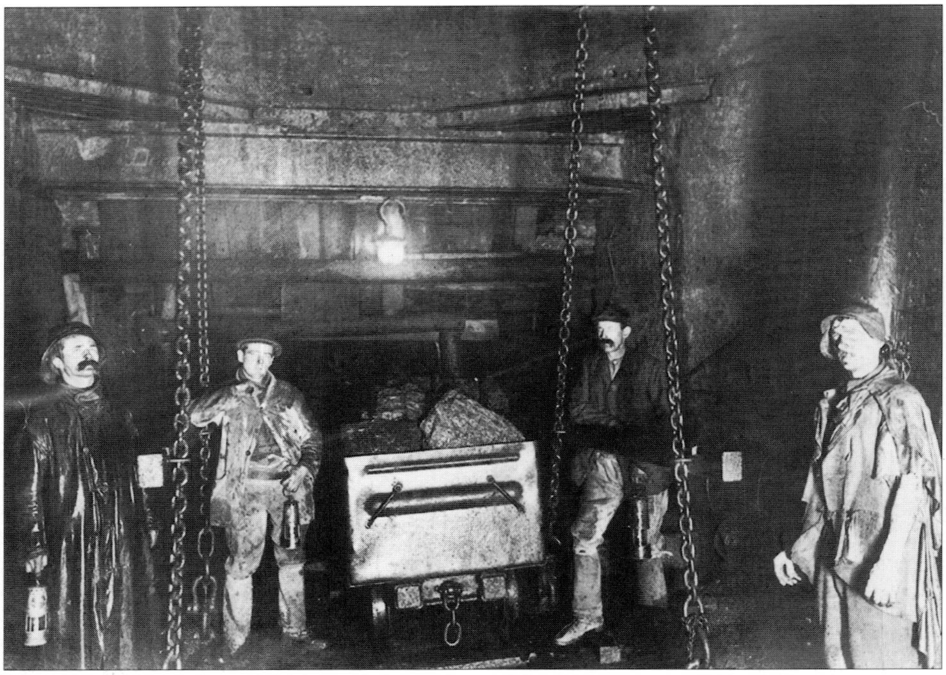

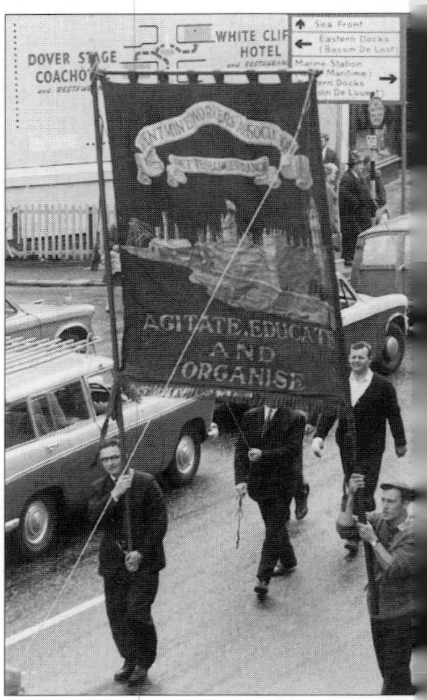


*Raising coal from Snowdown Colliery early in 1913. This was the first time that coal had been raised in saleable quantities.*
(Hollingsbee Collection – Tilmanstone WI)

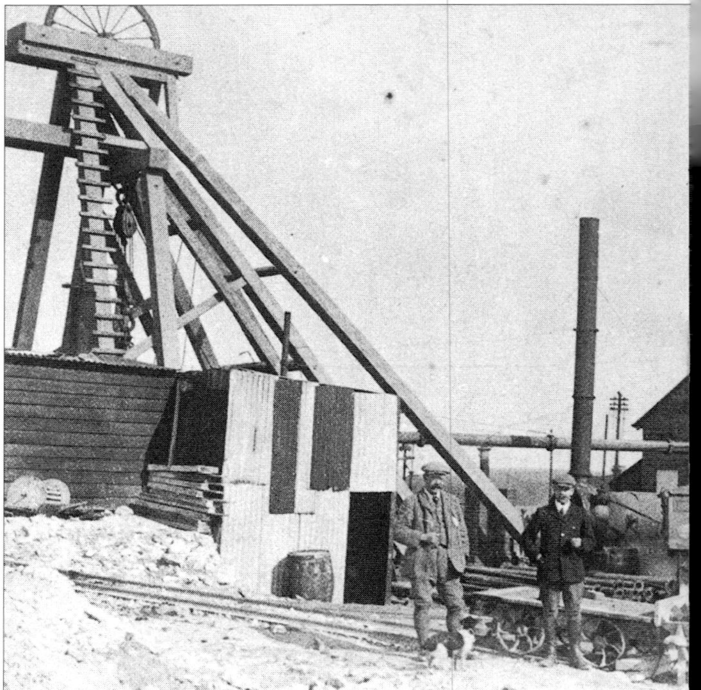

*Richborough Wharf in 1918, just after the war. It was a very busy place throughout the inter-war years, when ships this large could come up the Stour. It was developed by Pearson, Dorman Long who had their offices there, but these were moved to Dover after nationalisation of the mines in 1948 and the port then dwindled.*
(Audrey Lowley – Whitfield WI)

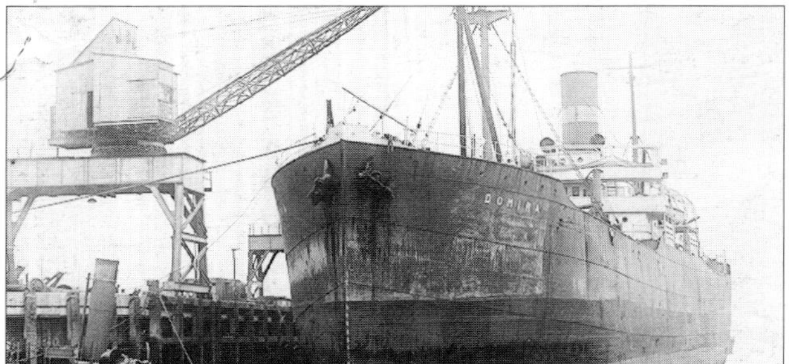

*Kent NUM members demonstrating in Dover with their Betteshanger branch banner during an industrial dispute some years before the coalfield closed.* (Hollingsbee Collection – Tilmanstone WI)

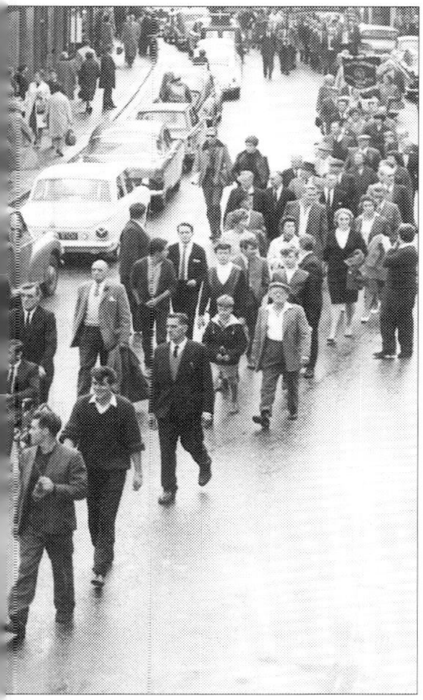

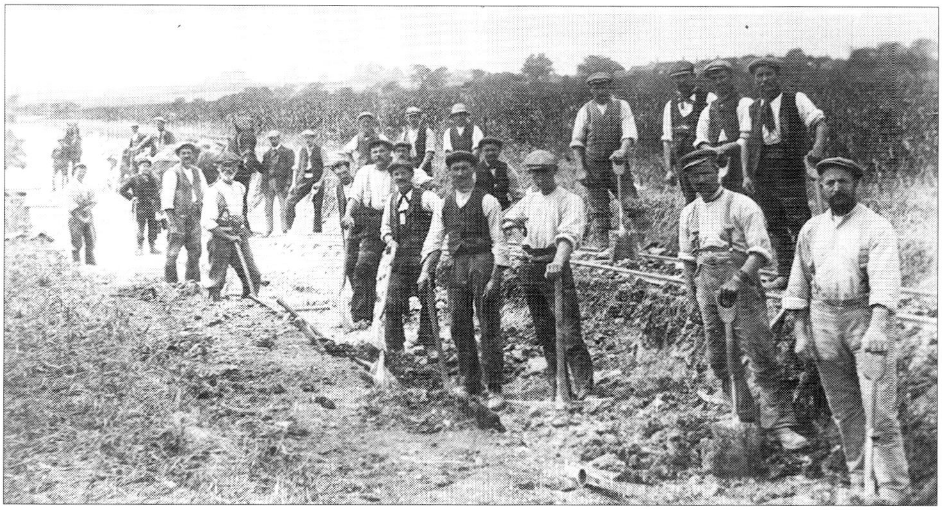

*Excavating the track bed for the East Kent Railway line near Eythorne. The narrow gauge track on the right was used to carry away spoil.* (Hollingsbee Collection – Timanstone WI)

***Below*** *The sinking of the first shaft at Tilmanstone Colliery in 1906. On the left is the headstock of the winding gear over the shaft and, right, the boilers and chimney providing the power.* (Hollingsbee Collection – Tilmanstone WI)

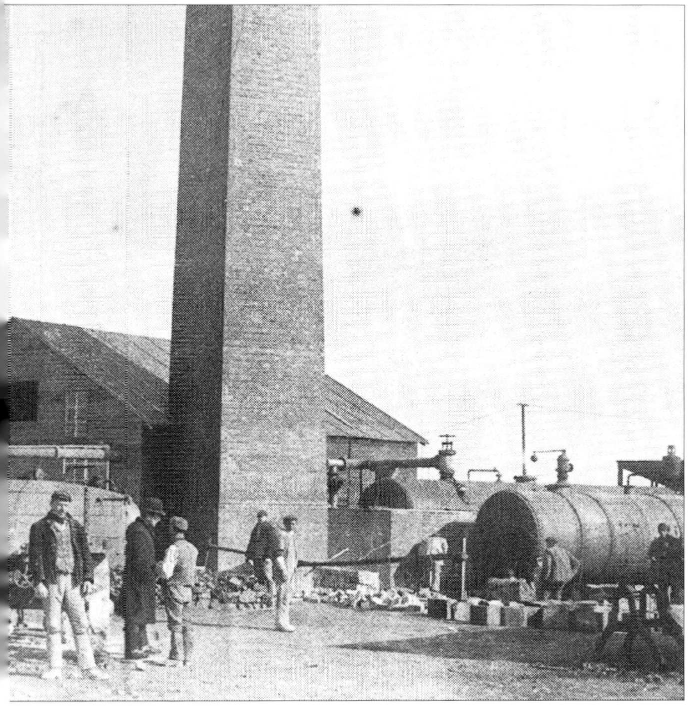

*President of the NUM, Mr Arthur Scargill, with Kent NUM members at the Snowdown Colliery during the industrial dispute that led to the eventual closure of the coalfield in 1987.* (Hollingsbee Collection – Tilmanstone WI)

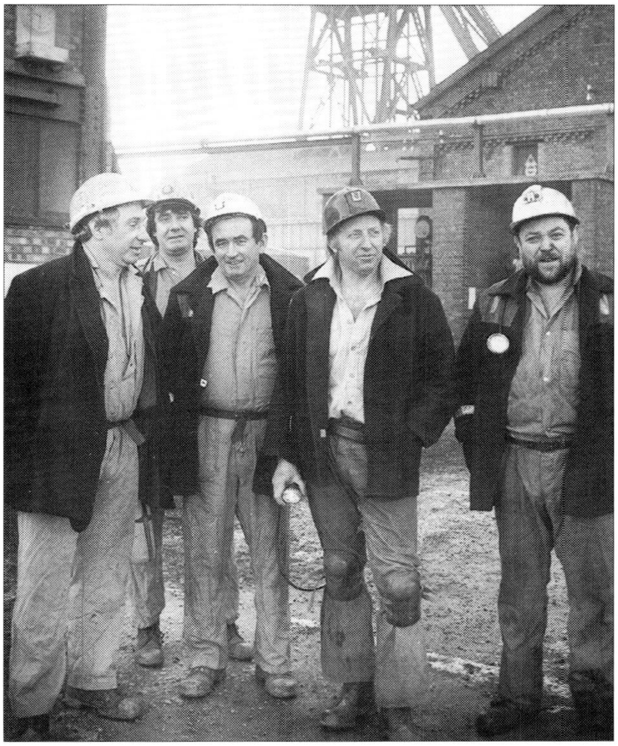

# BETWEEN THE WARS

## (1920 – 1938)

A Land Fit For Heroes had been the promise at the end of the war but returning servicemen, many of them disabled, found instead massive unemployment and a lack of housing. The Great Depression of 1929–31 also caused very real hardship. Council-built rented houses were part of the answer, many of which had running water and electric light, conveniences still lacking in the majority of homes.

Despite the depression, mass production brought more affordable consumer goods onto the market. This, in turn though, led to a decline in many of the small workshops. Cars became commonplace, and roads had to be improved accordingly. Young people found liberation from Victorian attitudes – no more chaperones for them – and discovered the liberation of lighter styles of dress. Cinema-going opened up new worlds of sophistication and entertainment, and Hollywood became a name familiar to all.

Women who had kept the factories and farms running during the war found themselves rewarded with the vote – though only for those over 30! It was 1928 before full equality with male voters was granted. Many women found a voice in national affairs through the Women's Institute. From its inception it has campaigned on matters such as housing, health and hygiene, transport, and the protection and preservation of the countryside. In the 1930s it was pressing for adequate school lunches and school milk, for public health and dental health services for children; and for the provision of telephone kiosks in isolated areas. In 1938 Hastingleigh with Elmstead WI called attention to the need for analgesia to be available for childbirth in rural homes.

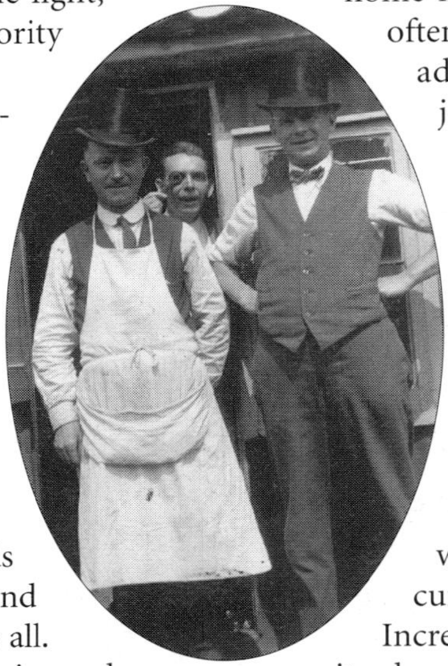

Children growing up between the wars had a freedom and security that later generations would sadly lack. They still played the games their parents and grandparents had played. Since they required so little equipment they were available to even the poorest child, and every game had its season, from marbles to conkers. On summer holidays they left home in the morning and would not return often until teatime, enjoying their own adventures and without care. Many joined their families in the hopfields in the autumn, when the annual picking was still a magnet for holidaying Eastenders and local people alike who relied on the money for their winter clothes.

In 1937 the Kent and Canterbury Hospital was opened. Doctors charged for their services though the 'Panel' was available to the very poor, and often families would go without medical care, home cures being much in demand.

Increased investment in the 1920s, much of it when Dorman Long entered the industry, brought expansion to the East Kent coalfields.

In 1923 the Southern Railway was formed and an improving rail service gave a substantial boost to the Kent coastal resorts. Margate, Ramsgate, Broadstairs, Herne Bay and Whitstable were just a few that flourished, with their famous seaside landladies, their piers and pierrots, and open air concert parties. Day trippers could get to the seaside from far inland, making a memorable treat for Sunday school and chapel outings. In 1927 the Romney, Hythe and Dymchurch Light Railway opened, a small gauge system that was later extended to Dungeness and is still running both as a tourist attraction and for commercial purposes.

*The carpenter, French polisher and stonemason (Mr Emptage from Margate) outside the carpenter's shop in Albert Road, Deal in 1930 – coffins were made on the spot.* (Mrs J. Davies – Walmer WI)

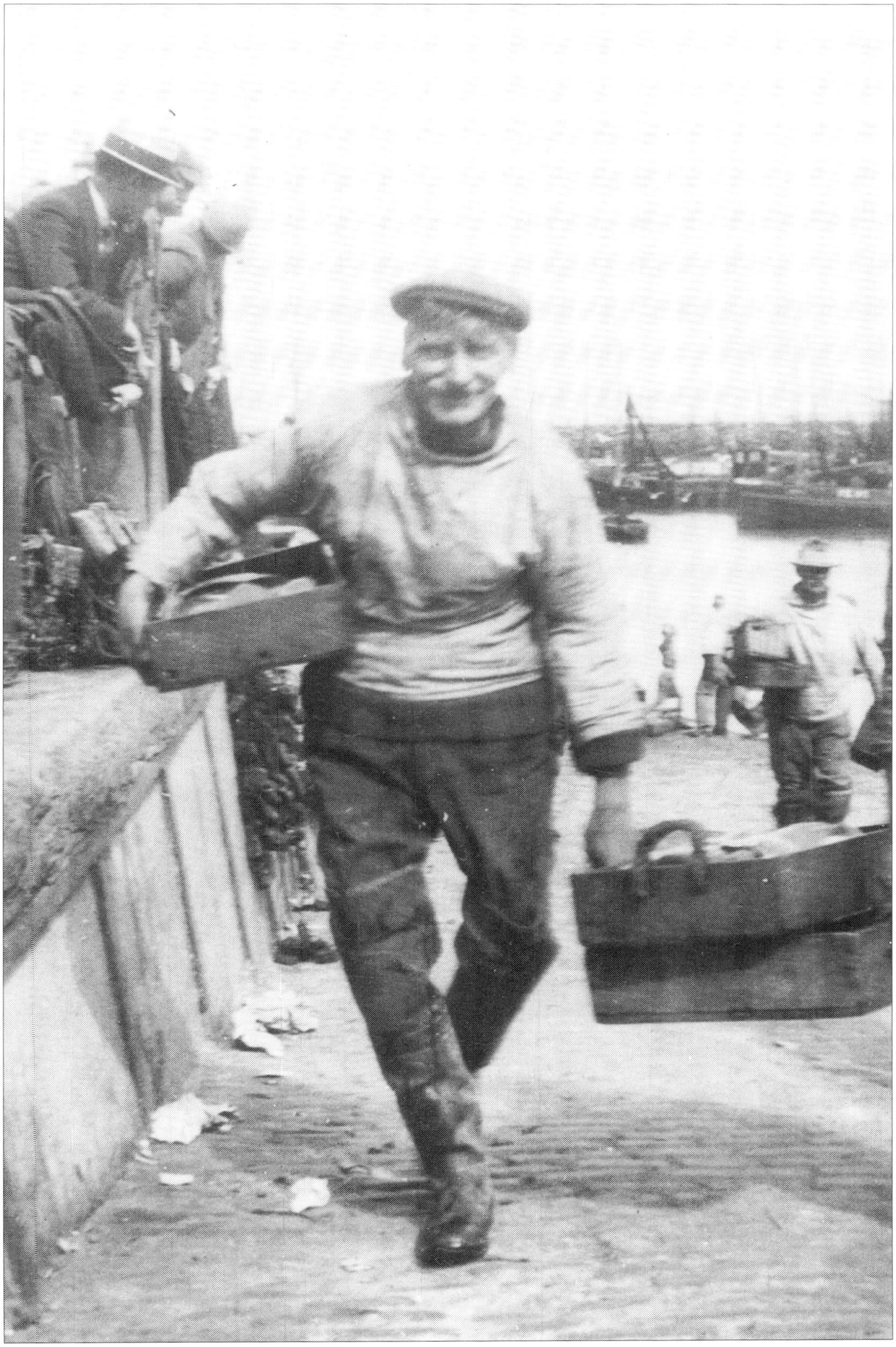

# 1920 – 1938

*Alfred May, fisherman and trawler owner, bringing part of the catch up the slipway at Folkestone Harbour in the 1930s.*
(Mrs A. Beaney – Hawkinge WI)

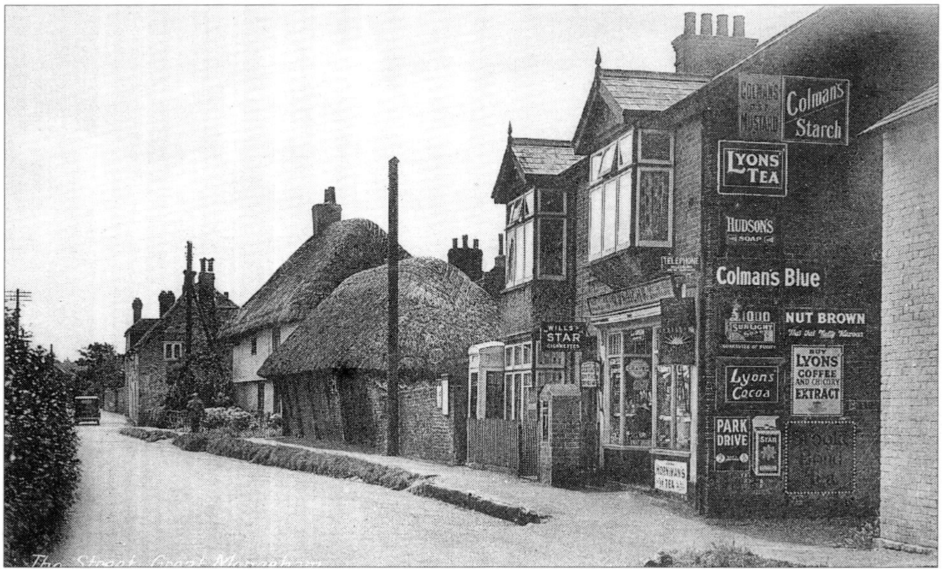


*The Street at Great Mongeham in the 1930s, showing the general store and sub post office, and a variety of advertising! The new telephone box stands discreetly to the side.*
(Mrs M. Court – St Martins WI)

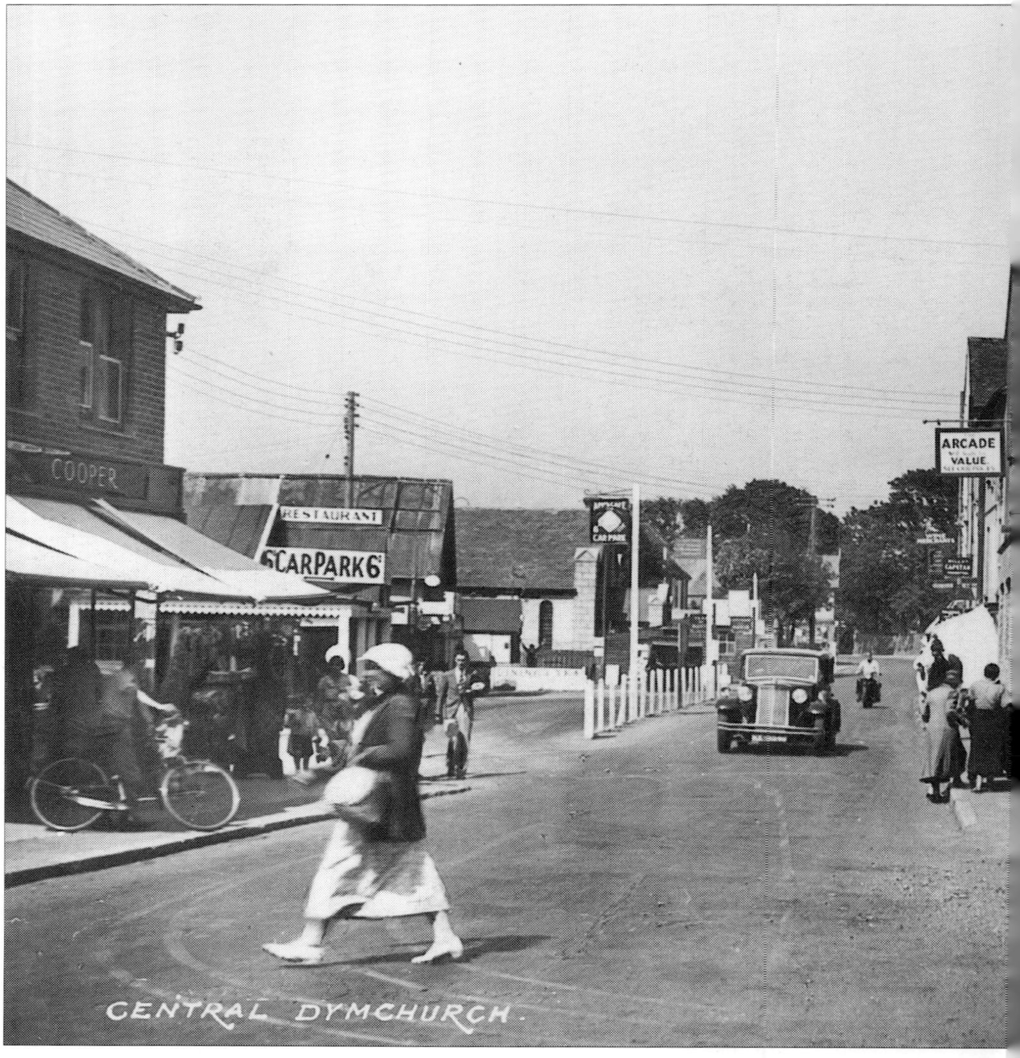


*Central Dymchurch in the 1930s. There are signs of the times in the notice 'Car Park' and in the early petrol pump outside the Central Cycle Stores.*
(Barbara Ware – Orlestone, Ham Street & Ruckinge WI)

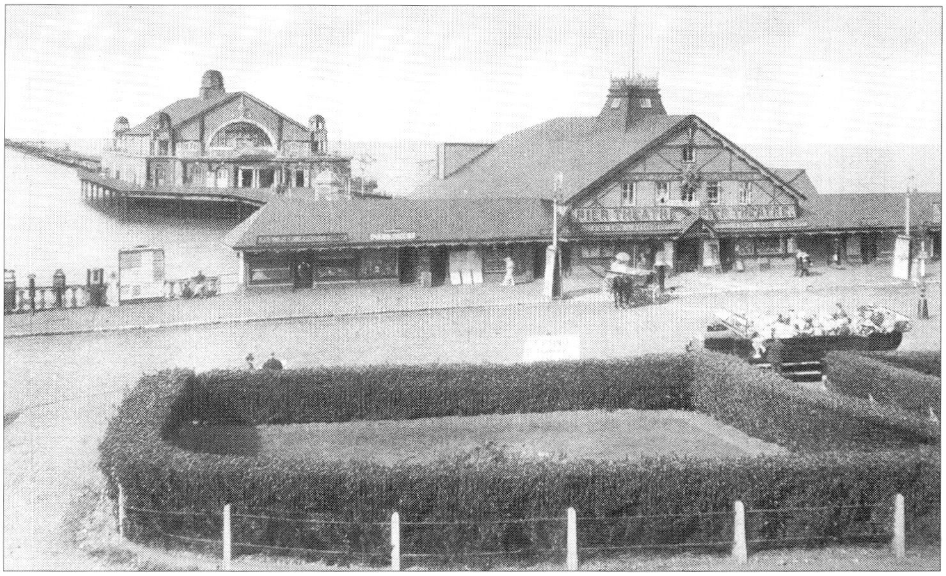


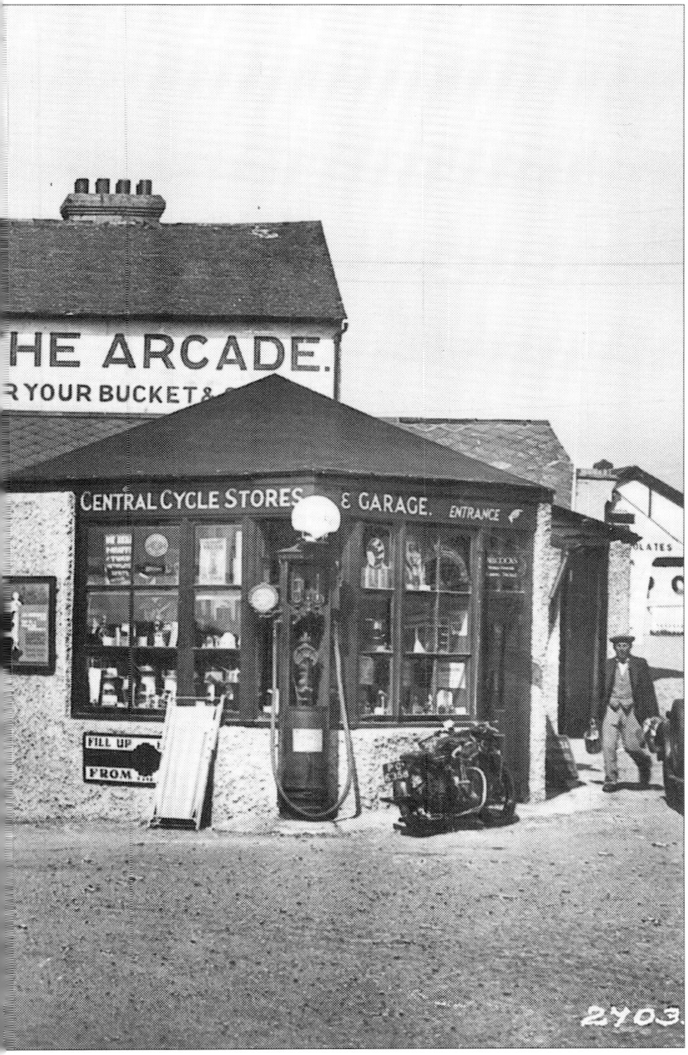


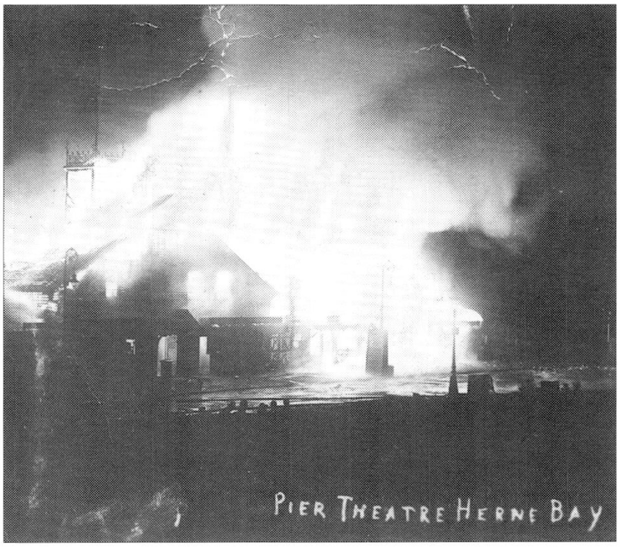


***Above*** *The Old Herne Bay Pier Theatre in 1920, and the scene on the night it was destroyed by fire, Sunday 9th September 1928. The glow from the fire could be seen for 30 miles.*
(Dorothy Martin – South Street WI & Pat Twyman – Herne WI)

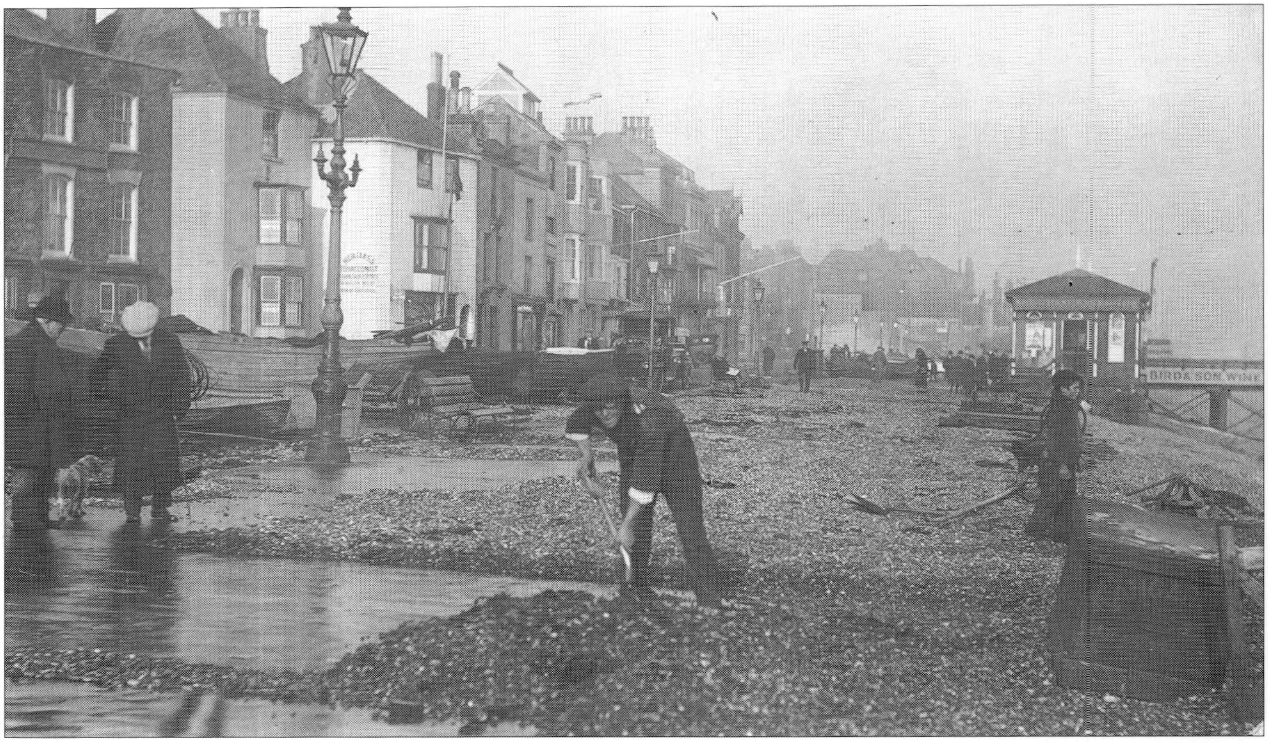

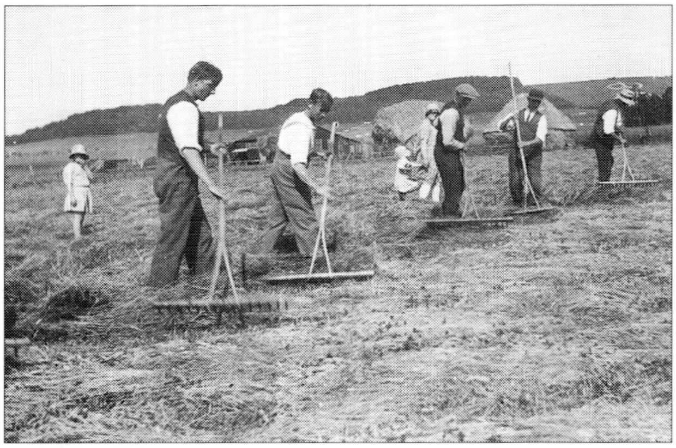

*The Brice family and others hay raking by hand at Wye in 1928. The scent of new-mown hay was one of the delights of summer and young and old would be seen out in the fields.*
(Mrs N. Tutt – Wye WI)

***Right*** *A load of threshed wheat straw being taken along Wey Street road on Romney Marsh in about 1920.*
(Mrs A. Hammon – Stowting WI)

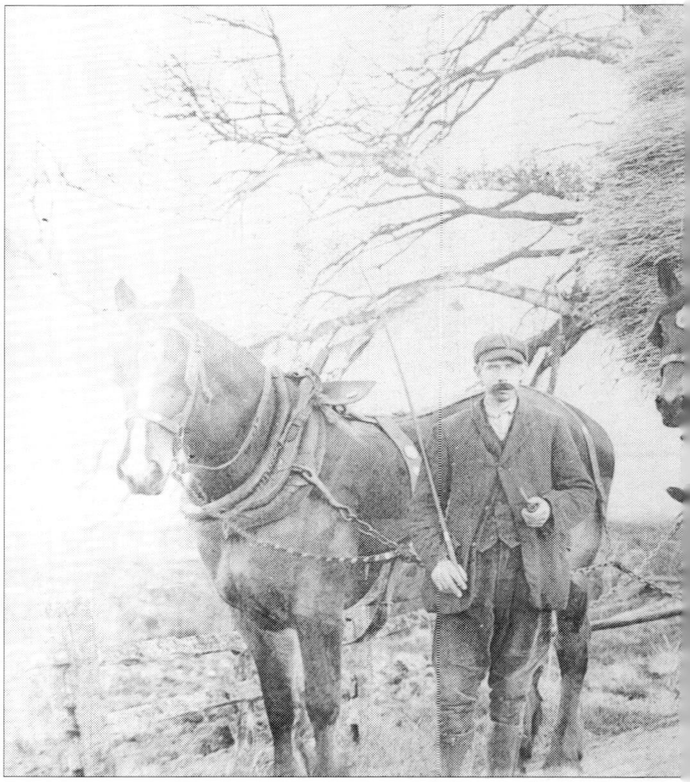

***Left*** *Storms and high tides pose a continuing threat to all coastal settlements and then as now, someone had to clear up afterwards. This was the aftermath of a storm at Deal in the 1920s.*
(Mrs W. Oram –River WI)

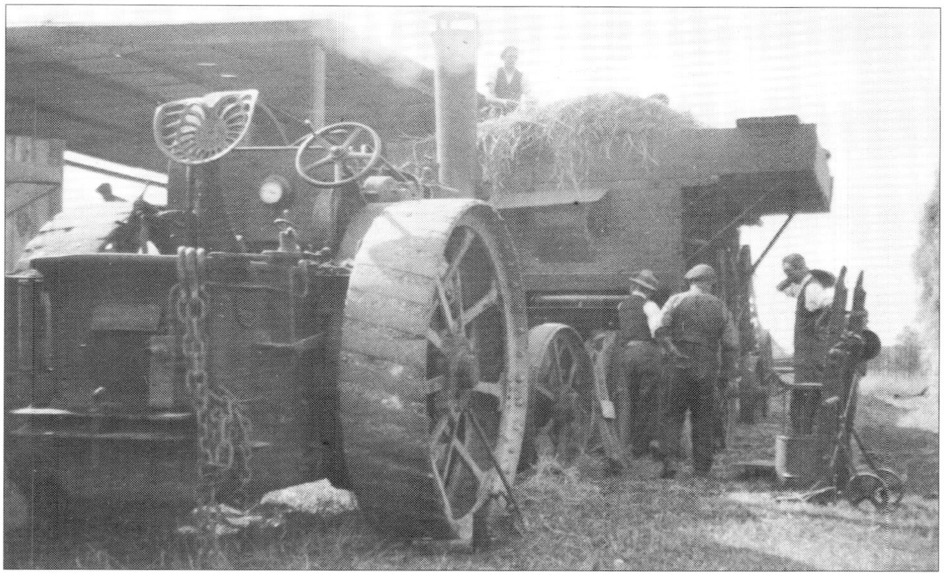

*Threshing in the 1930s meant the arrival in the farmyard of the local threshing machine. The man with his back to the camera was the operator of the machine and biked to and from Egerton. Farmers' wives prided themselves on their hospitality during this busy time and he became so fond of Mrs Vant's home-made wine that one day he never made it home, but had to sleep it off under the machine.*
(Joan Vant – Painters Forstal with Ospringe WI)

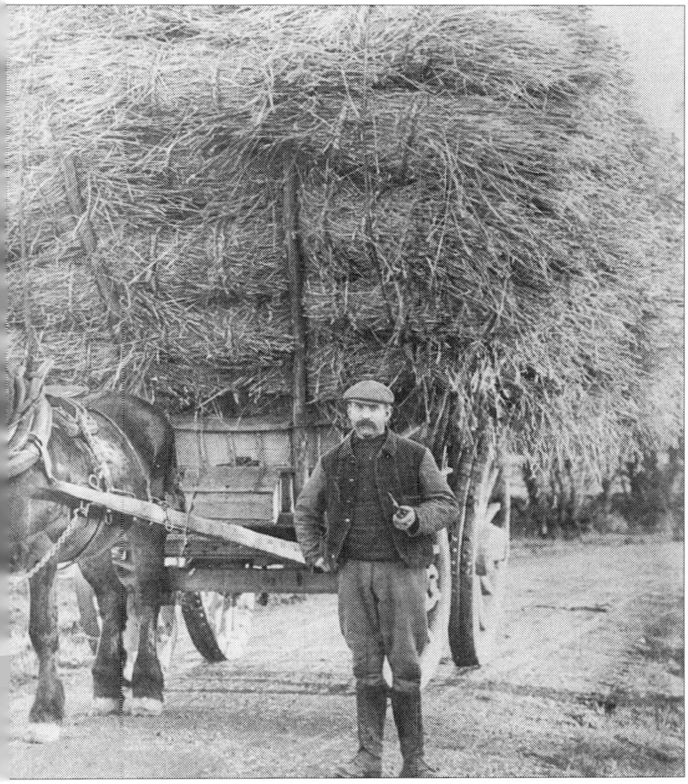

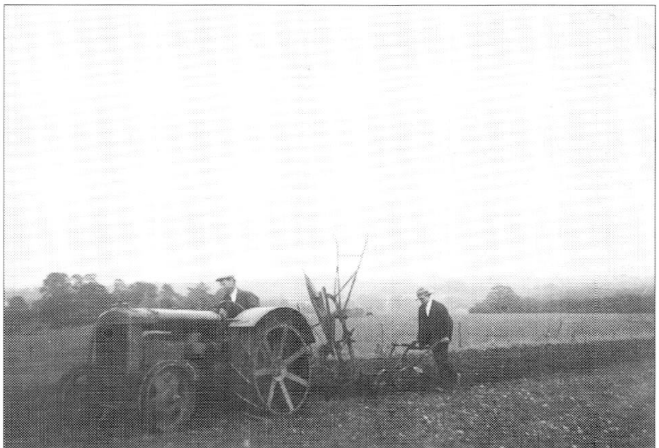

*Dick Vant driving the 1930s blue Fordson tractor at Stalisfield and George Hawkins steering the balancing plough, a combination of the old and the new at this time of transition from horses to machines.*
(Joan Vant – Painters Forstal with Ospringe WI)

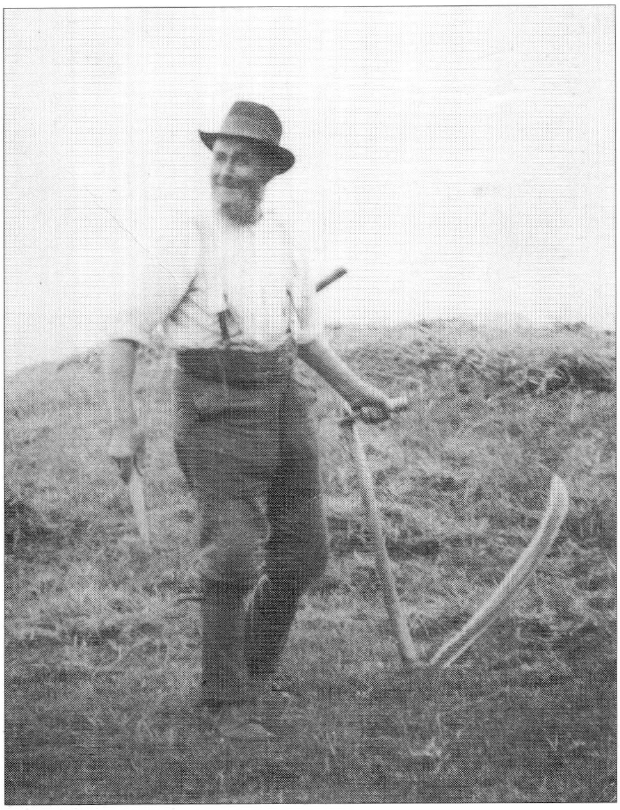

*Frederick Stannard, groundsman at Herne Bay golf links in 1938.* (Mrs P. Zergeang – Herne WI)

*The local 'big house' employed both indoor and outdoor staff – these chauffeurs on Sir Henry Dering's staff at Pluckley in the 1920s are posing by their master's car.* (Mrs J. Webb – Willesborough & Newton WI)

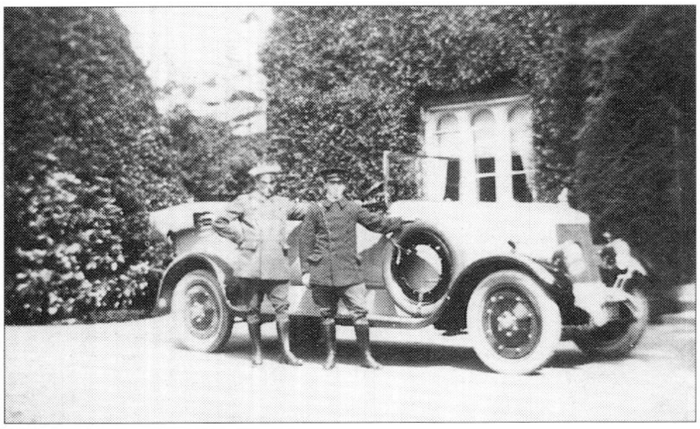

***Right** Young girls in 'training' for service in the late 1930s at the Northbourne Preparatory School for Boys, near Goodnestone, In their early teens, they worked from 7 am to 8 pm, sometimes longer, with two hours off in the afternoon and a half day once a week – all for 10 shillings a week, which most of them were expected to send home. They worked as maids, kitchen staff and cleaners.* (Mrs G. Wray – Goodnestone WI)

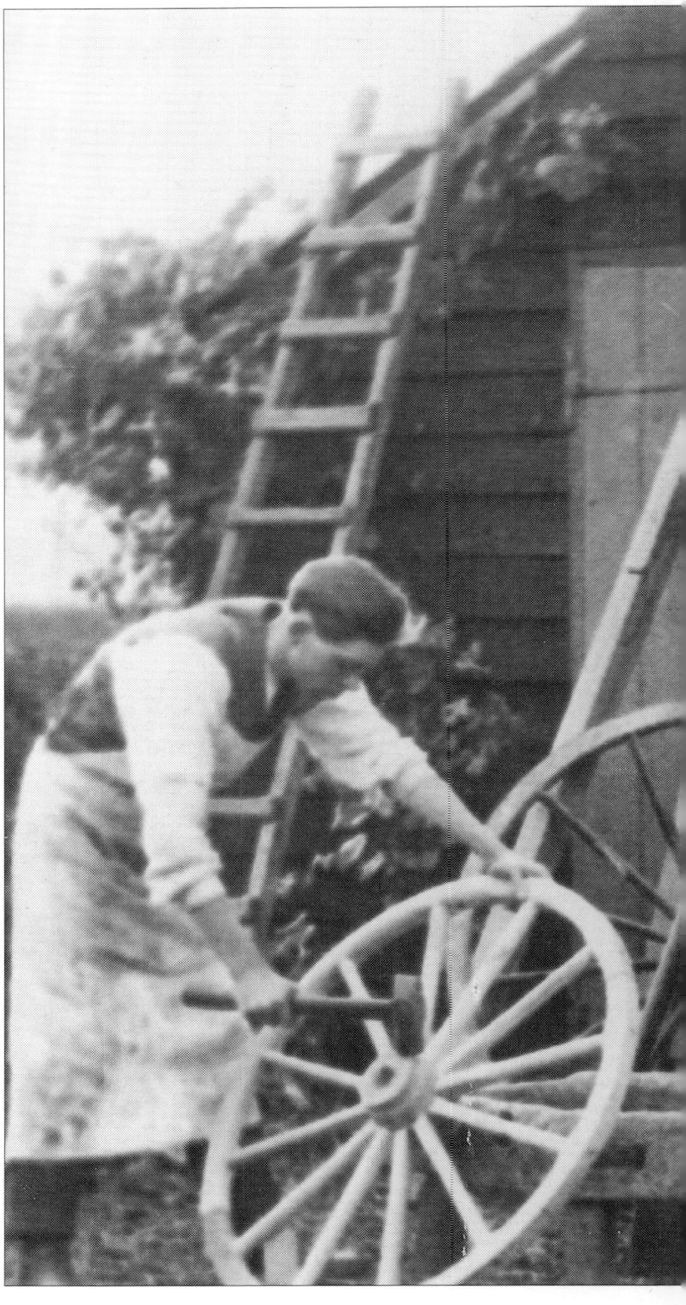

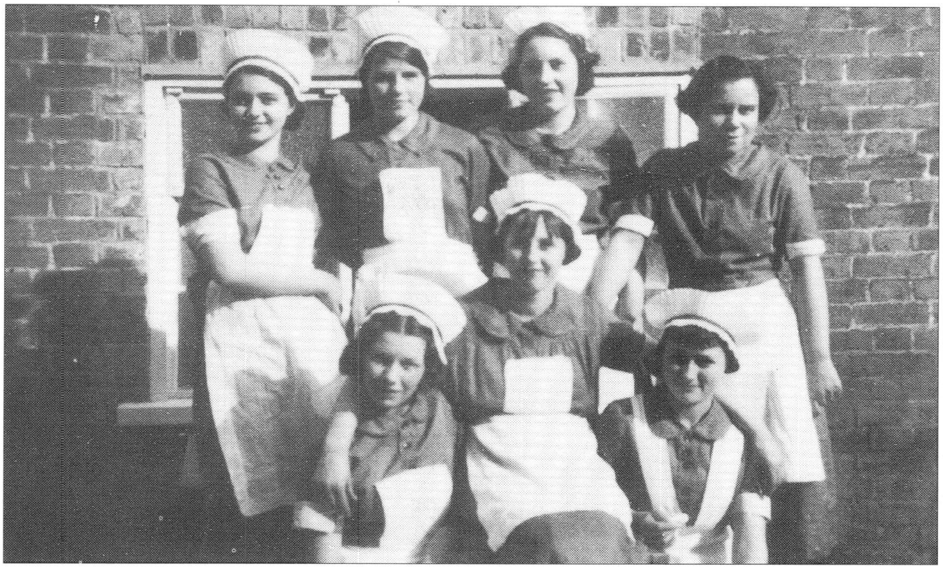

*Below* **Below** *The wheelwright's shop at Kingsnorth, near Ashford in 1925. Wheelwright A.E. Bailey, Mrs Terry's father, is on the right. The wheels would be finished with iron tyres at the forge.*
(Mrs P. Terry – Kingsnorth WI)

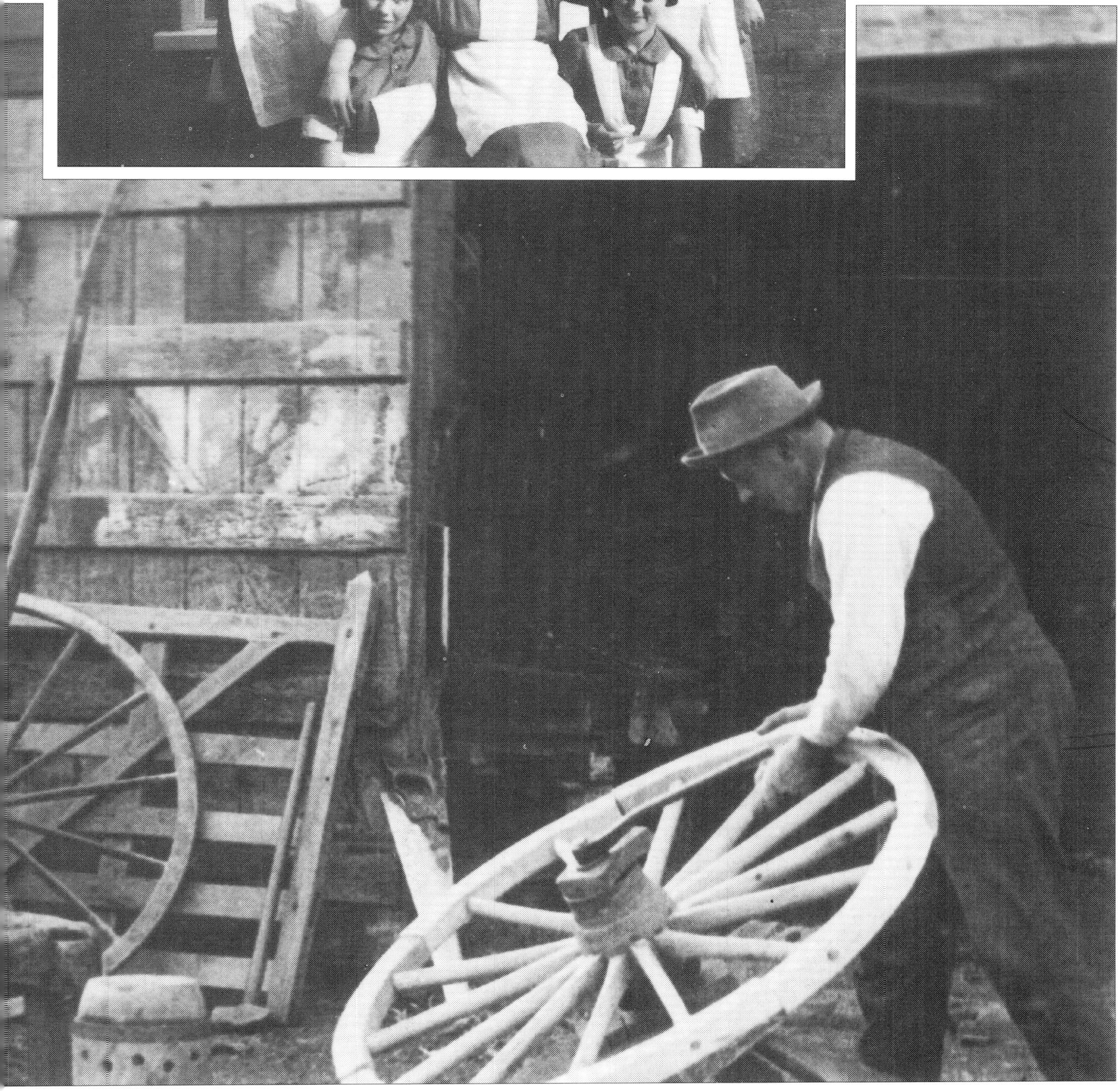

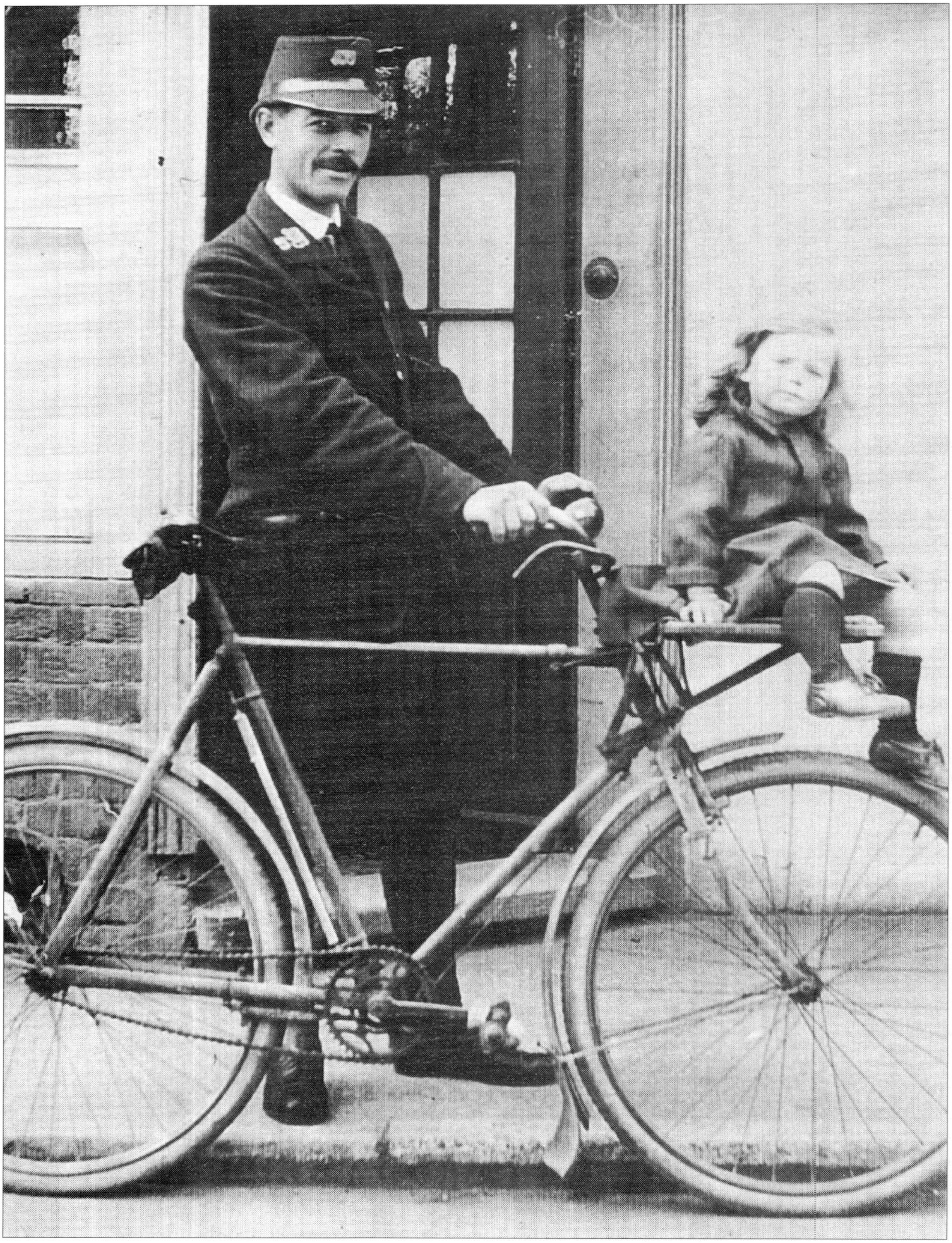

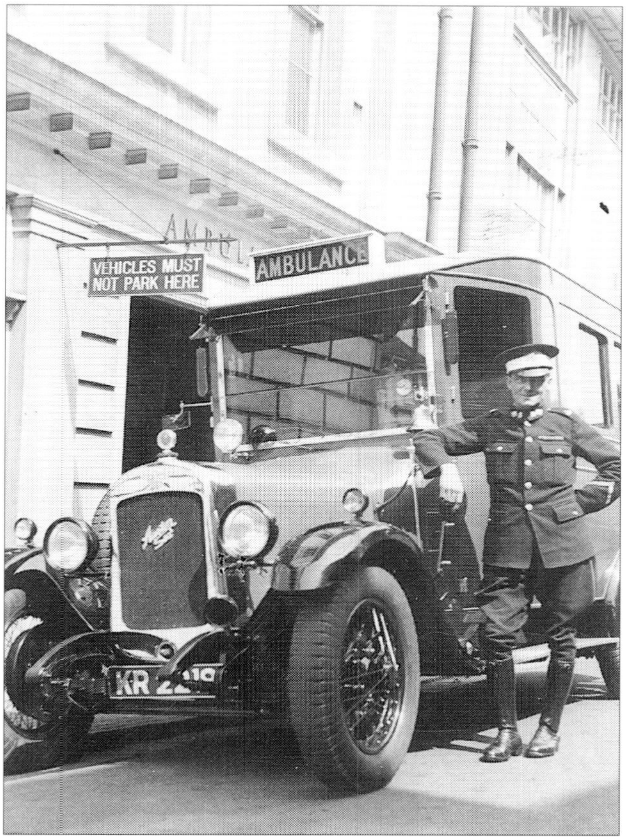


*The St John Ambulance Brigade was formed by Sir John Furley of Ashford in 1879, and the Ashford Corps is the earliest still in existence. They acquired their first horse-drawn ambulance in 1906, becoming motorised in 1909, and in 1927 George Thompsett became their first full time driver, at £3 a week. He was on call night and day. Here he is standing by his first ambulance outside the ambulance station in Middle Row, Ashford.*
(Grace Thompsett – Kennington WI)

*A postman from the Eastry sub post office in the early 1920s.*
(Mrs M. Court – St Martins WI)

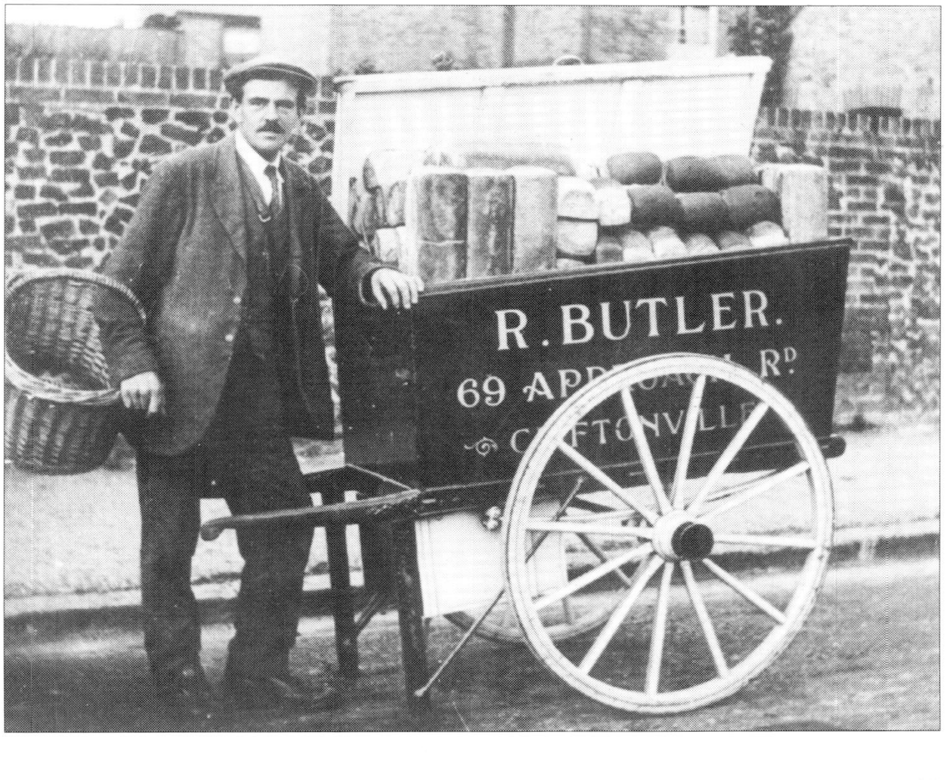


*Vincent Pritchard delivering bread in 1923 at Cliftonville. Local tradesmen brought fresh produce direct to your door; he made two deliveries a day, carrying a normal load of 217 loaves each time.*
(Janet Robinson – Grenham Bay WI)

*Early petrol pumps at Brenzett Garage in the 1920s.*
(Barbara Ware – Orlestone, Ham Street & Ruckinge WI)

*Whitstable Fire Brigade in 1929. New motorised transport meant fire crews could get to fires with greater speed than in the days of hand or horse-drawn engines.*
(Jean Camburn – Swalecliffe with Chestfield WI)

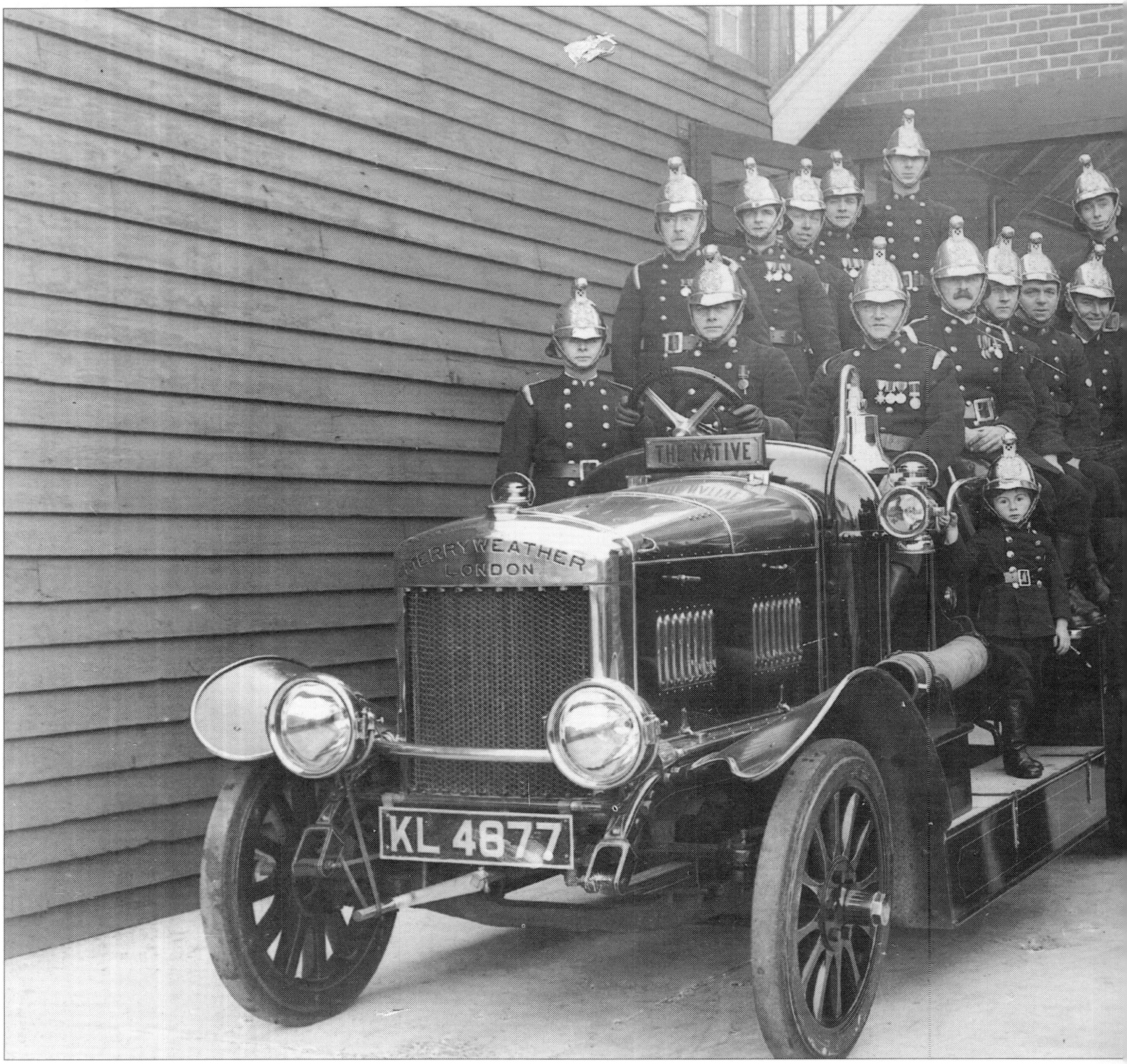

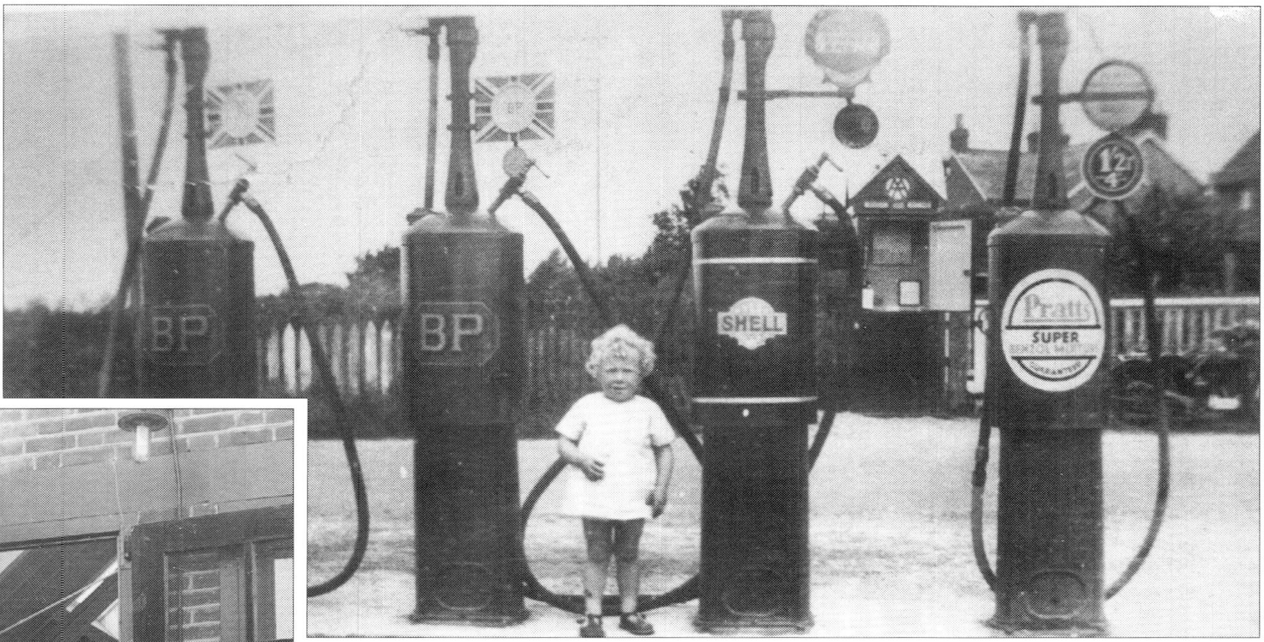


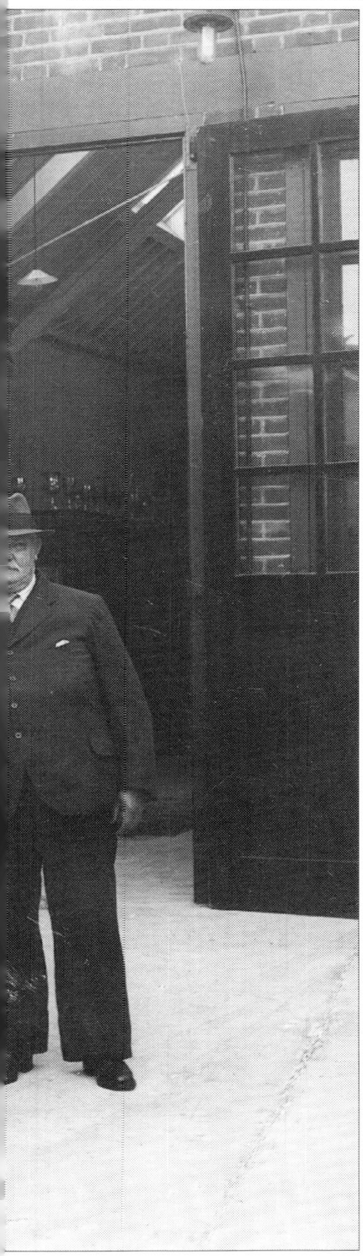

*An array of cars outside the garage of the Bell Hotel at Sandwich Barbican. The reason for the gathering is not known, but a chauffeur stands beside each car at a time when motoring was still only for the wealthy. The garage was pulled down in 1926.*
(Audrey Lowley – Whitfield WI)

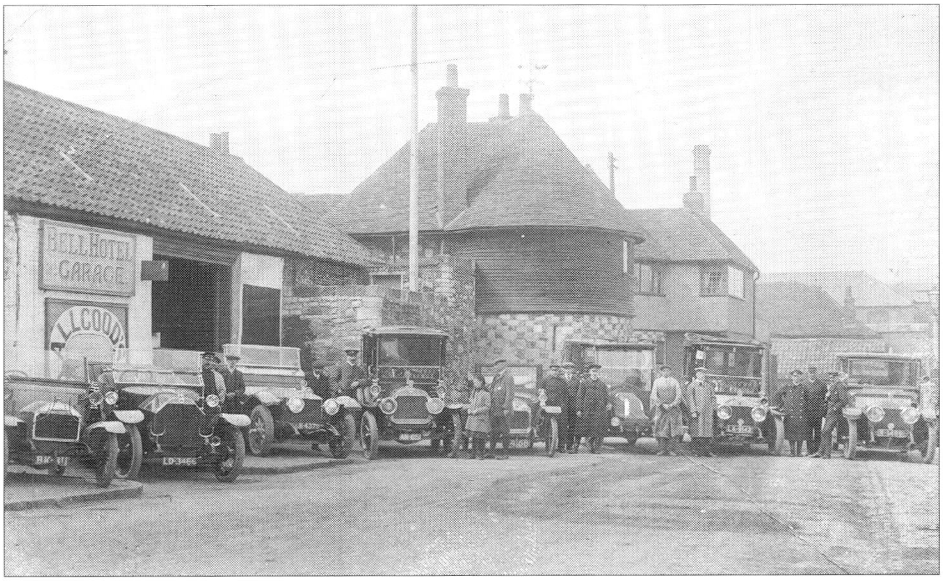

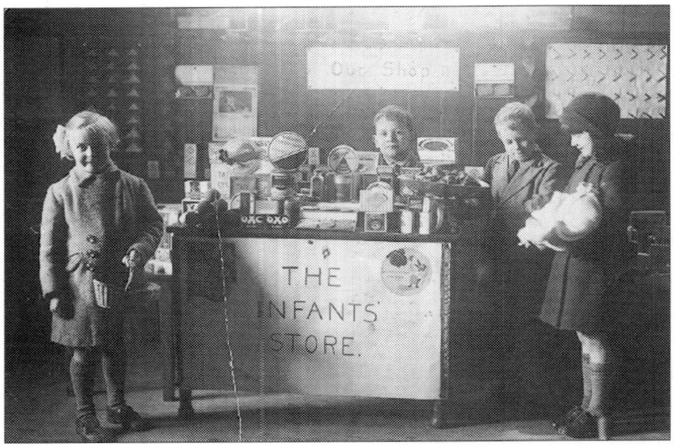


*The school shop at Egerton primary school in the late 1930s. Sadly, many of the items 'on sale' in their store would soon be rationed.* (Priscilla Harper – Egerton WI)

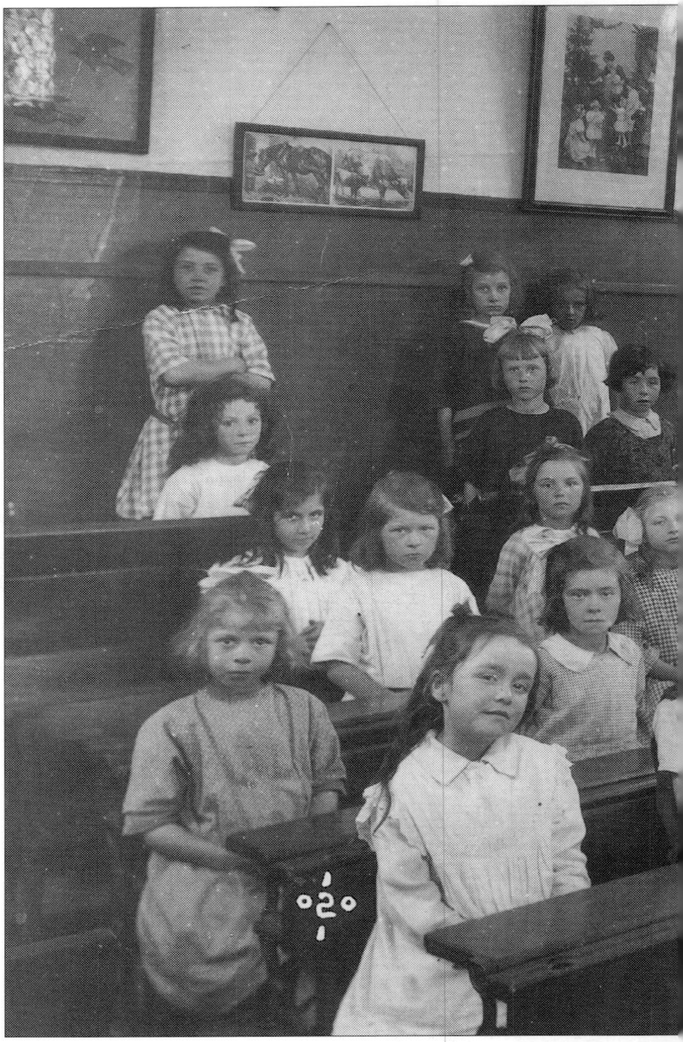

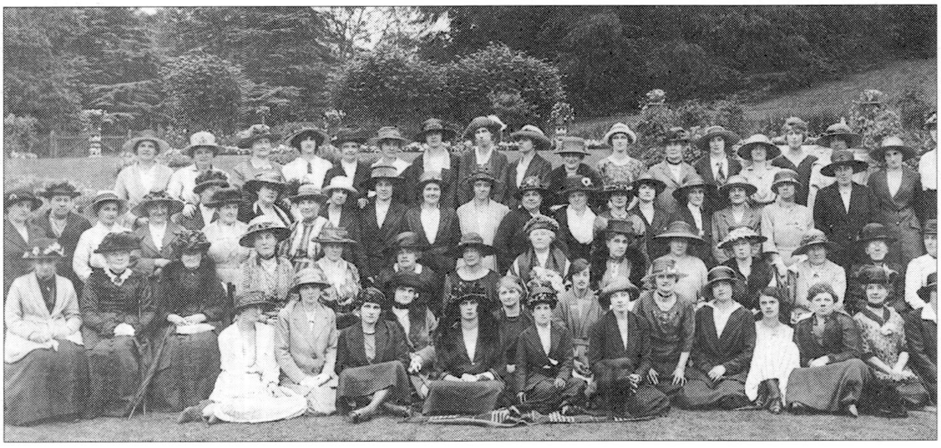

*Members of Wye Women's Institute in September 1922. Wye WI, formed in 1917, was the first Institute in East Kent and one of the first twelve in the whole country. The group includes three County Chairmen, present and future – Mrs Dunstan (2nd row down, 6th from l.); Mrs J. Loudon (3rd row down, 8th from l.); Miss Dorothy Erle-Drax (seated, 9th from l.).* (Mrs A. Findlay – Wye WI)

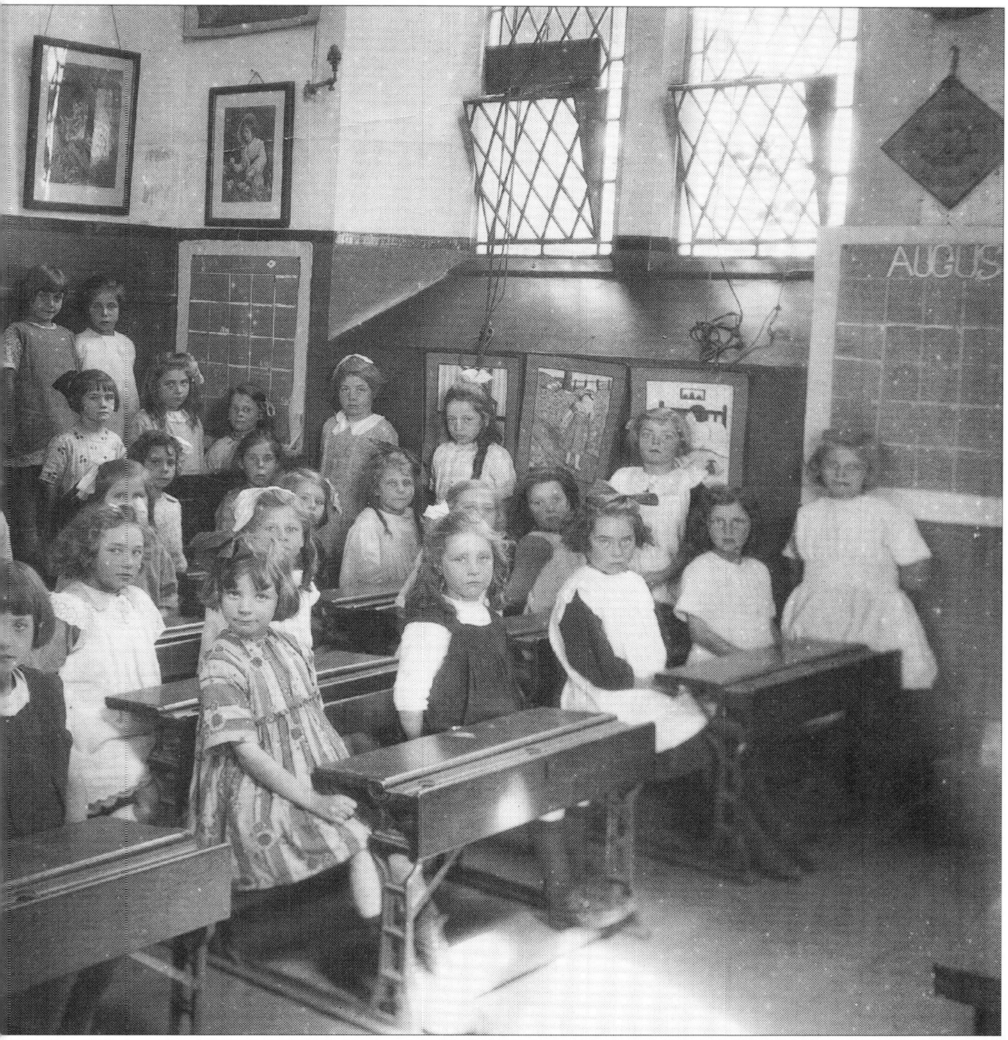

*Newtown Girls' School (infants) in 1924. The railway came to Ashford in 1842 and the company built a 'Newtown' for the employees to live in. The school was built in 1852. By 1924 another school had been built next door for girls after the age of seven. Today the school has been turned into flats and the railway workshops are gone.*
(Grace Thompsett – Kennington WI)

*William Fuller, general dealer, with his pony and trap and a cab that he hired out for village fetes and weddings. He is pictured coming down through Appledore on his way home to Snargate in 1936.*
(Mrs J. Fuller – Brenzett WI)

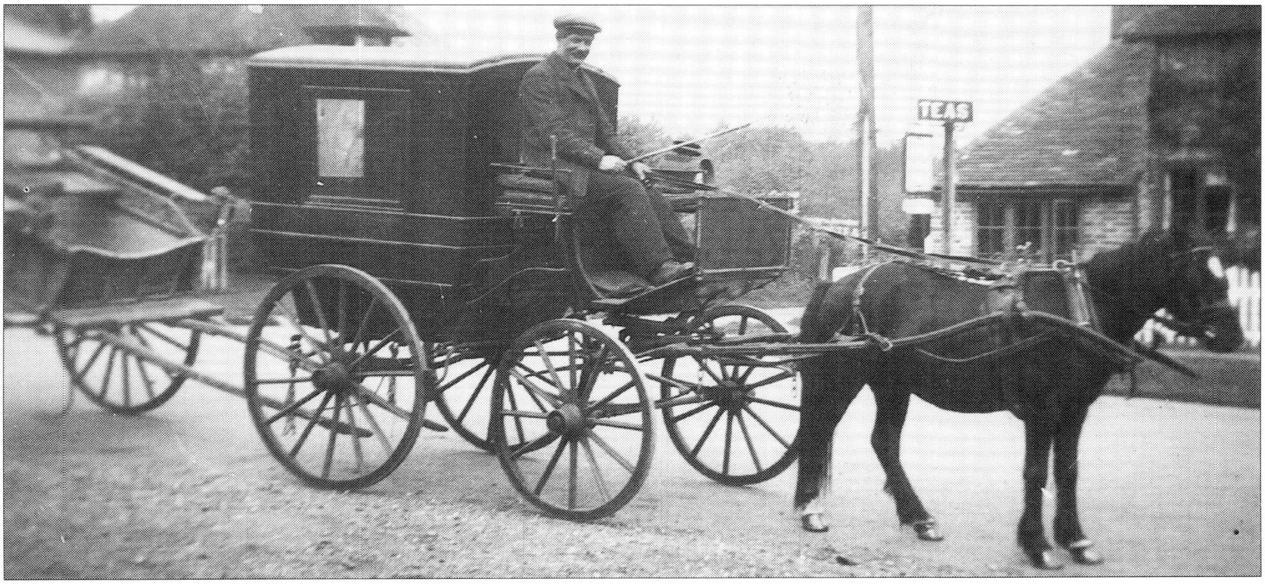

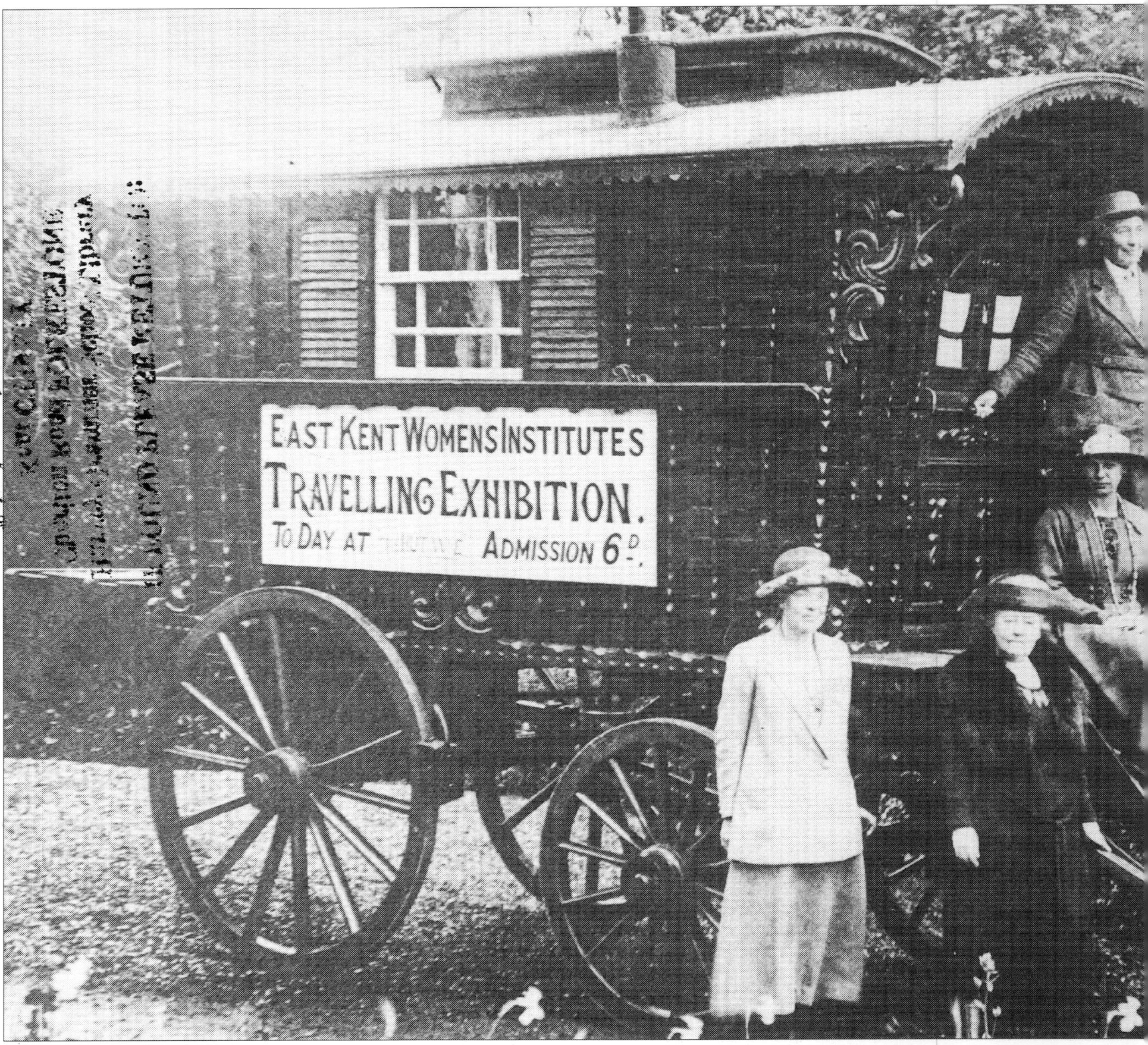


*The East Kent Federation of Women's Institutes was formed in 1919 and the WI 'Travelling Exhibition', which visited all parts of the county over the next few years, is pictured here at Wye, 1921. L to r: Mrs Barnard (Federation Chairman 1930–4), Mrs Dunstan (the first Chairman), Miss Gwen Newnham, Miss Florence Beard, and Miss Dorothy Erle-Drax.*
(Anne Findlay – Wye WI)

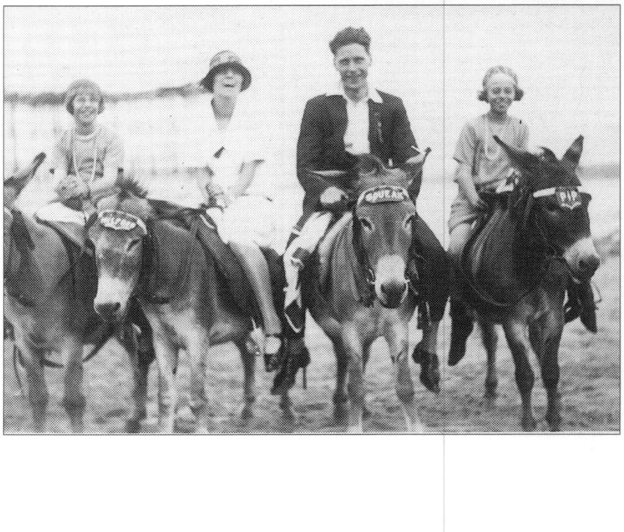

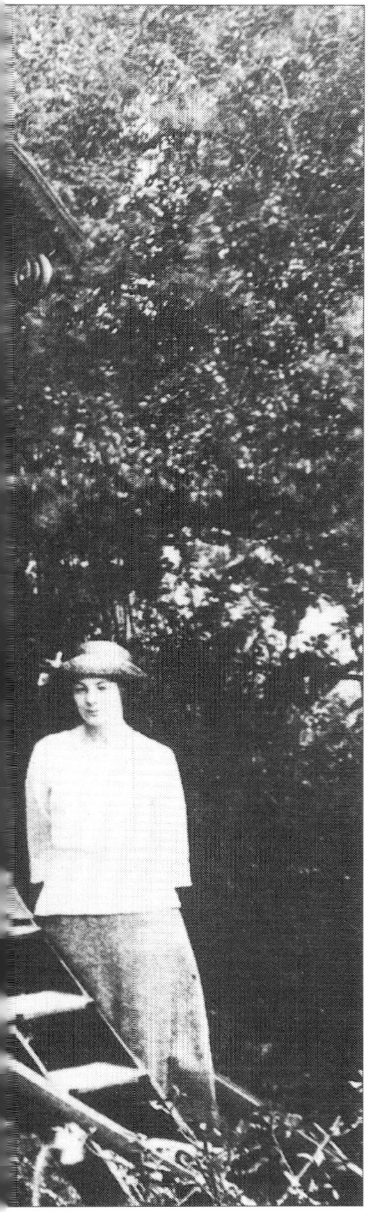

A donkey ride was part of the fun on holiday and could be enjoyed at Westgate, Margate, Broadstairs and Ramsgate. Interrupted by the war, they were started up again in the late 1940s and continued to delight youngsters of all ages. This quartet were at Ramsgate in 1924.
(Ivy Streatfield – Swalecliffe with Chestfield WI)

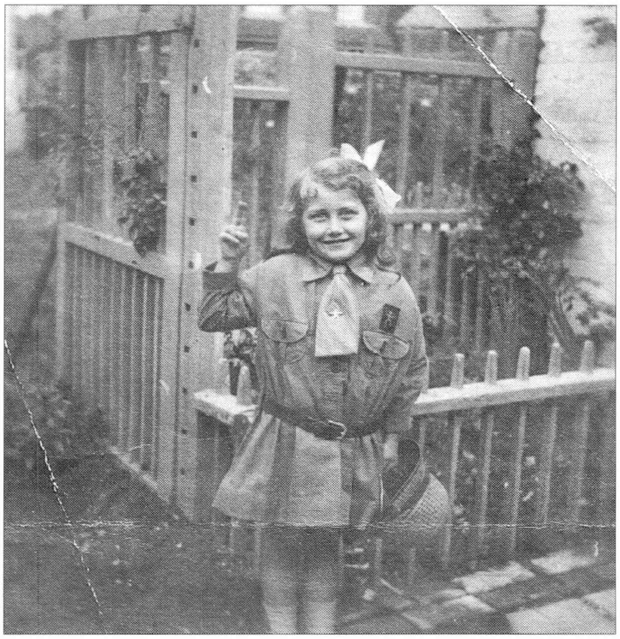

*A proud member of the Brownies in 1927 at Deal.*
(Mrs J. Davies – Walmer WI)

IF FOUND PLEASE RETURN TO:
Harvey Grammar School Library
Cheriton Road FOLKESTONE
Kent CT19 5JY
Telephone: 01303 252131

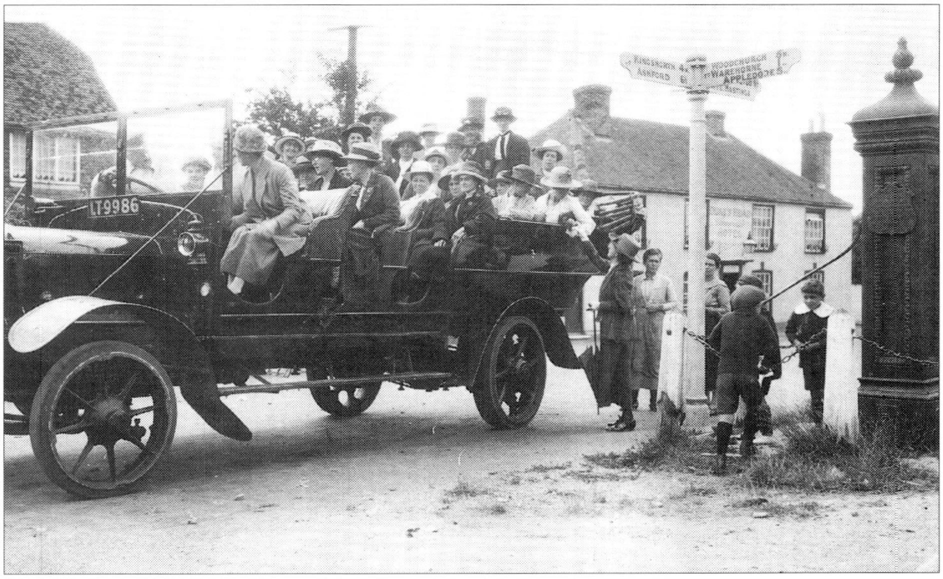


*A stop by the village pump at Ham Street for refreshment for this ladies' outing from Brooklands in the 1920s. Many villages continued to rely on pumps and wells for their water until after the Second World War. Charabancs were popular forms of transport for group outings, travelling at about ten or twelve miles per hour along the country lanes. The hood at the back could be pulled over if it rained.*
(Barabara Ware – Orlestone, Ham Street & Ruckinge WI)

*On the sands at Broadstairs in 1930.*
(Mrs A. Webb – Hernhill WI)

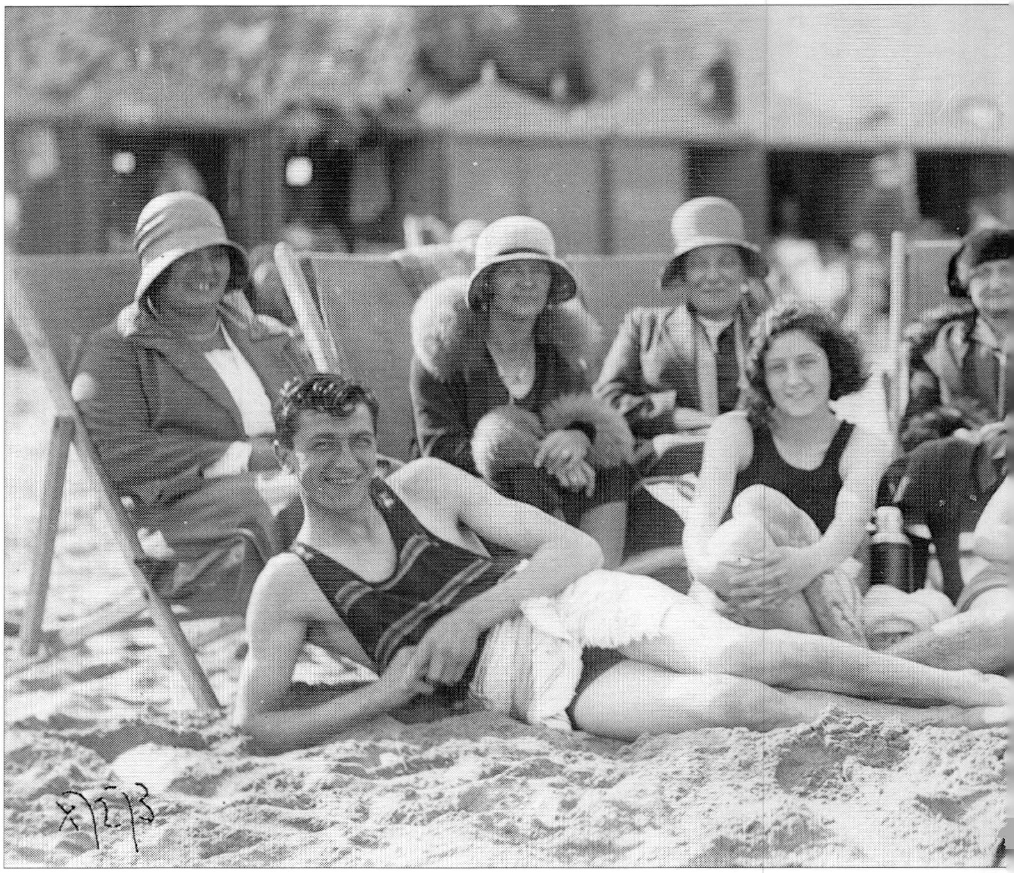

*On the greasy pole at Whitstable Regatta in the summer of 1938.*
(Mary Williams – Kennington WI)

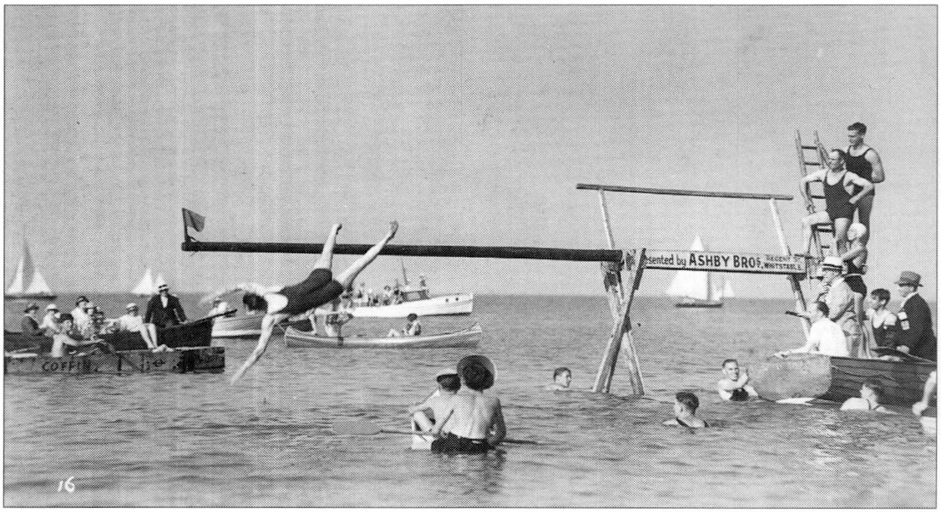


***Right** On another Royal day in the 1930s, the children of Preston having a good time on George VI's Coronation Day, 1937.*
(Mrs J. Tong – Preston, Elmstone & Stourmouth WI)

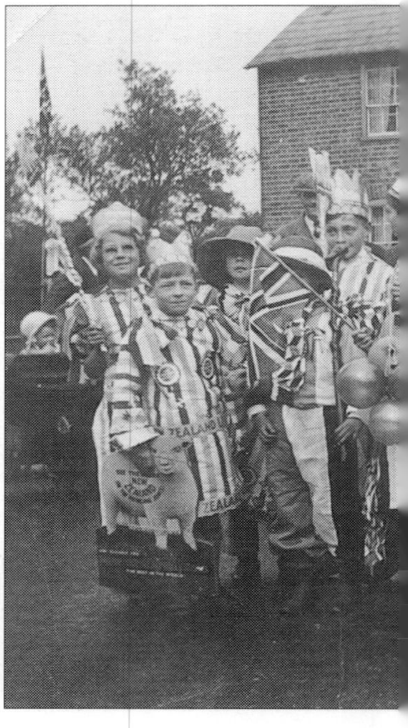

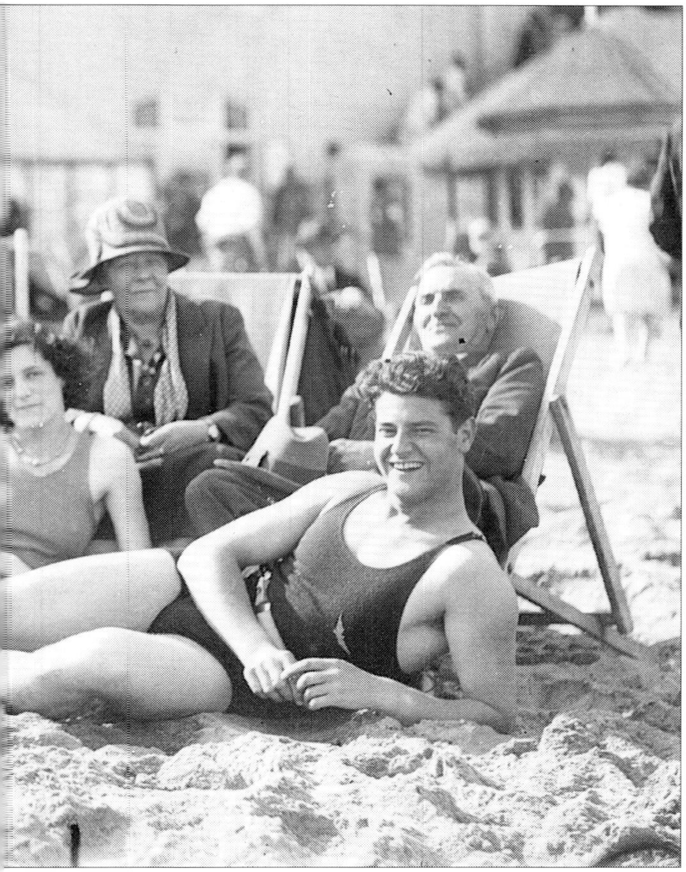

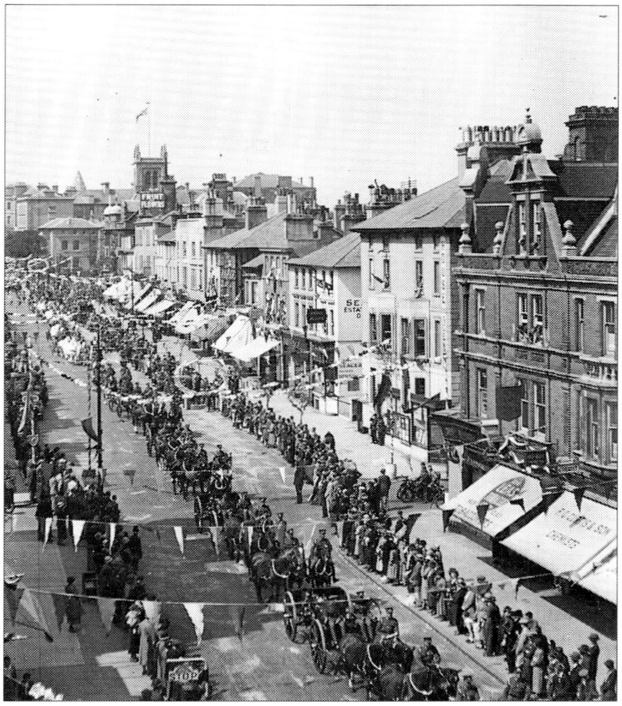

***Below*** *Lea Front, Herne Bay as it was in the 1920s. The diving boards were there until the war when they were removed and never replaced.* (Wendy Penn – St Nicholas at Wade WI)

*The procession down Sandgate Road, Folkestone for George V's Silver Jubilee celebrations in 1935.* (Mrs P. Tiddy – South Street WI)

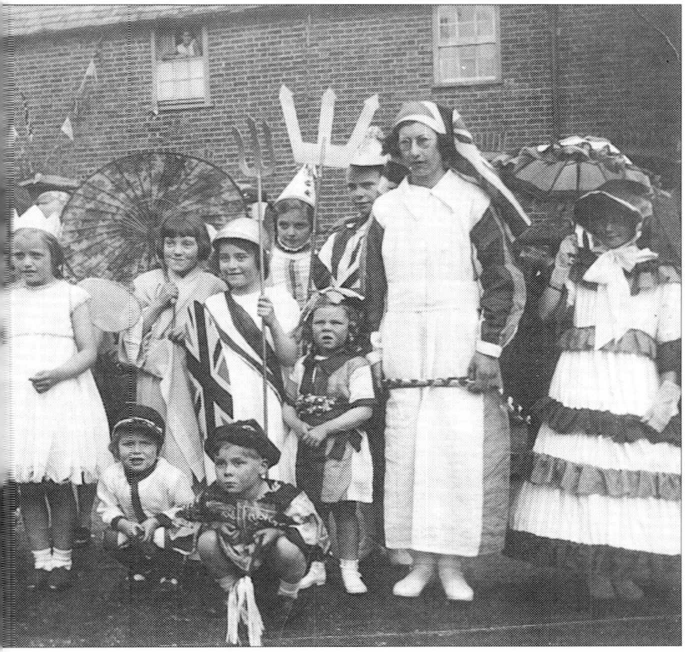

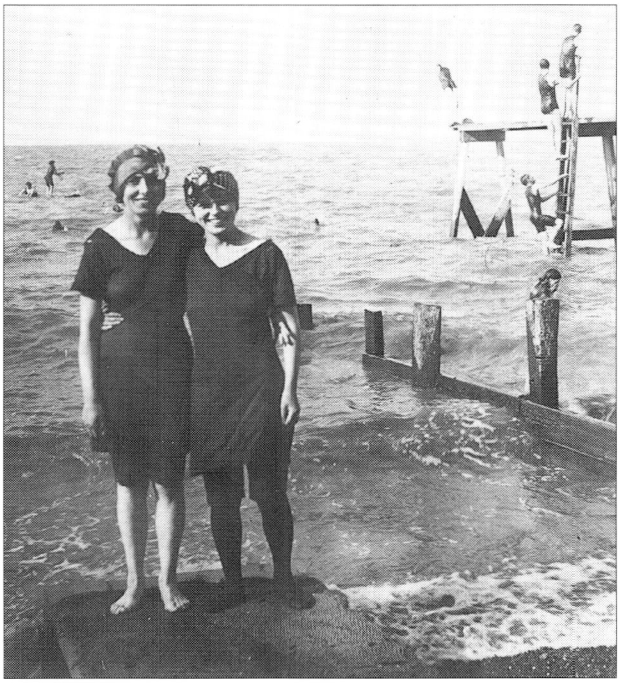

# The Second World War

## (1939 – 1945)

In 1939 the British Expeditionary Force embarked at Dover and Folkestone for France: once again we were at war and this time East Kent would feel the full ferocity of modern armaments.

At first it seemed to be a 'phoney war' – buildings were sandbagged, blackouts imposed, sirens tested, air raid shelters built and gas masks issued, but little happened. Then came the evacuation from Dunkirk in May and June 1940 and we realised fully the dangers that faced us. Many of the armada of little boats that saved a major set-back from becoming a disaster were from East Kent, and the troops brought back from France were landed on these shores. Trains ran non-stop to get them away to safety and local hospitals and volunteers worked tirelessly to give what assistance they could.

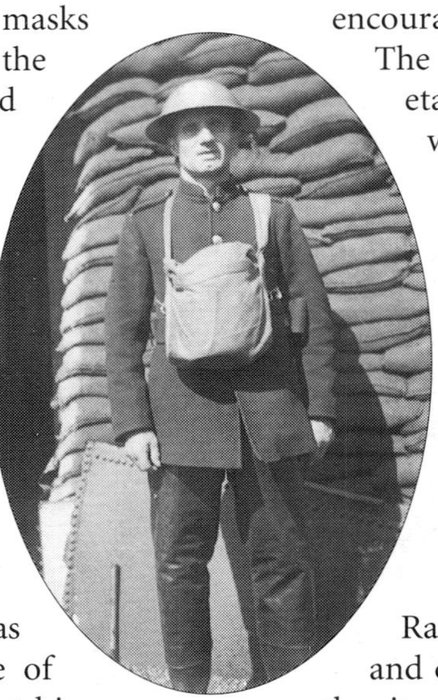

As Winston Churchill warned, the Battle of Britain had begun. It was fought over the heads of the people of Kent that summer, with local people watching the dogfights between RAF and Luftwaffe pilots and hastening to the scene of crashed aircraft. The airfields at Manston, Hawkinge and Lympne were frequently and heavily attacked, with nearby residents suffering. The radar stations that controlled the battle, with their WAAF operators, were situated in East Kent.

We prepared for invasion and the coastline became a restricted area. Houses were commandeered and soldiers billeted in nearby villages. Secret preparations were made to train underground resistance fighters. Dover was bombarded both from the air and by big guns mounted on the Calais coast. There were clashes in the Channel between MTBs based in Dover and German E-boats.

As the war dragged on, young and old joined in the war effort. Civilians volunteered for the Home Guard, Civil Defence and fire-fighting. Women who were called up or volunteered chose between the Services, munitions work and the Women's Land Army. Rationed food was supplemented by home-grown produce and the Dig For Victory campaign encouraged people to use every foot of land. The government called for fruit and vegetable preservation and by 1942 there were 88 WI Preservation Centres in East Kent – in that year alone they produced over 46 tons of jam, two tons of pickles, 31,242 cans and 4,423 bottles. The Produce Guild also encouraged pig clubs, spinning and growing vegetables. Seeds and canning machines came from the USA, and Mrs Roosevelt, the President's wife, visited East Kent WIs to see them in action.

In 1942 the so-called 'Baedeker Raid' on Canterbury killed 115 people and destroyed much of the eastern part of the city. Air raids continued to haunt the county and in 1944 came the V1 'doodlebug' rockets. Their principal route was over Kent, and many were shot down by guns at the coast or by fighter planes overhead, with 2,400 falling in Kent, which was 200 more than landed in London. That year too came the preparations for the Normandy landings, with massive troop concentrations in parts of East Kent. Sections of the Mulberry Harbour were built on the Faversham marshes.

Then at last it was over. In villages and towns all over Kent people lit bonfires, rang the church bells that had been silent for so long, and pooled rations to give children a treat. They thought with grief of those who would not be coming back, and waited with anticipation for loved ones to return at last.

*George Richards, part time fireman, outside a sand-bagged Whitstable fire station in 1940.* (Mary Williams – Kennington WI)

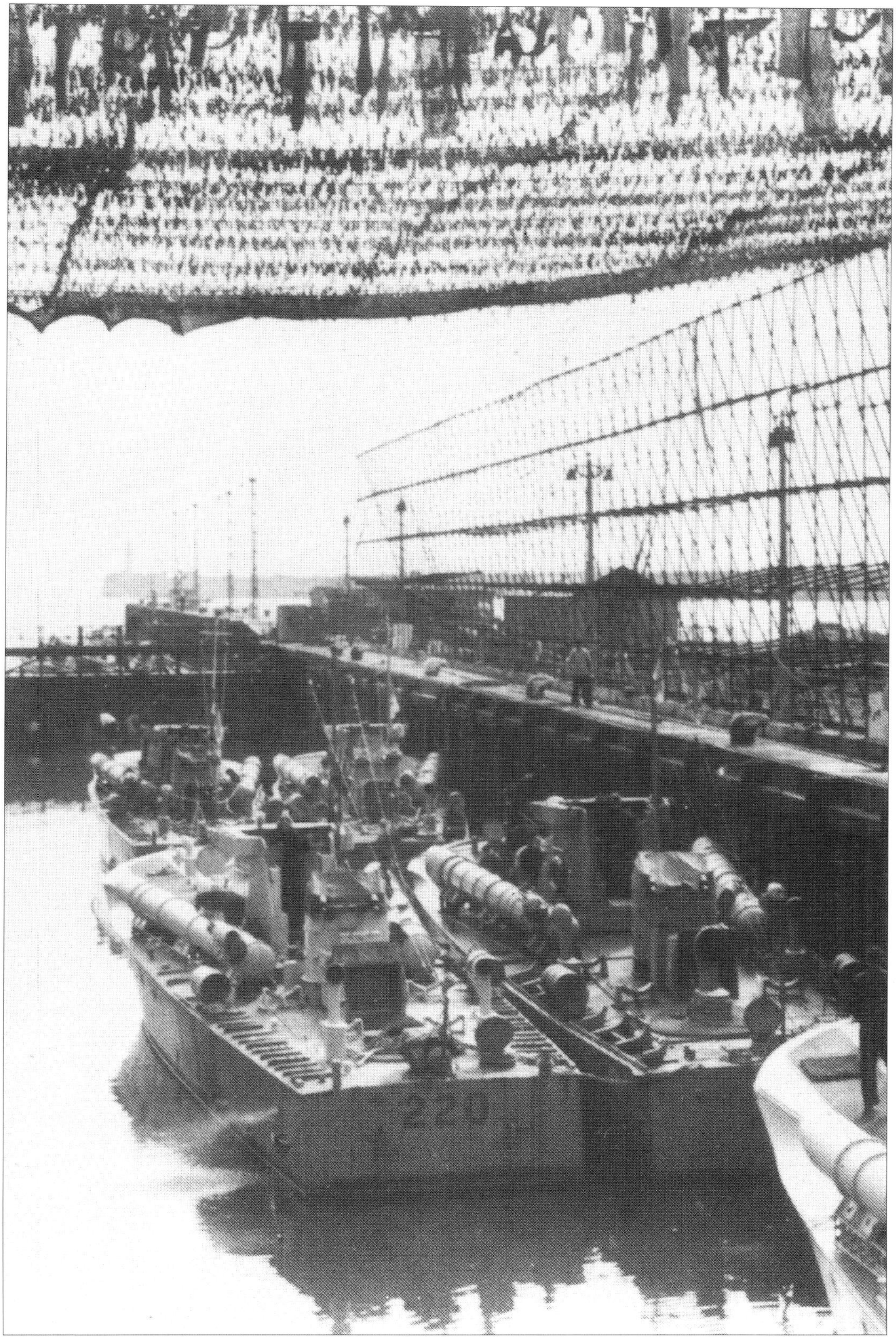


1939 – 1945

*The camouflaged train ferry berth in the Western Docks at Dover that was used as a base for MTBs and RAF rescue craft. They saved the lives of many pilots downed in the Channel.* (Hollingsbee Collection – Tilmanstone WI)

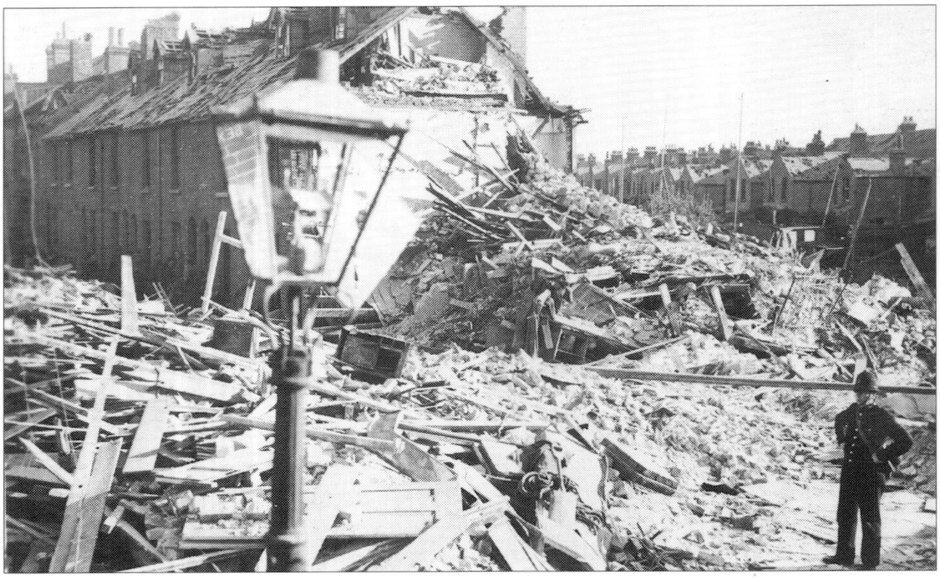

*A scene of devastation in Whitstable in the summer of 1940: the bombed out remains of Tilleys fish and chip shop on the corner of Victoria Street and Regent Street. Towns and villages all over East Kent suffered terrible damage under the almost continuous onslaught by German bombers.*
(Mrs E. Hopkins – Herne WI)

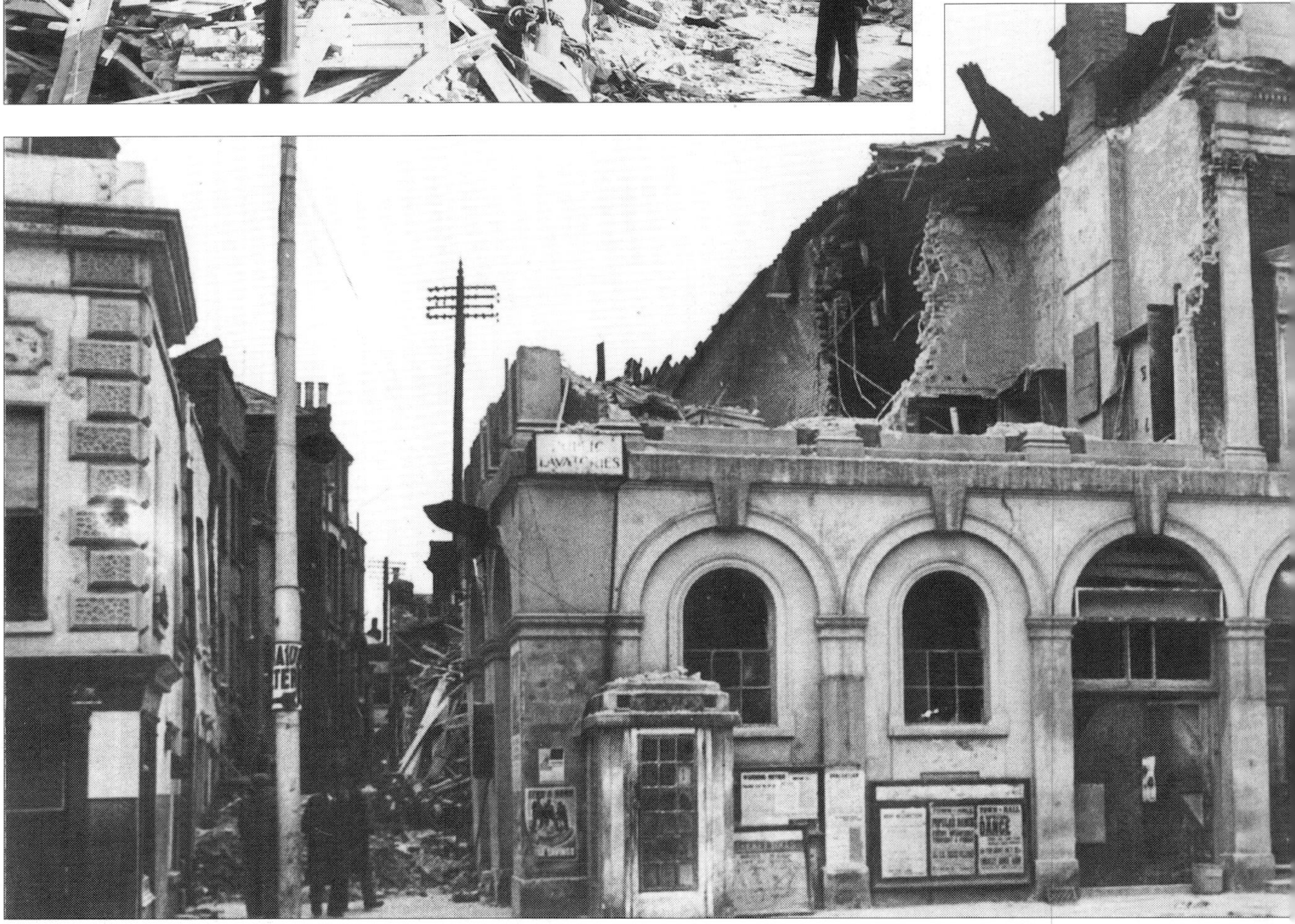

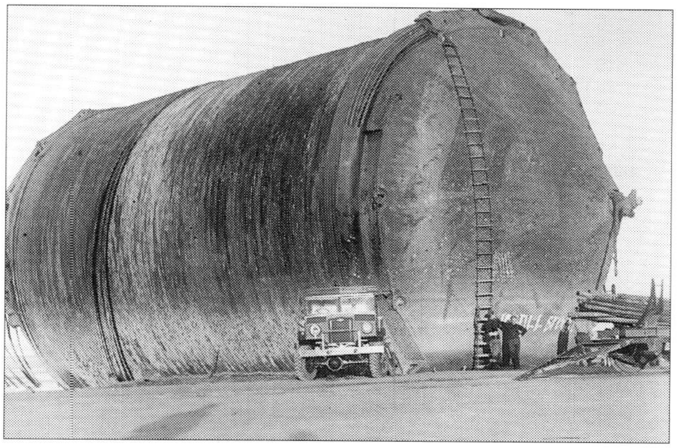

***Left*** *PLUTO (Pipeline Under the Ocean) was an ingenious scheme for carrying fuel under the sea to the Allied forces across the Channel. This drum carrying part of the PLUTO oil pipeline was lost at sea, and stranded on the shore at Littlestone in 1944.*
(Betty Blackford – Wye WI)

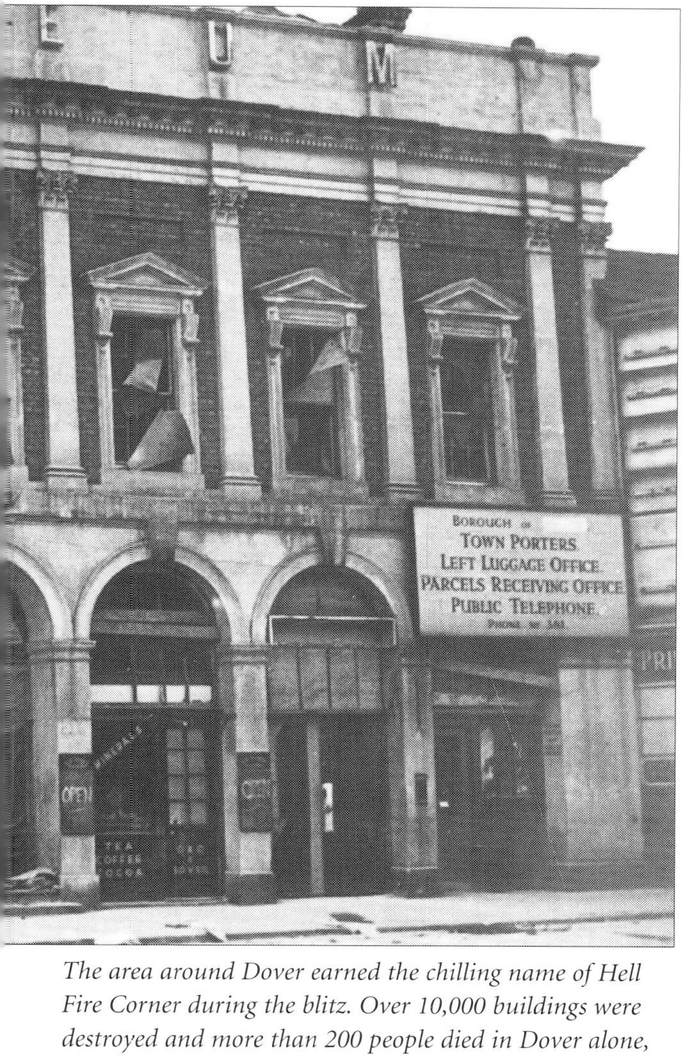


*The area around Dover earned the chilling name of Hell Fire Corner during the blitz. Over 10,000 buildings were destroyed and more than 200 people died in Dover alone, with many more injured. The old Market Hall and Dover Museum suffered two direct hits by bombs. Luckily, on the occasion of this picture the only casualties were stuffed animals and birds.* (Hollingsbee Collection – Tilmanstone WI)

*Even the elements seemed to be against us at times and the sea often brought its own dangers. The Dutch coaster* Nora *hit a mine off the coast at Deal in January 1940. The stricken vessel then dragged her anchor in bad weather and crashed into the pier, demolishing some 80 yards of the structure and leaving the pier cut in two. The pier, built of iron in 1864, was not repaired, as part of the anti-invasion measures, but in 1957 it was rebuilt in concrete and reopened.* (Mrs W. Oram – River WI)

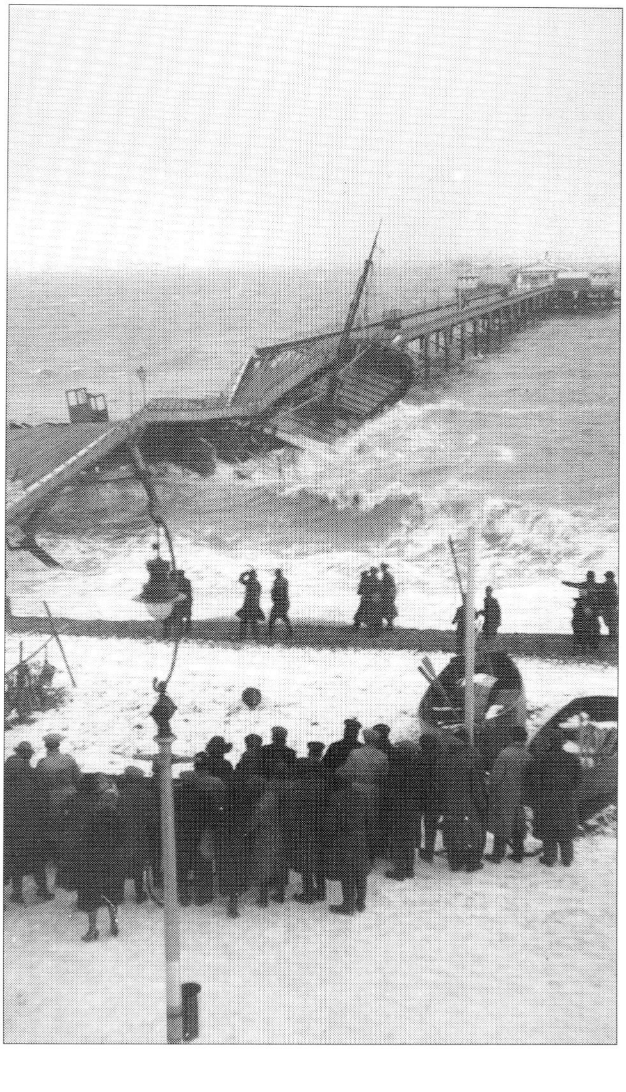

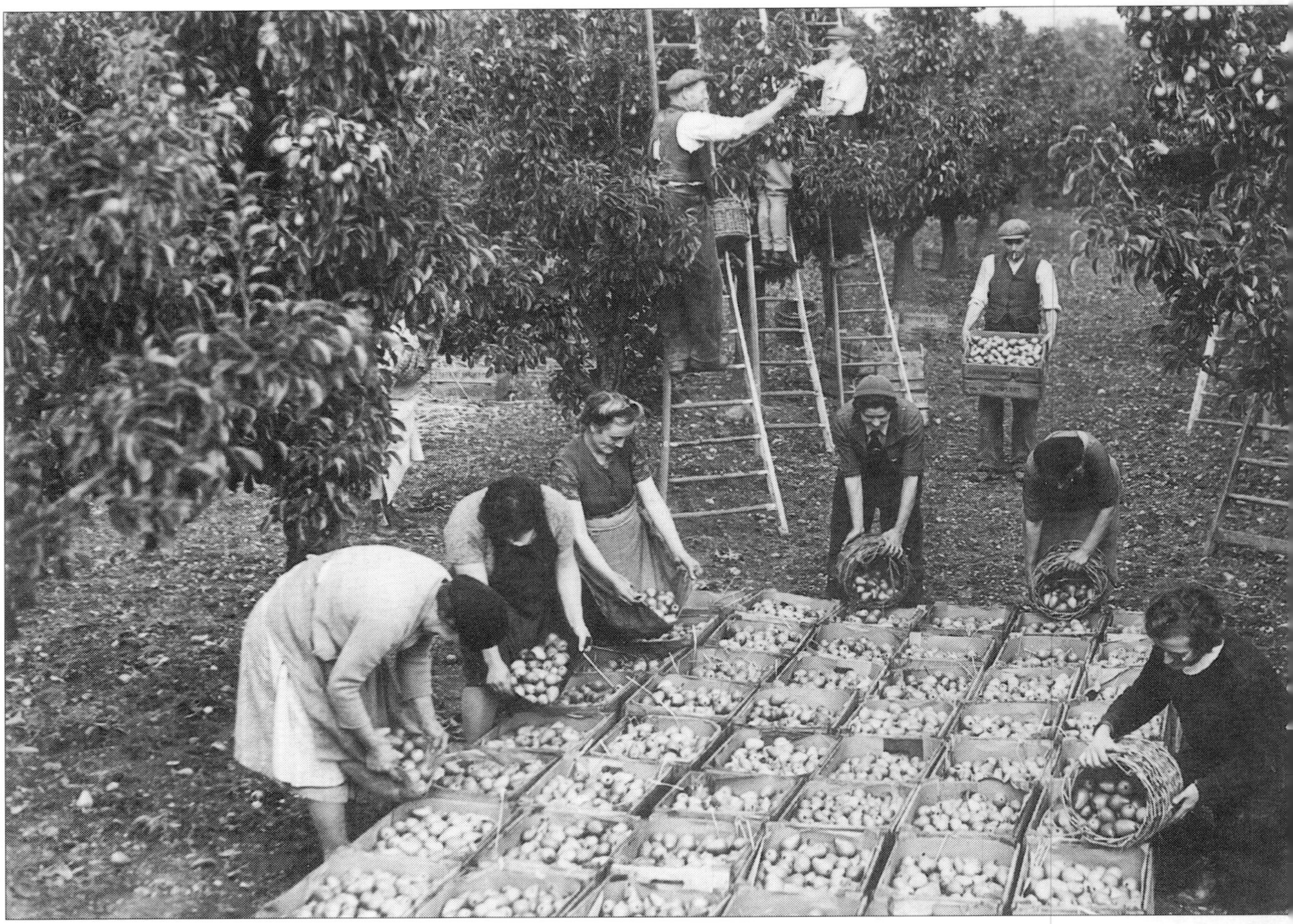

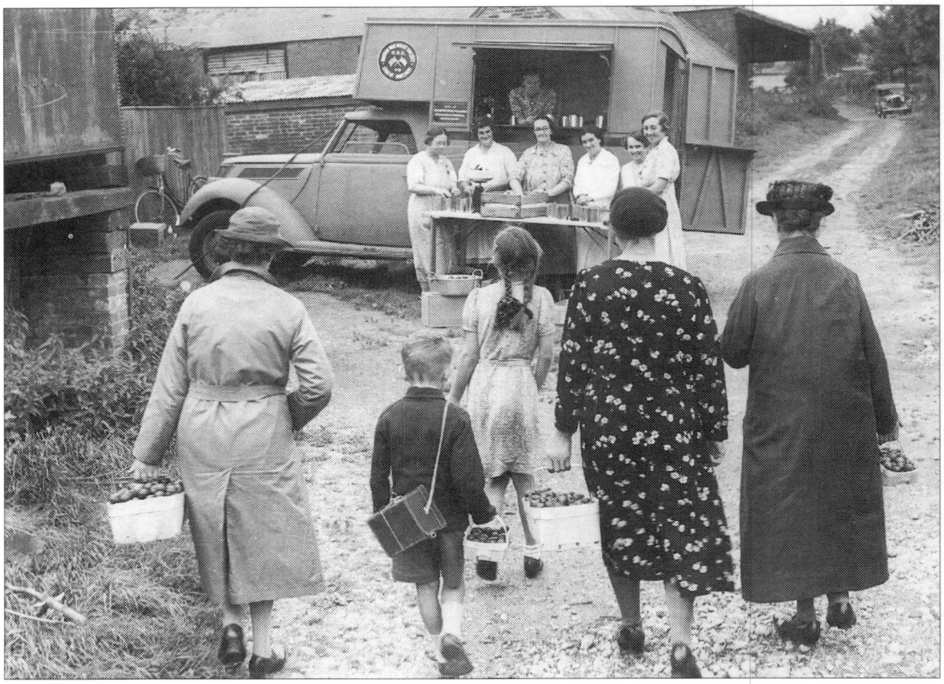

*Kent's ability to produce quality fruit and vegetables for a rationed home market was an essential part of the war effort. This photograph of the apple and pear harvest in September 1944 was taken for official publicity purposes so the orchard could be identified only as 'somewhere in Kent', wartime press restrictions preventing any more detailed information being given.*
(Mrs D. Barnes – Sellindge WI)

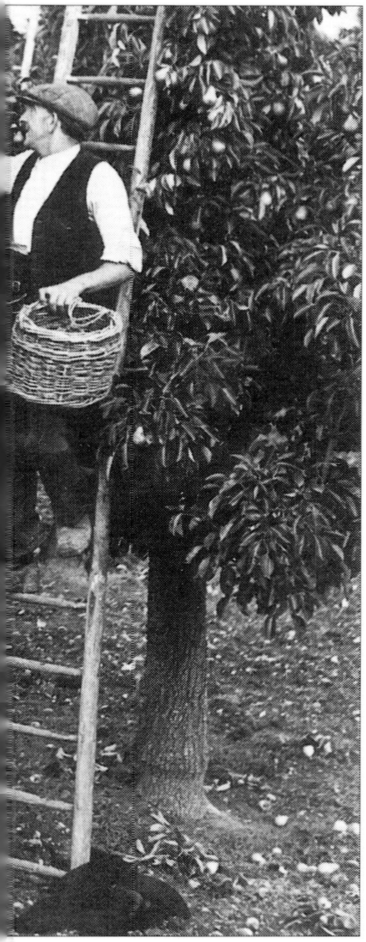

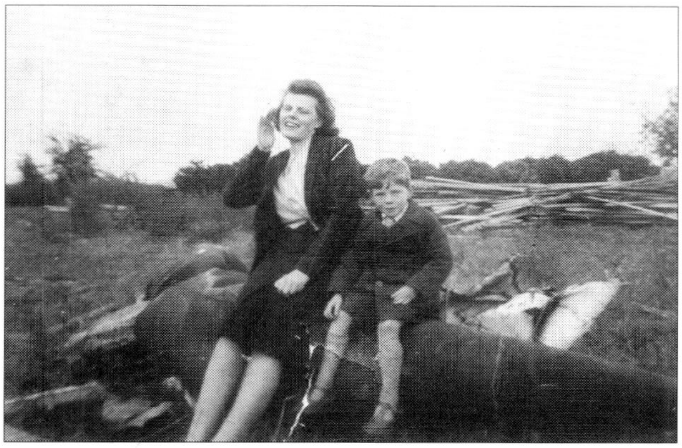

*Eileen and Patrick O'Brien sitting on a doodlebug which crashed on 28th July 1944 at Bankside, killing one person and injuring three. Kent received 2,400 'hits' from these deadly weapons – 200 more than London!*
(Mrs A. Hammon – Stowting WI)

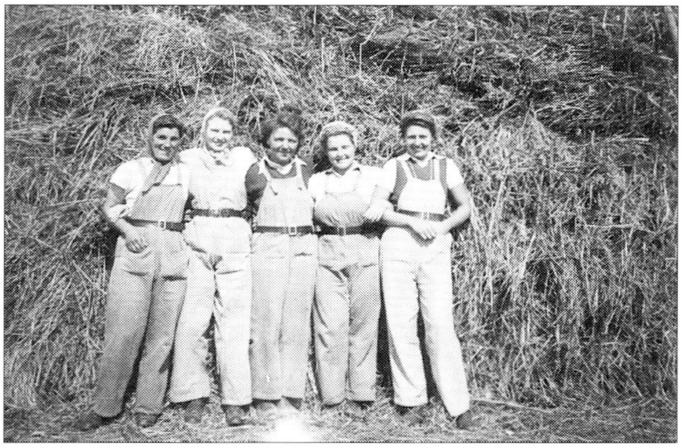

*The Women's Land Army was one option open to young women who were called up and Helen Parker (second from the left) came to Kent from Lofthouse in Yorkshire in 1944, aged 18, as a land girl. She never went back to Yorkshire, having met her husband-to-be on a local smallholding.*
(Helen Markwick – Eastry WI)

*Land girls worked on every aspect of farming and fruit growing. Phyllis Usher, Win Duncan, Gladys Cook, Phyllis Cutting, Joan Usher and Jo Harvey were pruning fruit trees on Mr Gaskain's farm at Selling in 1942.*
(Betty Recton – Selling & District WI)

*Using a van donated by the British War Relief Society of the USA, members of Hawkinge, Acrise & Paddlesworth WI await the arrival of more local fruit.*
(Anne Beaney – Hawkinge, Acrise & Paddlesworth WI)

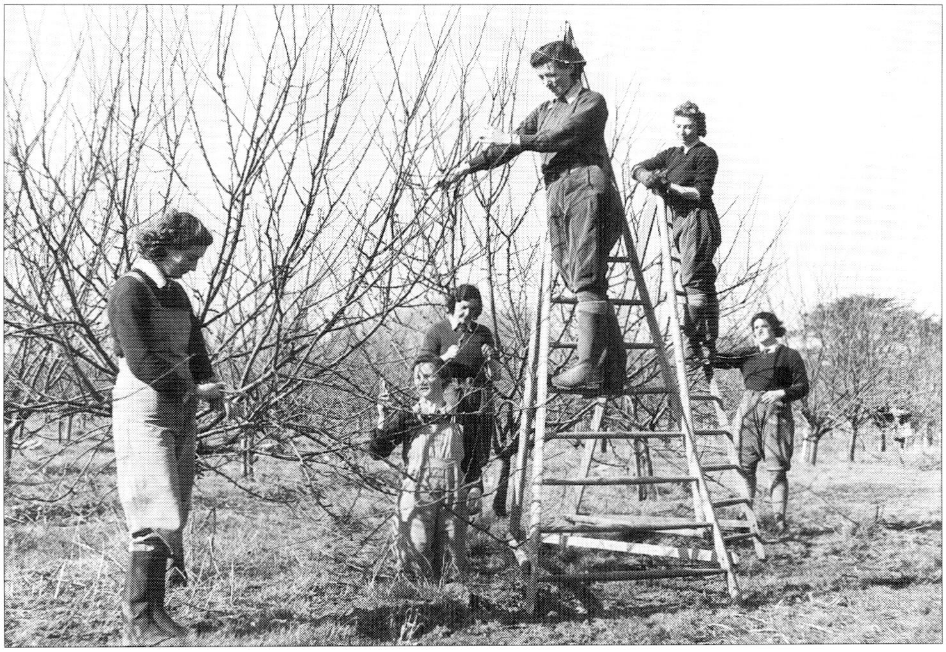

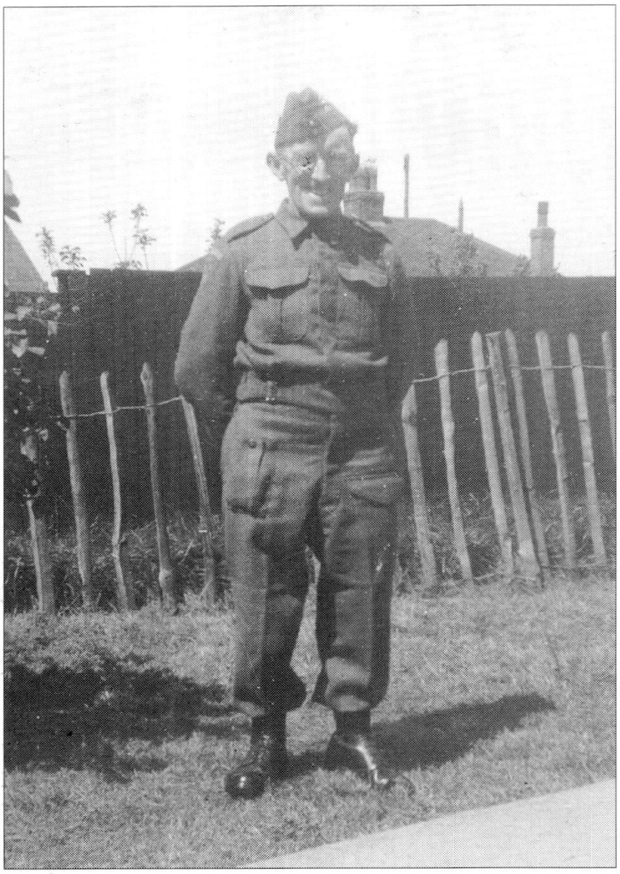

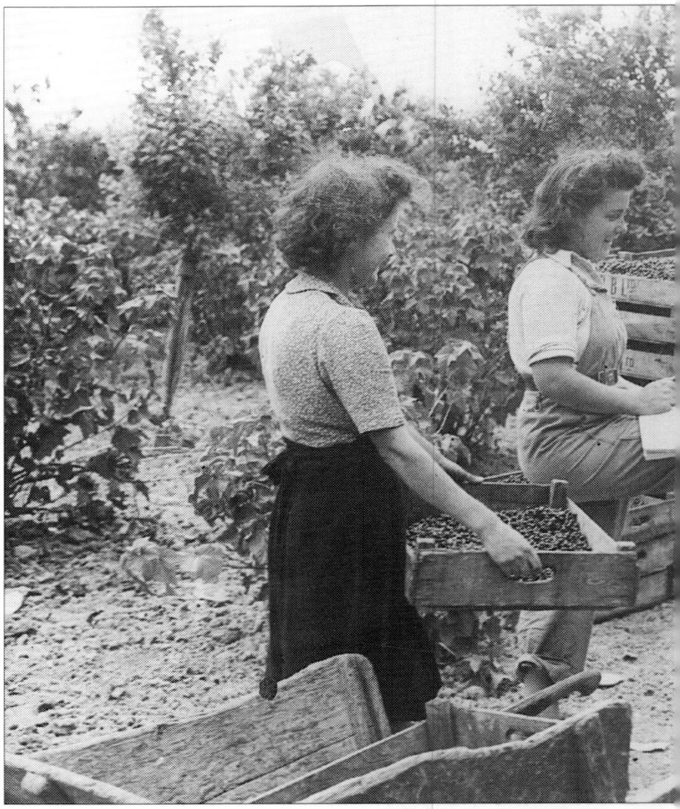

*Weighing morello cherries on Manor Farm at Icklesham in 1944.* (Mrs E. Brown – Stone cum Ebony WI)

*Men who were too old or too young for the Forces, or working in reserved occupations, were stalwarts of the Home Guard. Men such as Richard Bedford, who worked as a lorry driver for a firm transporting sandbags from Whitstable beach up to London, were willing to fight to the death should the threatened invasion reach Kent's shores. Mr Bedford posed proudly in his Whitstable Home Guard uniform in 1940; it was his daughter's job to clean all his buttons before he went on parade!* (Mary Williams – Kennington WI)

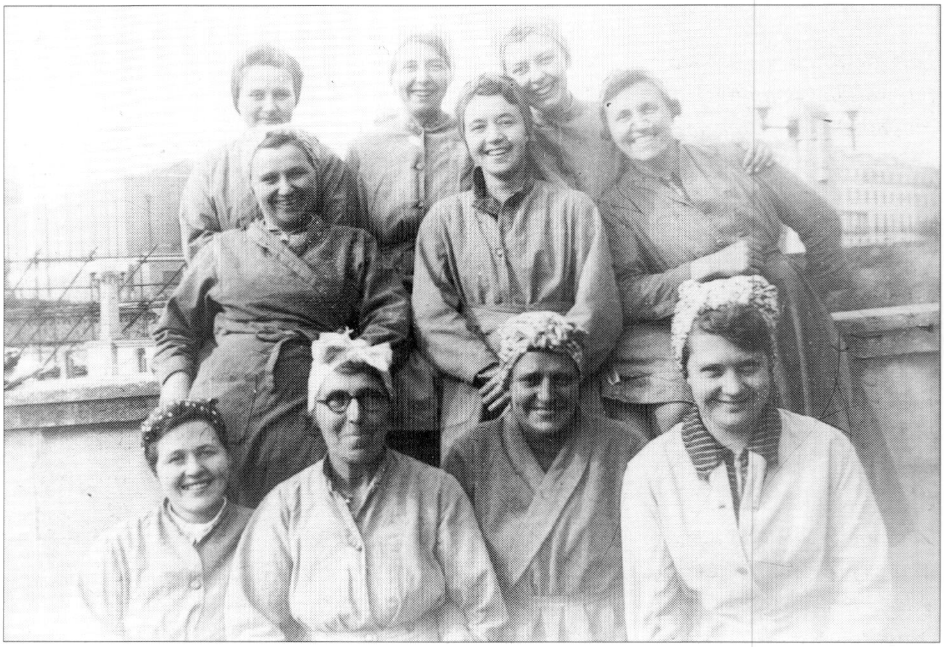

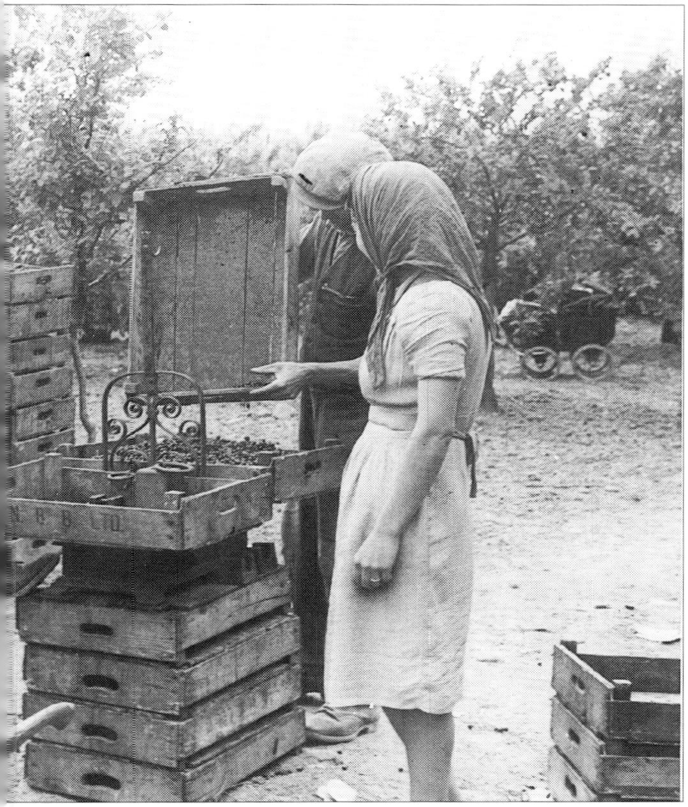

*October 22nd 1940 and the wedding of Hugh Grosvenor and Marjorie Ansell – the last to be held in St George's church, Ramsgate before all ceremonies had to be moved to the crypt of the church for safety. All the family had donated coupons to buy the material for the bride's dress. The air raid sirens had sounded just before the ceremony, but neighbours and friends braved the danger to support the young couple. Best man Ernie had been rescued from Dunkirk only a few months earlier, one of those brought back to Kent's shores by the bravery and daring of the 'little armada'.* (Mrs M. Heatlie – Thanington Without WI)

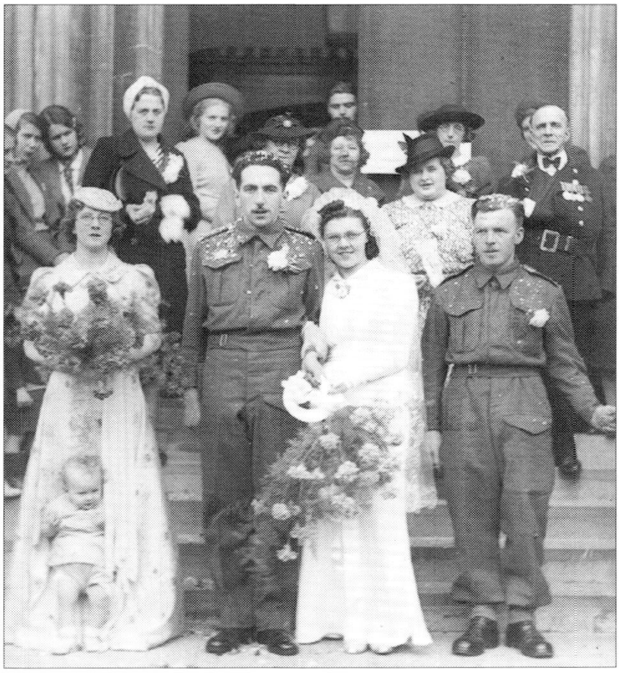

***Below*** *Troops were billeted in and around many local villages and often participated in local community activities – this RAMC unit put on an entertainment for the villagers of Etchinghill.* (Mrs D. Arnold – Cheriton WI)

***Left*** *Women also did their bit, working in munitions and other essential factories. This group of workers were from the factory at the Pier Pavilion, Herne Bay which made camouflage netting during the war. At one time over 200 women worked there. (l to r from the top row – Nelly Ridgen, Phyllis Shelley, Floss Bomber, Ethel Finch, Dorothy Searle, Connie Marsh, Maisie Chambers, Mrs Kennard, Margery Stroud and Hilda Wickens)* (Floss Bomber – Beltinge WI)

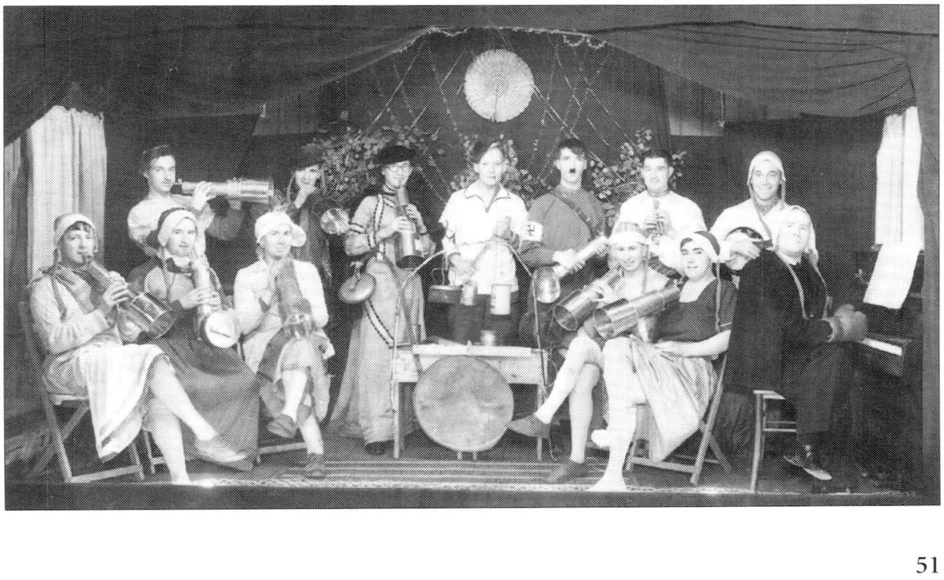

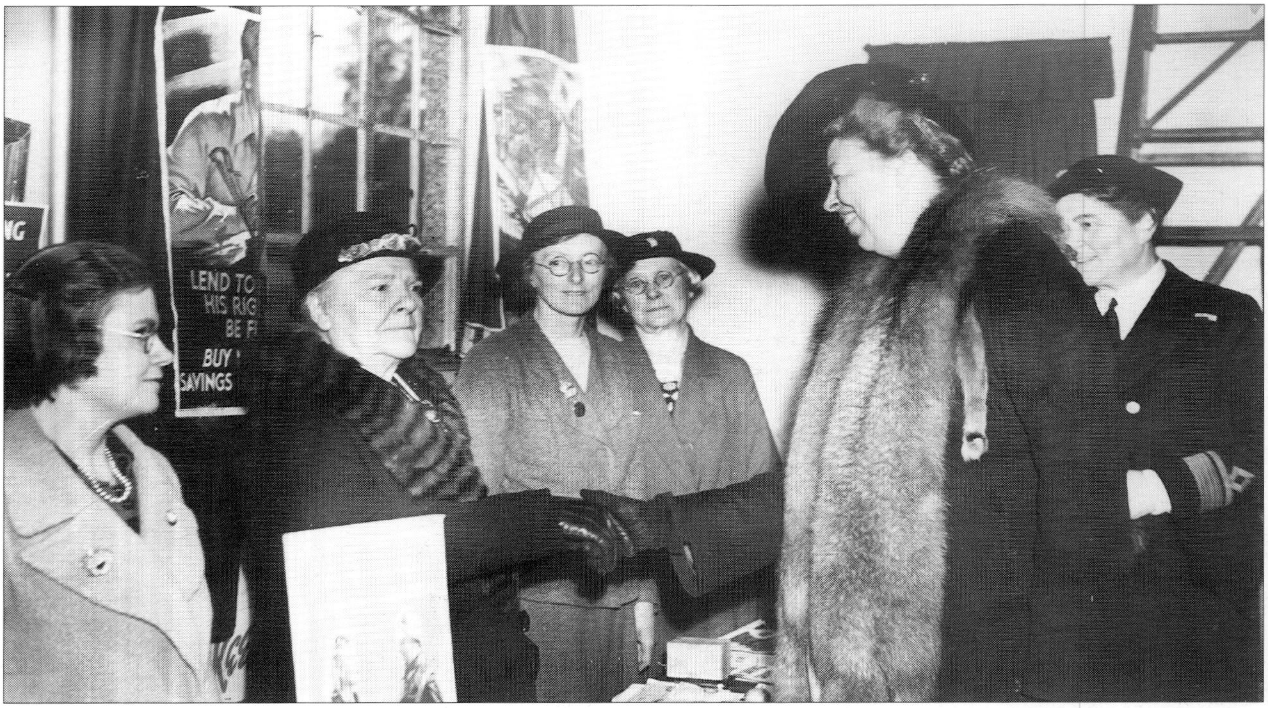
LEND TO
HIS RIG
BE F
BUY
SAVINGS

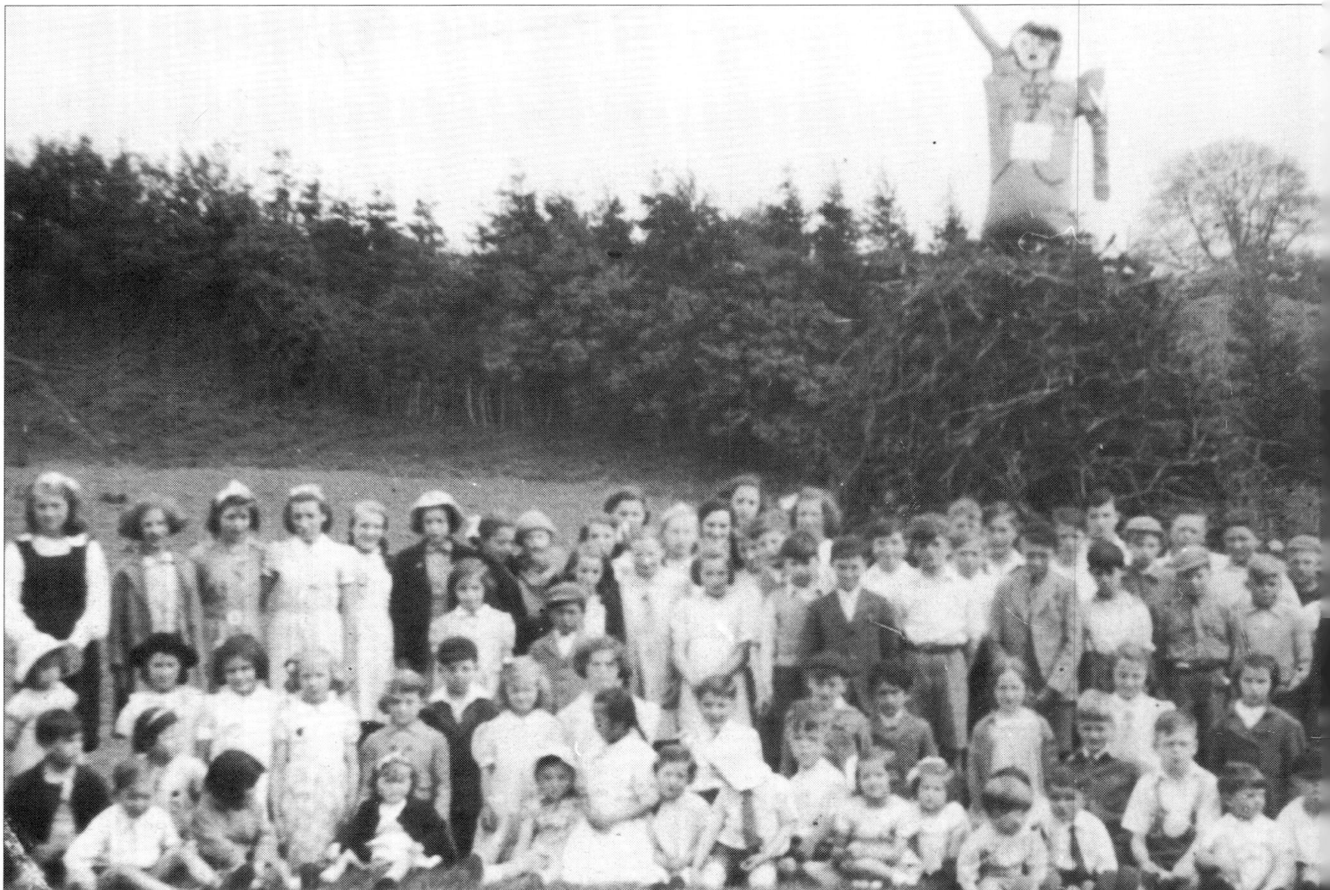

*Mrs Eleanor Roosevelt visited Barham Women's Institute in October 1942, accompanied by Mrs Churchill. The stalls were toured and questions asked. On seeing the piglet held out for inspection, Mrs Roosevelt asked its name and a quick-witted member replied, "Franklin, ma'am, we hope you don't mind." Mrs Roosevelt then turned to the doe rabbit and said, "I suppose this is Eleanor?" She is pictured shaking hands with Mrs Eliza Fox, the oldest member of the Barham Institute.*

(Freda Jackson – c/o Cheriton WI & L. Ross – Barham WI)

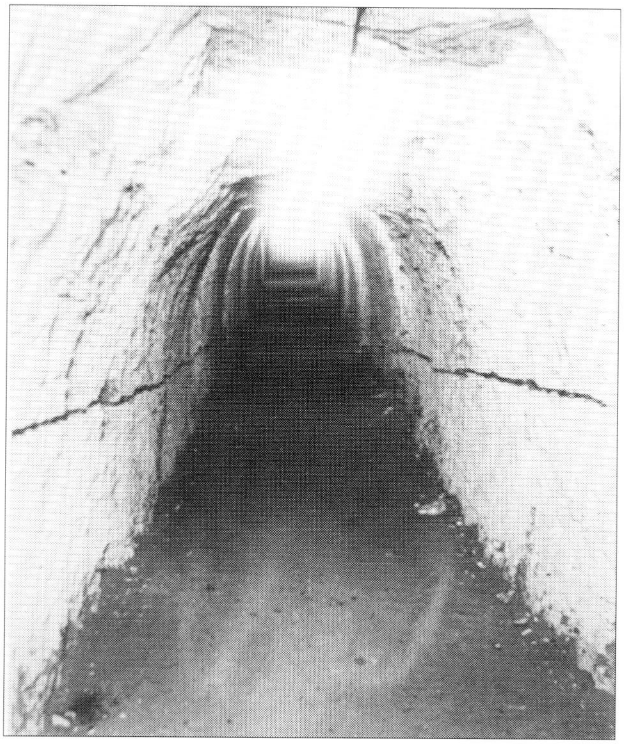

*Many lives were saved in Ramsgate by the 70 ft deep tunnels cut in the chalk which acted as air raid shelters. Three and a half miles long, with 17 entrances connecting all parts of the town, including schools and the hospital, they cost £60,000 to build and could hold 60,000 people, double Ramsgate's population. Being well signposted, it was possible to walk underground from one end of the town to the other in safety.*

(Peggy Belsey – Sandwich WI)

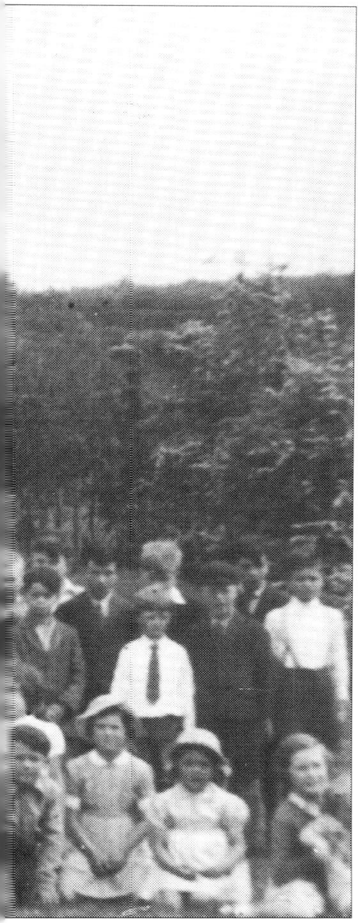

*The children of Egerton gathered on the recreation ground for the village VE Day celebrations in May 1945. At last the war was over – and Hitler was on the bonfire!*

(Priscilla Harper – Egerton WI)

*We all got used to the frugalities of Make Do and Mend. One Women's Institute scheme organised the spinning of wool gathered from the hedgerows. The tufts of sheeps' wool were carded and spun, sometimes mixed with dog or rabbit hair. Mrs Winifred Simpkins took classes in spinning all over East Kent – this photograph was taken at Sir Edward Hardy's house in Boughton Aluph.*

(Mrs J. Simpkins – Swalecliffe with Chestfield WI)

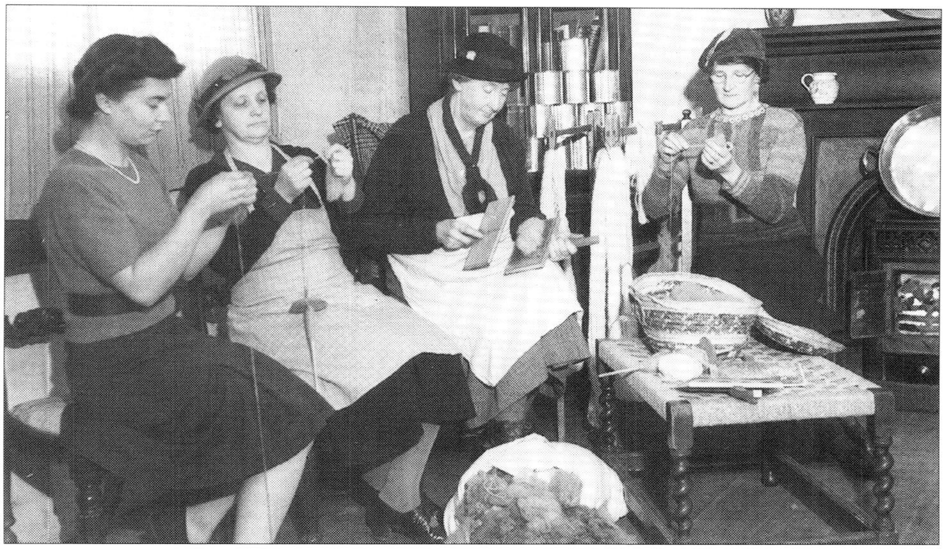

# Then & Now
# Dover Harbour

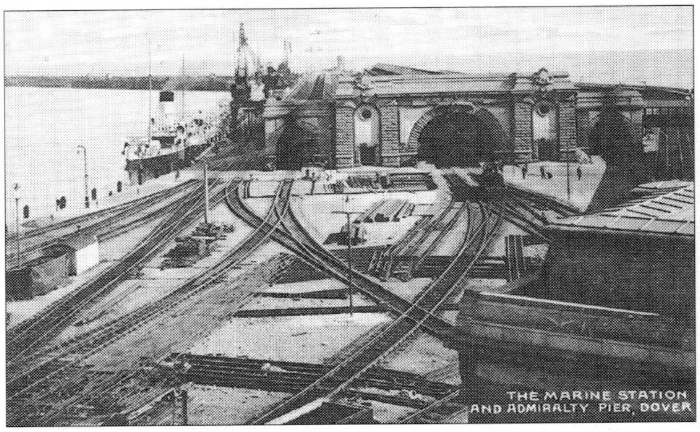


*Dover Marine Station in the Western Docks in 1914. Far and away the greatest number of travellers to the Continent arrived at this station and walked to the ferries alongside.*
(Temple Ewell WI)

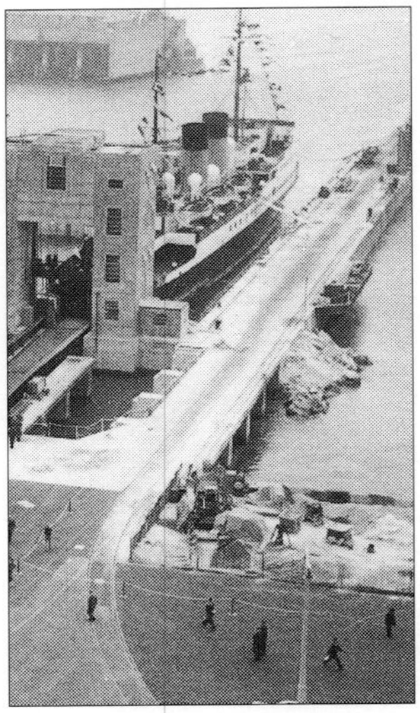

*In 1953 the first roll-on, roll-off berths were opened in the Eastern Docks. This picture also shows the submarine pens that were built to protect submarines during the First World War, which were not demolished until 1990.*
(Pamela Blaxland – Temple Ewell WI)

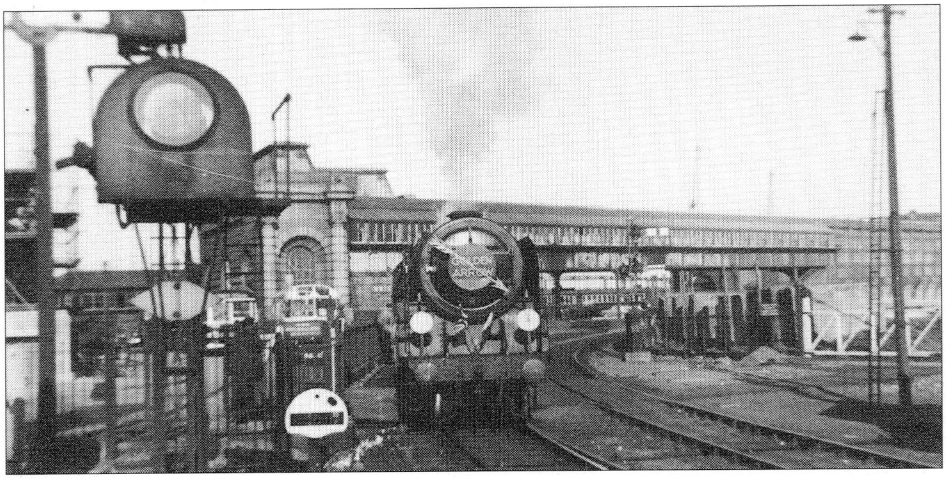


*The rich could travel by the Golden Arrow, shown here arriving at Dover Marine in 1950, and were driven, train and all, onto a special ferry so that those with sleepers could sleep all the way from London to Paris. This service continued until 1972.*
(Jennifer Dunkley – St Margarets at Cliffe WI)

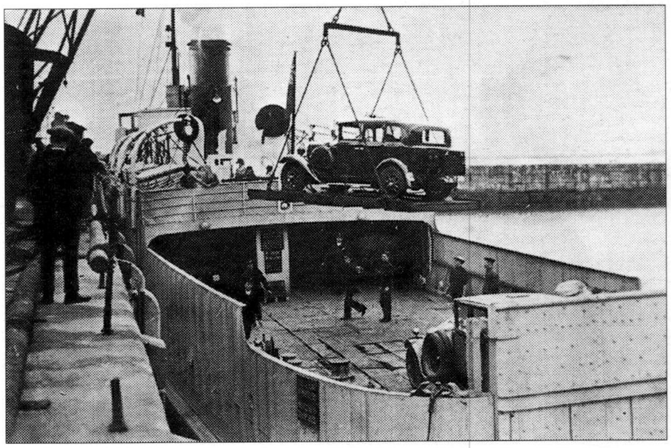

*It was possible to take cars to the Continent but, until the 1950s, each one had to be hoisted individually into the ship. Among the early users of this service were the British starters in the Monte Carlo Rally.*
(Hollingsbee Collection – Tilmanstone WI)

*In 1966 a small hovercraft made an experimental beaching on the sand. A completely new Hoverport with its beaching ramp and terminal buildings has now been created in the western side of the Harbour adjacent to the Western Docks, hovercraft using the western entrance to the port. Another recent development is a high-speed catamaran called Lynx, which has come into service for cars and passengers.*
(Audrey Lowley – Whitfield WI)

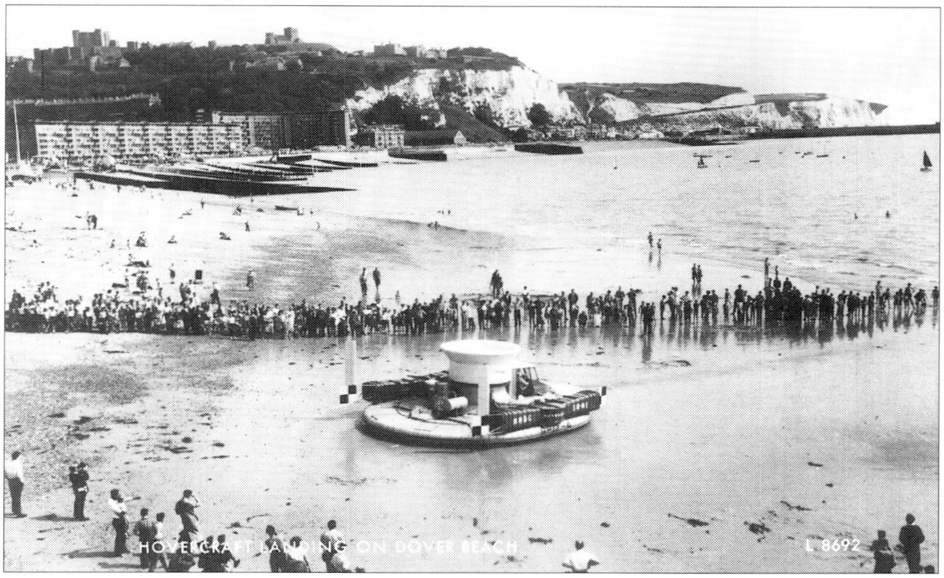


***Below** The Eastern Docks in 1996. There are now seven roll-on, roll-off berths used by three separate ferry companies with sailings every few minutes, in addition to the hovercraft and catamaran services. In 1996 over 19 million passengers travelled to the Continent from Dover Harbour.*
(Dover Harbour Board)

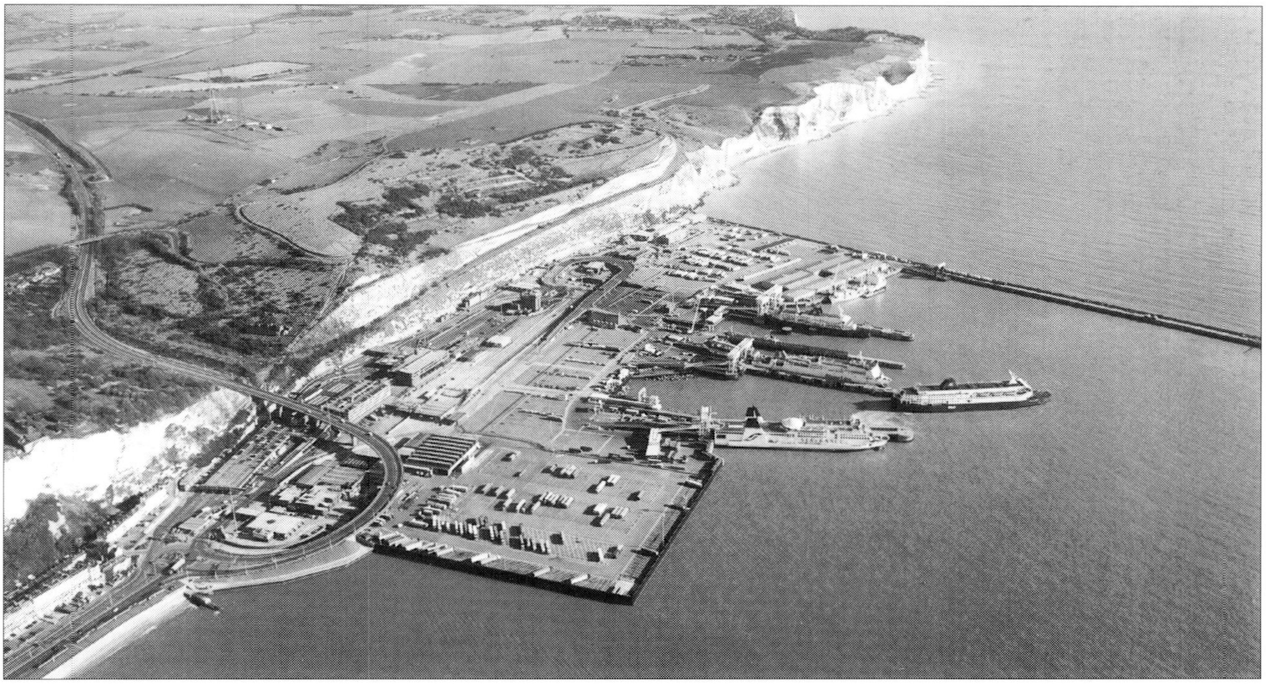

# THE POST-WAR YEARS

## (1946 – 1959)

Even before the war was over, thoughts had turned to the kind of society the future would hold. There was wide support for the Beveridge Report, and the post-war Labour government implemented the Report's recommendations for a Welfare State. Essential industries such as coal mining and the railways were nationalised, and the National Health Service created. Winston Churchill lost his premiership, but the hero of the wartime government was warmly welcomed by the people of East Kent in 1946 when he was made Lord Warden of the Cinque Ports.

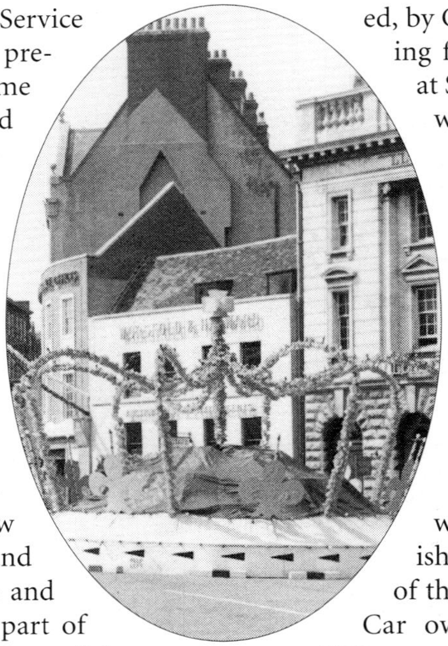

With so much destruction from bombing raids, new homes were urgently needed and 'prefabs' were quickly erected. Rationing had to continue for some time, and this time of austerity was a long and hard struggle for many families. But eventually it passed and in came the 'New Look', a celebration of femininity and fabric! Fridges, washing machines and Hoovers were soon to become a part of every home and not just the preserve of the wealthy. The 'teenager' was born and young people began to behave and dress in ways baffling to their elders.

In 1947, in one of its most inspired actions, the WI bought a large country estate in Oxfordshire, every Institute making a contribution. It was converted into a residential college named after their founding Chairman, Lady Denman. It has flourished to such an extent that it now takes no less than 6,000 students a year, attending an astonishing variety of courses ranging from Renaissance art to surfing the Internet.

The weather brought hardship on occasion. During the winter of 1947 the severe cold froze the sea in several places, and in early 1953 exceptional high tides caused widespread flooding in the Thames estuary and along the Kent coast. Thanet almost became an island again, Margate lighthouse was pounded, and railway lines were washed away.

In 1954 the Dover British Legion was presented, by Calais, with a piece of armour plating from the German long-range guns at Sangatte, recording that 2,226 shells were fired at the town and harbour during the war. The plate was erected on the sea front. In 1959 the Royal Naval establishment at Sheerness was closed.

The ever increasing power and versatility of farm machinery resulted in a considerable loss of manpower on the land. Horses were needed no longer and soon were hardly to be seen in the fields. One growth industry in the area was tourism – holiday camps flourished and the beaches were soon freed of their wartime barbed wire.

Car ownership grew tremendously; in 1958 over four million private cars were registered. Greater ease of personal travel meant that houses, shops, offices and factories could be more widely sited, and changed the pattern of leisure activities. It also brought traffic problems. In the late 1950s roads were opened to bypass Maidstone, Ashford and the Medway towns. Congestion was a particular problem in East Kent, due to the increase in cross-Channel traffic.

The death of King George VI was a sad time, for many recalled the leadership he and Queen Elizabeth had given during the war. However, the coronation of Queen Elizabeth II in June 1953 was celebrated with great enthusiasm – a New Elizabethan Age was

*Coronation decorations in Market Square. Dover, in 1953, part of the great celebrations held across the county for the coronation of Queen Elizabeth II.* (Pamela Blaxland – Temple Ewell WI))

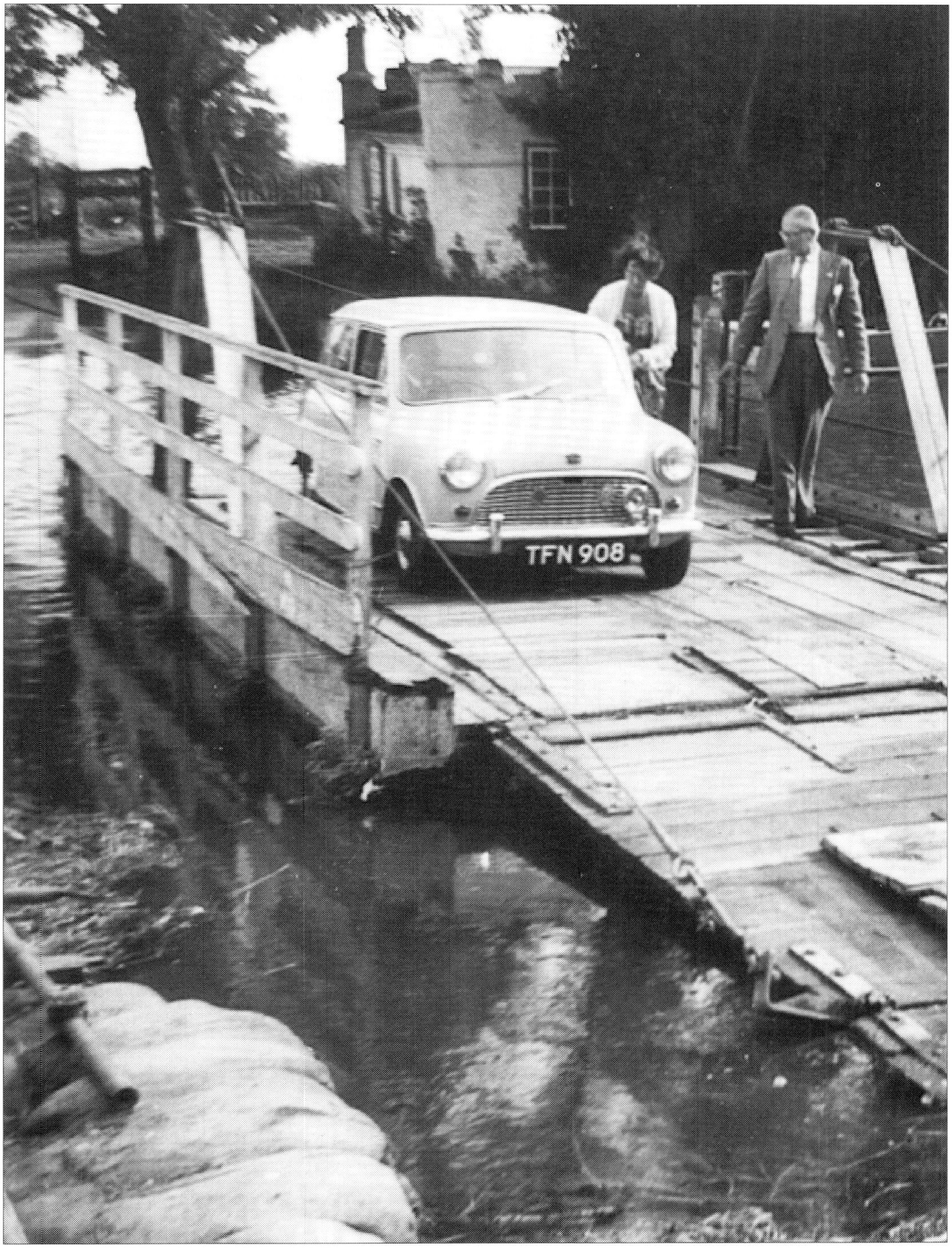


1946 – 1959

*Grove Ferry in the late 1950s. The Mini was the first to be seen in Ramsgate – bought for £395. It was so new that Knights Garage insisted on keeping it in their showrooms for a few weeks before the family were allowed to have it.* (Eileen Bean – Cliffsend Evening WI)

dawning. Two years before, the Festival of Britain had given the country a taste of the future. On Coronation Day itself, the announcement was made that Everest had been conquered by the British Everest Expedition and a wave of patriotic fervour swept the country. The showing of the Coronation ceremony live incidentally gave a great boost to television, and by 1959 some 60% of households had a set.

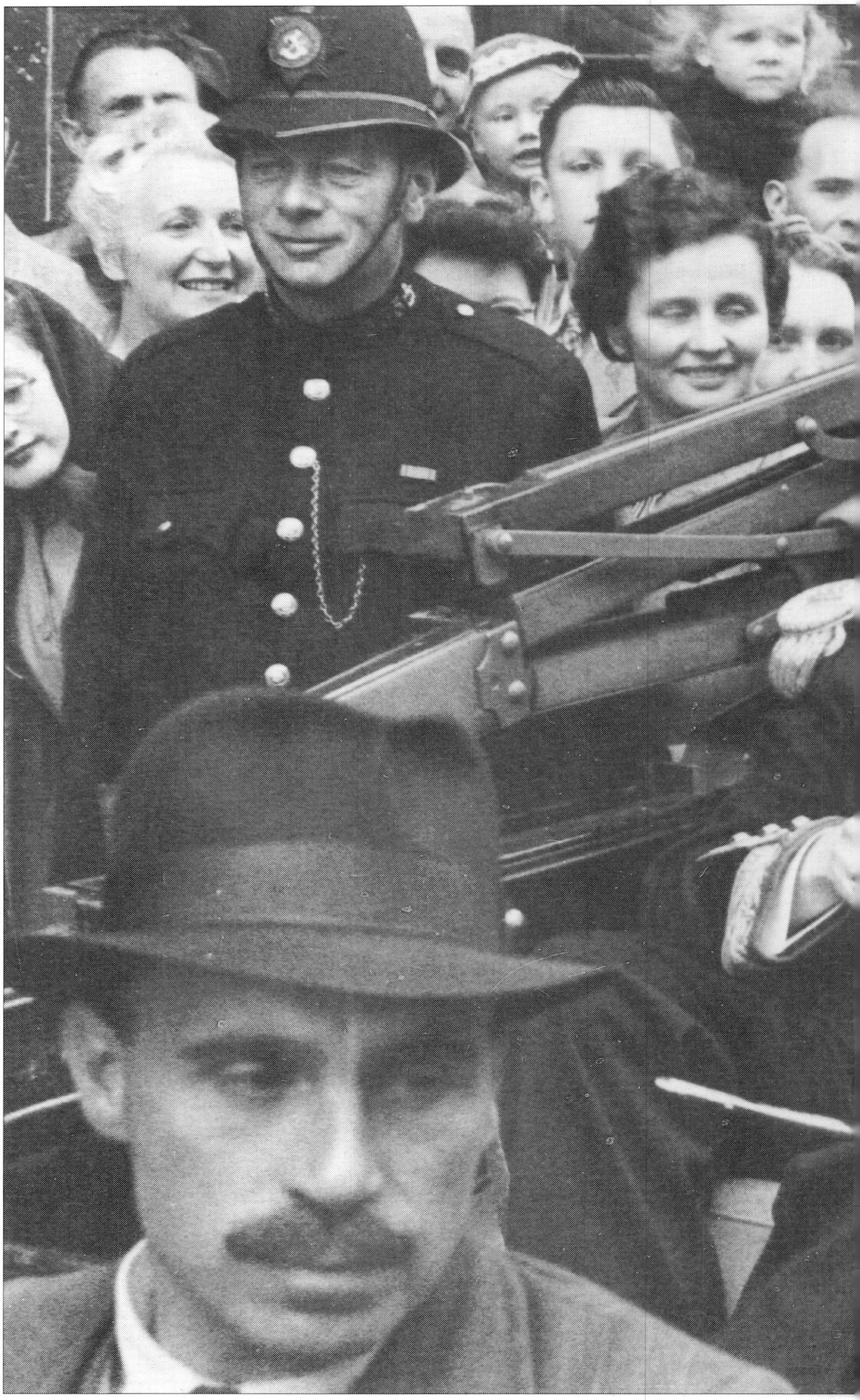

*Winston Churchill at Dover Town Hall on the occasion of his installation as Lord Warden of the Cinque Ports on 14th August 1946. Though the Conservatives had lost the general election the year before, Churchill himself retained widespread respect and affection as a great wartime leader.* (Julie Danson – Temple Ewell WI)

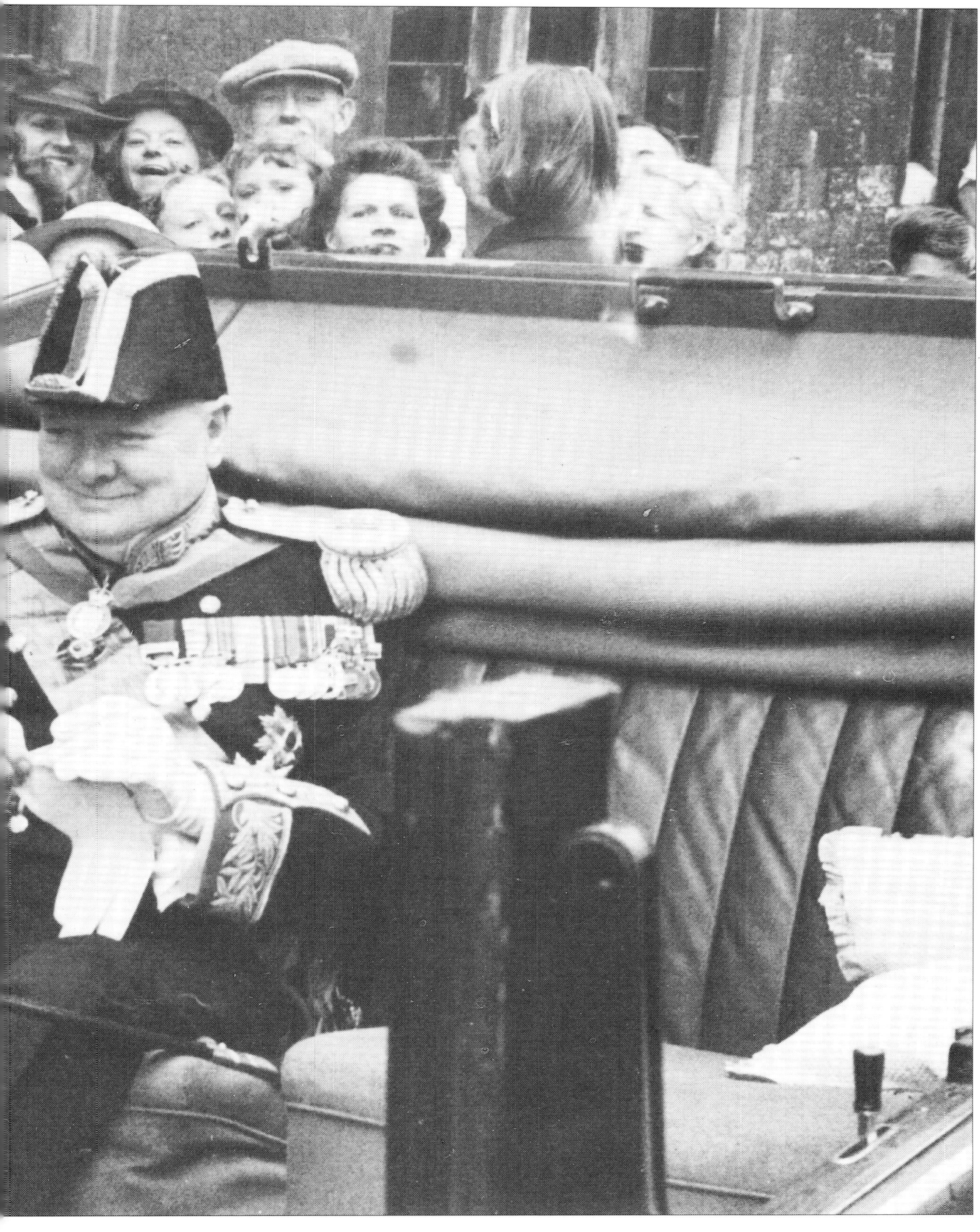

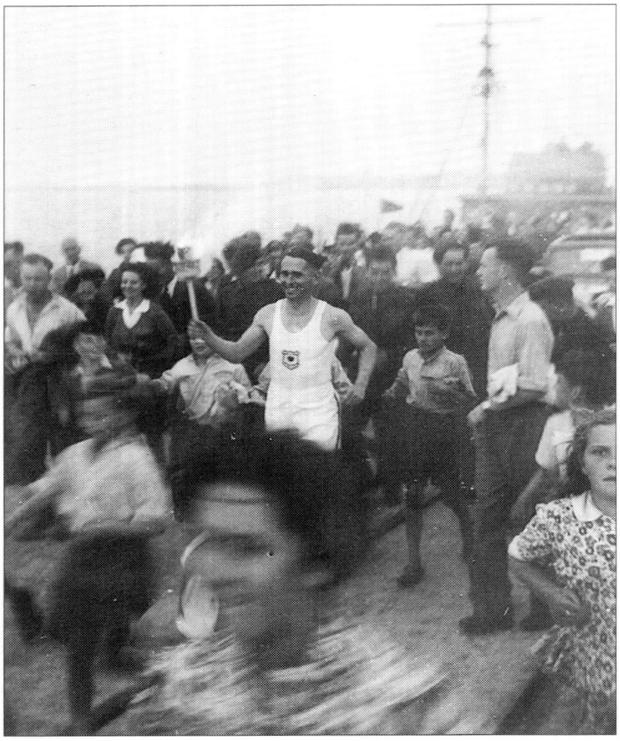

*In 1948 the Olympics were held in London, and crowds turned out at Dover to see the arrival of the Olympic flame, brought across the Channel on the destroyer HMS Bicester. It was carried for the first two miles on British soil by local man Sidney Doble.*
(Audrey Lowley – Whitfield WI)

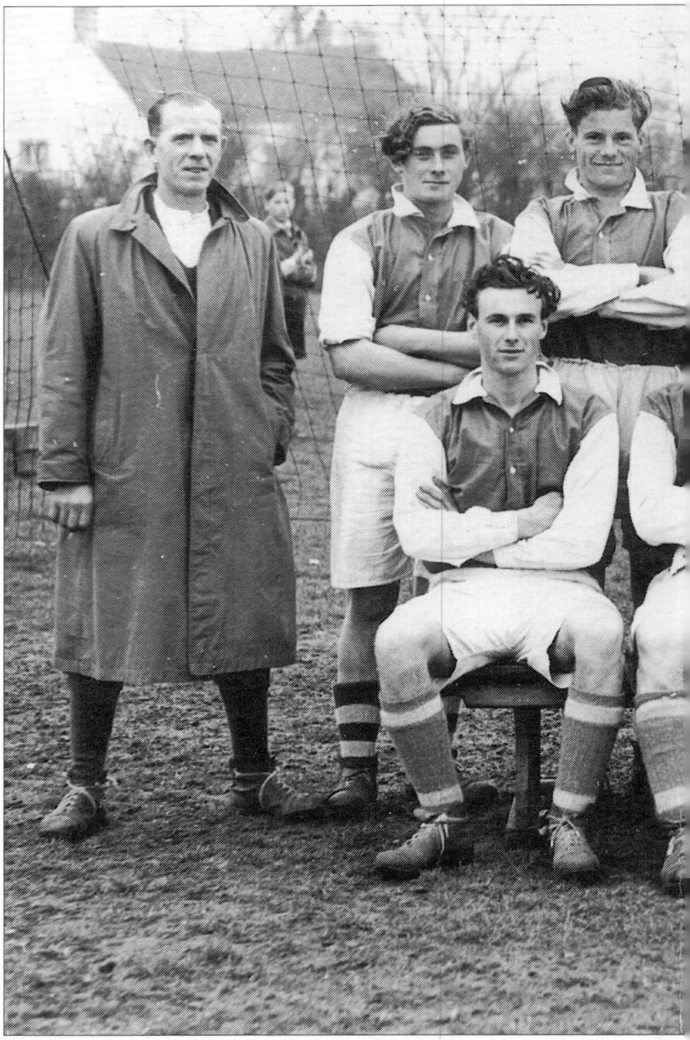

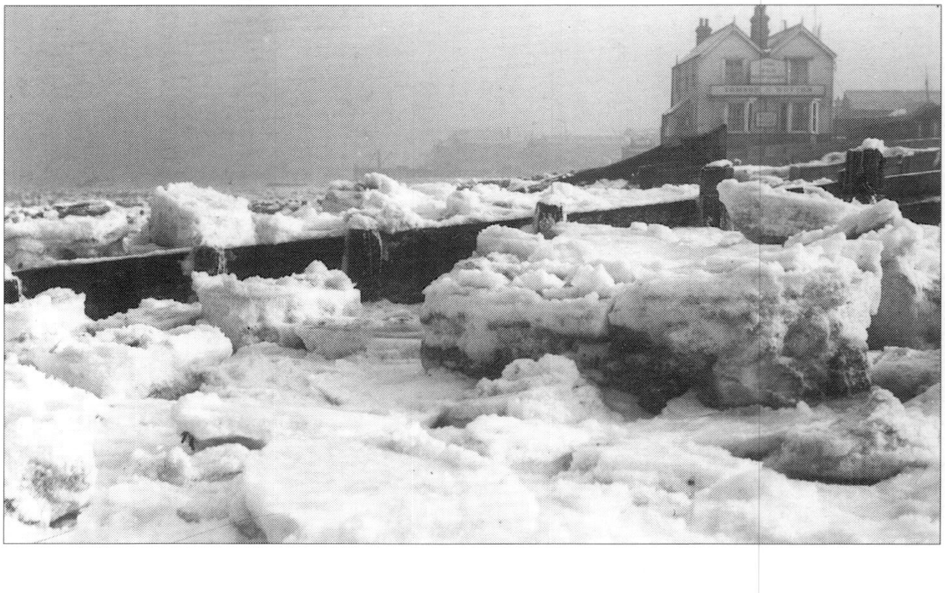

*Post-war austerity seemed to be symbolised by the Big Freeze of 1947. Bitterly cold weather lasted for months and food and coal were still in short supply. At many places around the Kent coastline the sea froze solid – here at Whitstable on 25th February.*
(Jean Jordan – South Street WI)

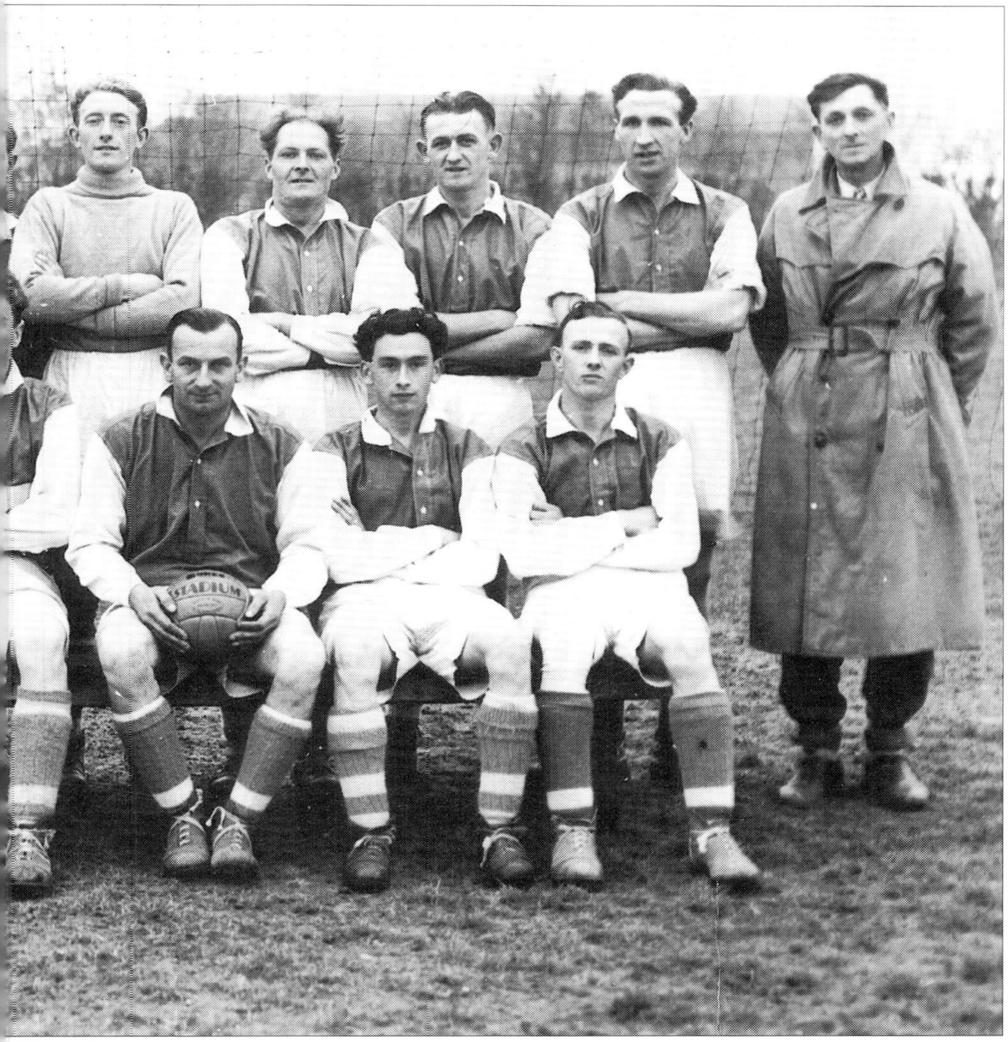


*The post-war football team of Preston village, in about 1946. Most of the players had recently come out of the Forces.*
(Mrs J. Tong – Preston, Elmstone & Stourmouth WI)

*A village cricket match at Alkham in the 1950s – such a good, flat pitch!*
(Susan Lees – Alkham WI)

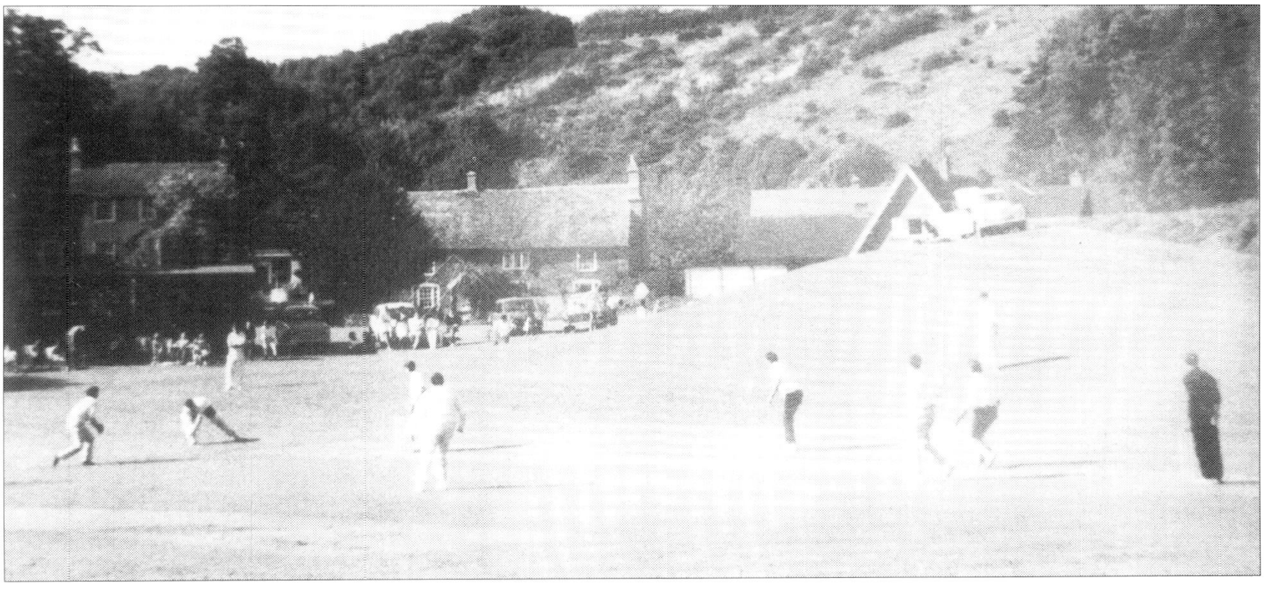

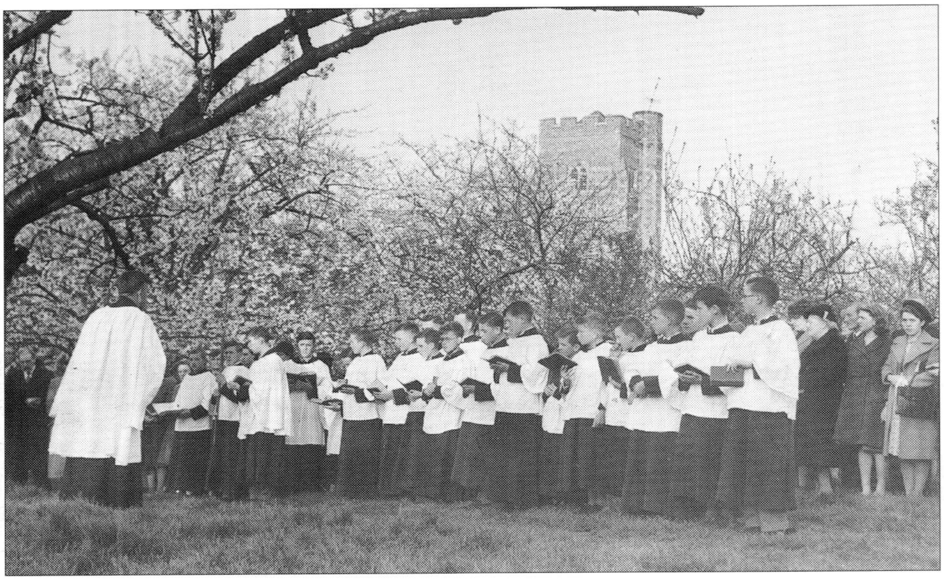

*Blessing the cherry orchards at blossom time, a service conducted by Rev A.H. Lance in 1948 at Newington by Sittingbourne. This followed the ancient ritual of blessing the trees to ensure a good crop.* (Newington WI)

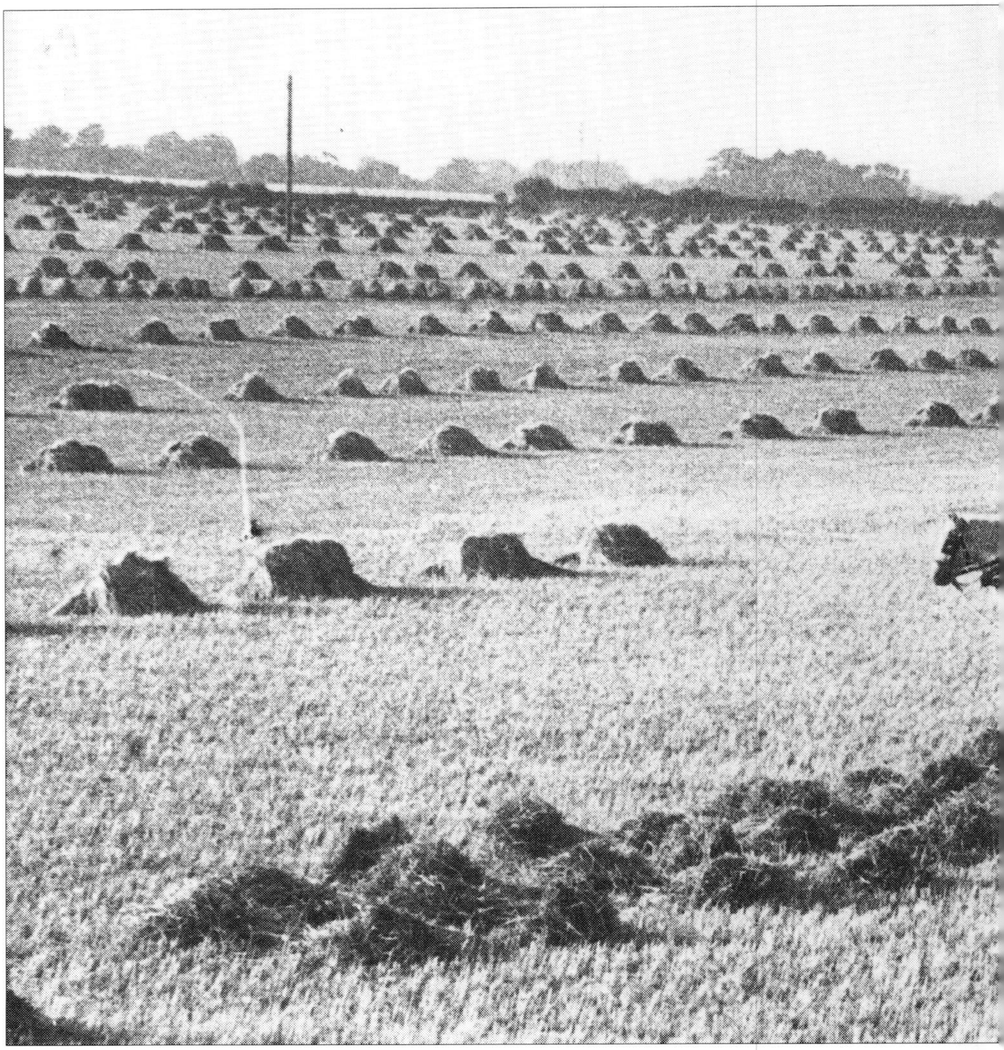

*Despite encroaching mechanisation, traditional scenes such as this were still common in the East Kent countryside. This was harvest time in the 1950s at Tilmanstone, between Lower Street and Barville. Loading sheaves onto a cart drawn by carthorses Prince and Nobby were Wilf Elgar, Horace Birch, Bill Friend and Vic Jarvest.* (Hollingsbee Collection – Tilmanstone WI)

*Threshing in the late 1940s – the Miller family owned the threshing machine.* (Mrs B. Miller – Bethersden WI)

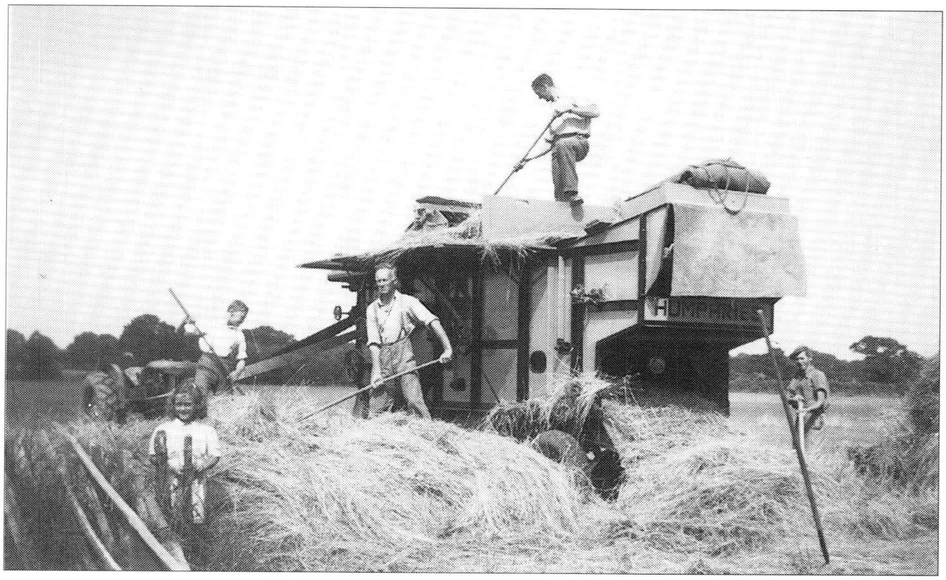

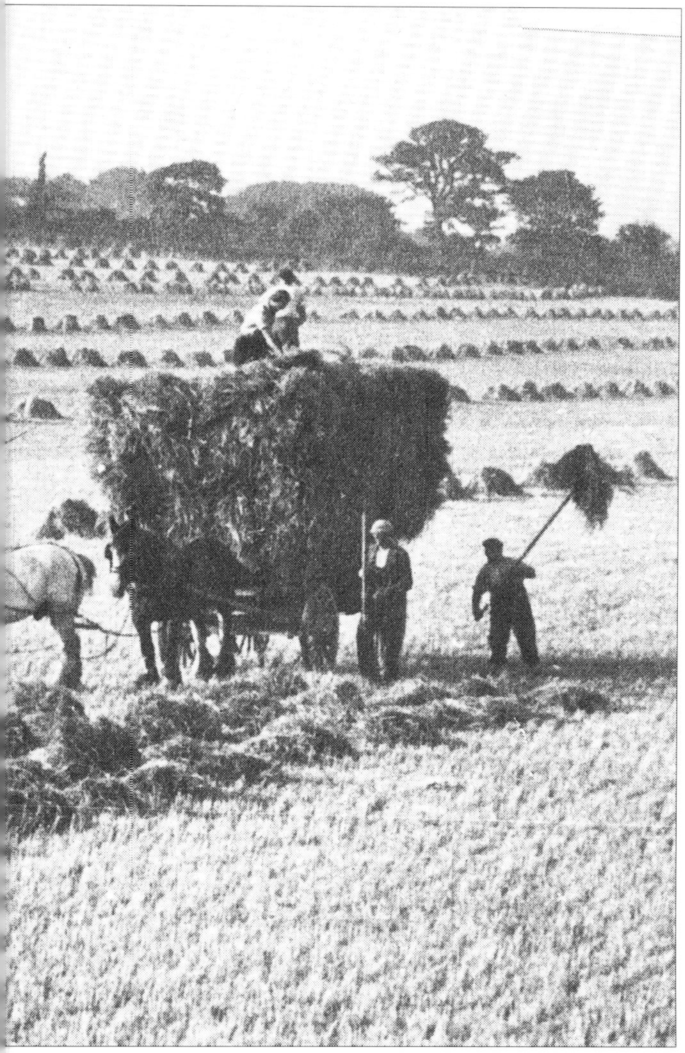

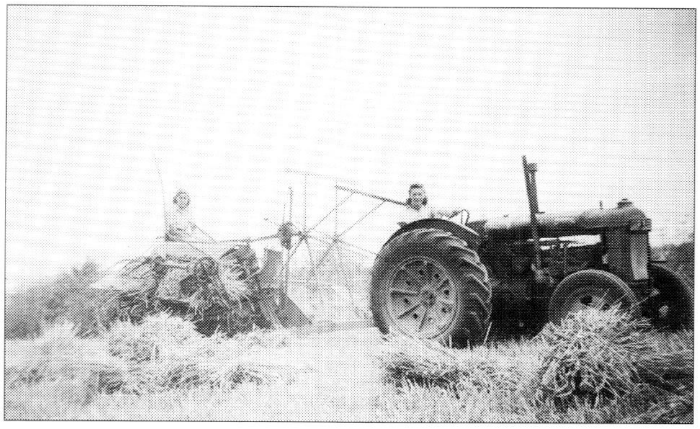

*Members of the Women's Land Army worked on after the war, as many foodstuffs continued to be rationed and scarce. Land on the Sandwich Marshes had been taken over to grow corn and the combine harvesters shown working here in 1947 were among the first to be seen in the country.* (Mrs M. Trice – Godinton WI)

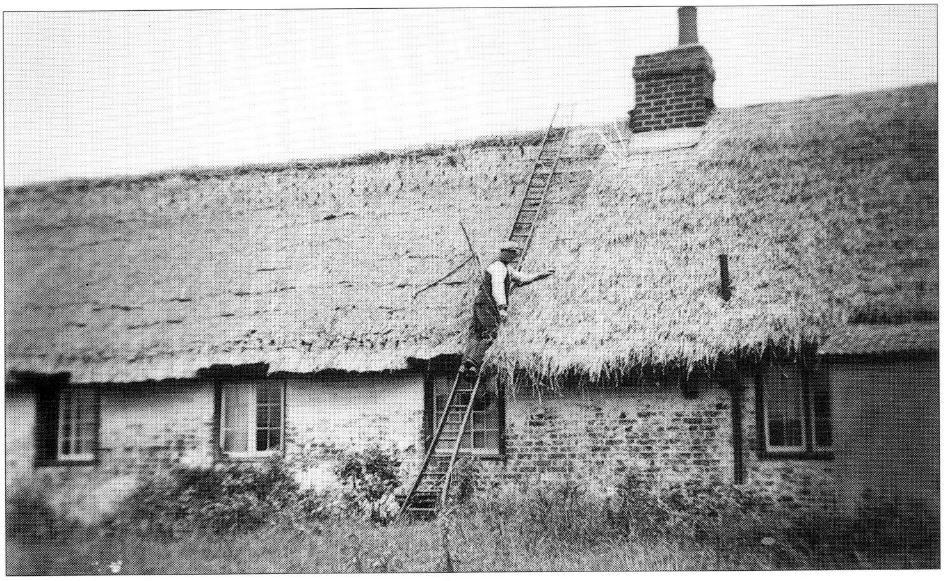

*'Dutch' Coleman thatching cottages at Crockyard Farm, Wingham in the 1950s.*
(Mrs E. Coleman – Wingham WI)

***Below*** *A shooting party in 1950 on the Orlestone estate, owned by the Oliver family. Estate workers were allowed to shoot at the end of the season.*
(Barbara Ware – Orlestone, Ham St & Ruckinge WI)

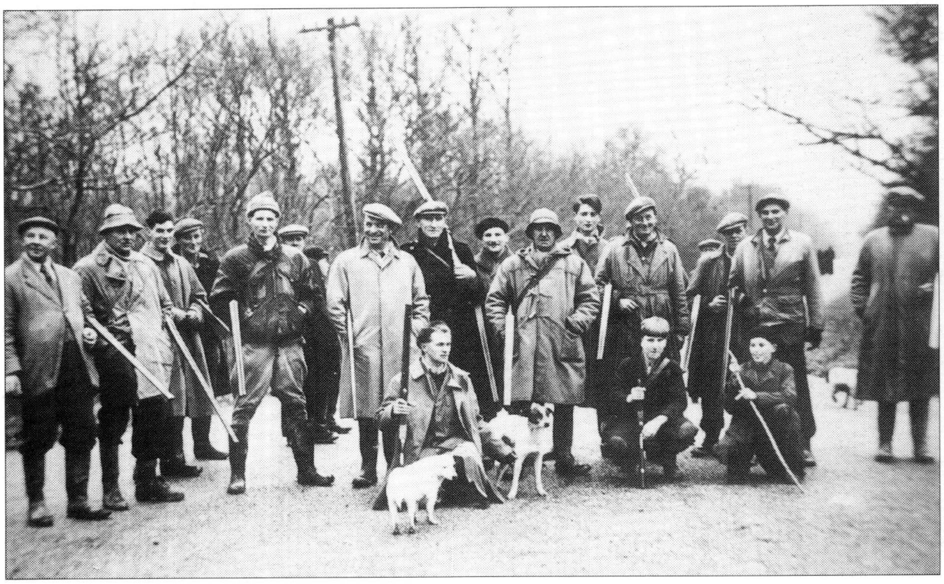

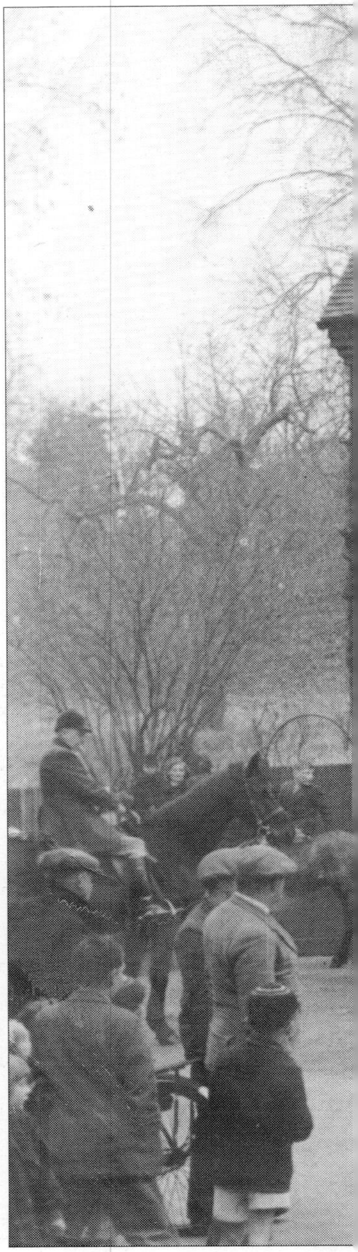

*The local hunt meeting at the Dublin Man of War pub, River, on 1st March 1952.*
(Mrs J. Simpkins – Swalecliffe with Chestfield WI)

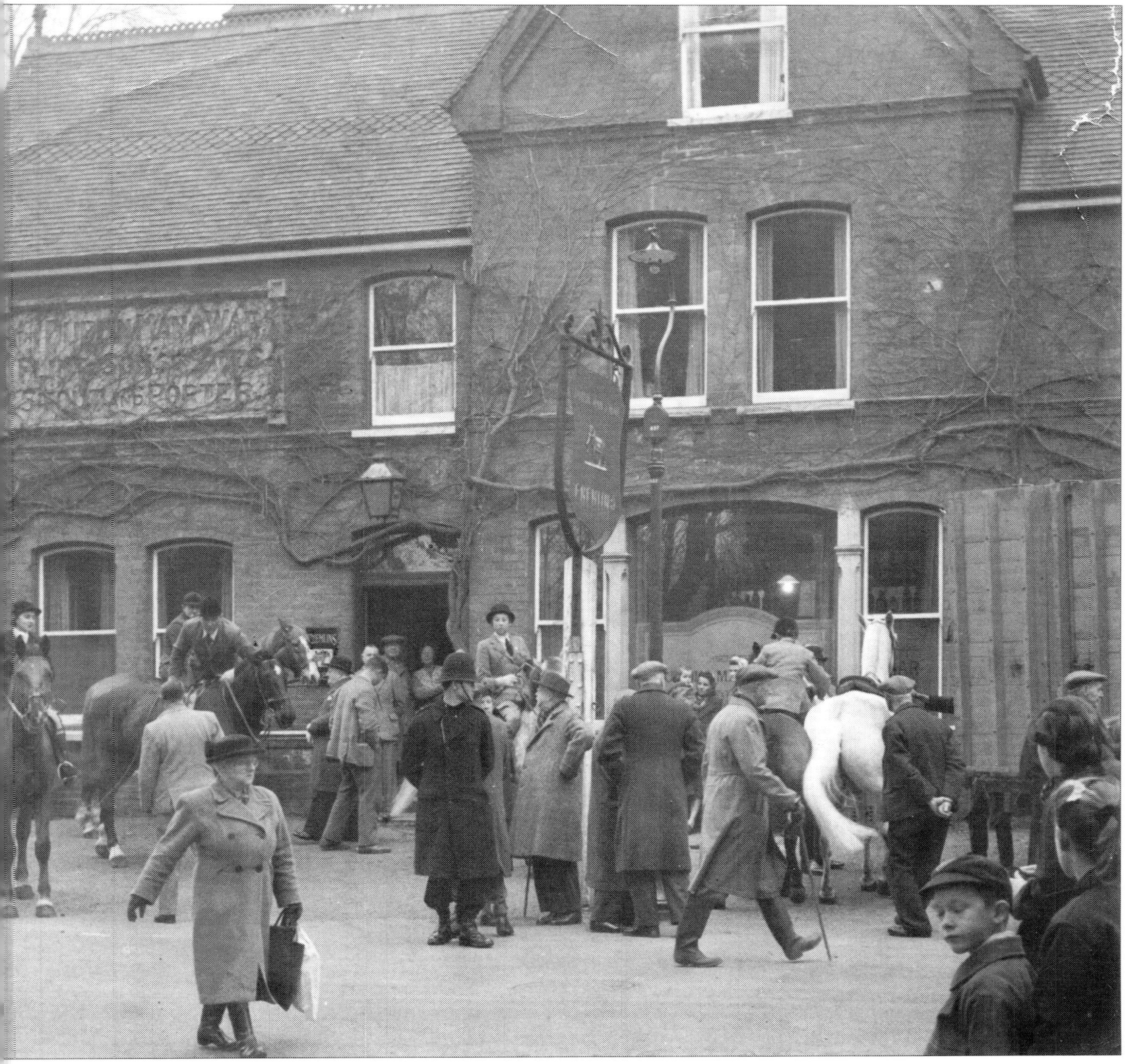

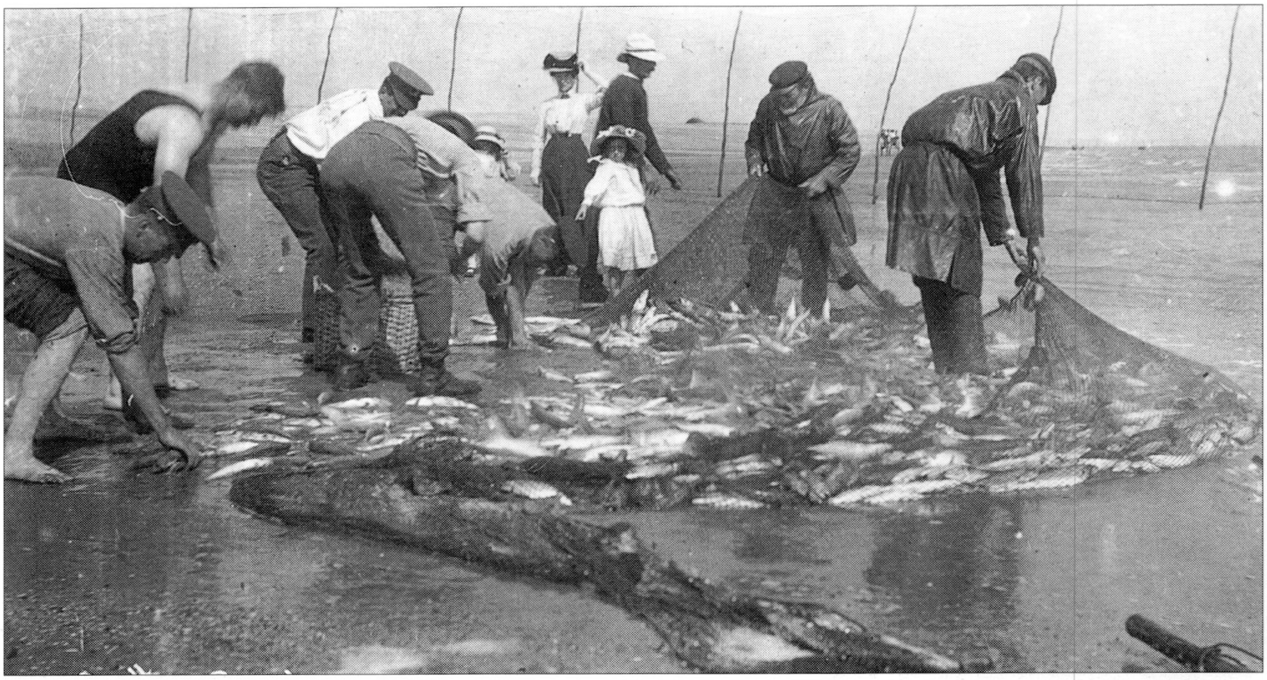

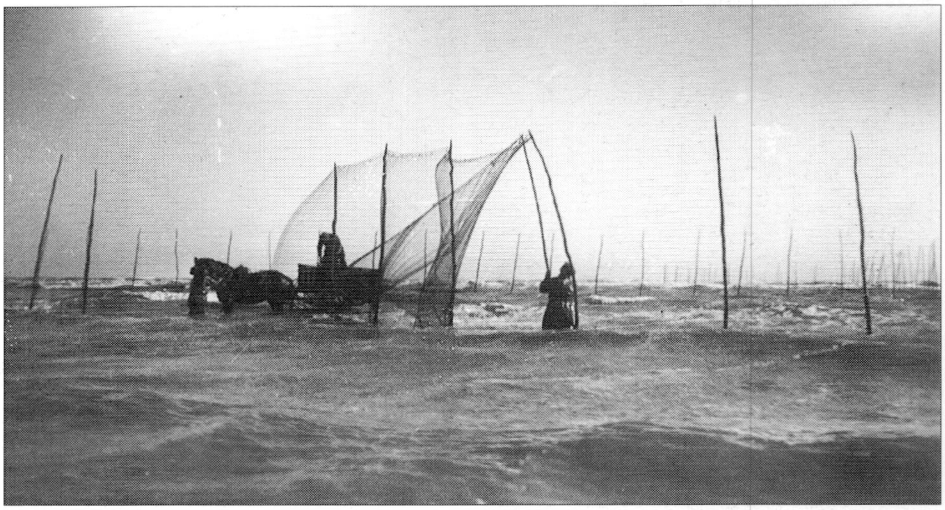

*THEN & NOW: The use of kettlenets for catching mackerel is unique to this part of the coast. A row of poles some 15 feet in length were embedded in the sand, set at right angles to the shore and hung with nets. At the end of the line was a circular ring of nets, the 'bight', with an opening on the landward side. The Gillett family fished at the Midrips for many years: the early photograph shows them c1912 with some of the catch, while the view of the nets was taken in 1949. They continued fishing into the late 1950s, a part time occupation which was dependent on the season and the tides, when they could no longer provide the horse and cart needed to carry the nets and bring in the catch. The family had passes to get through the army ranges to the beach but today this part of the coast is not accessible to the public.*

(Mrs F. Gillett – Lydd WI)

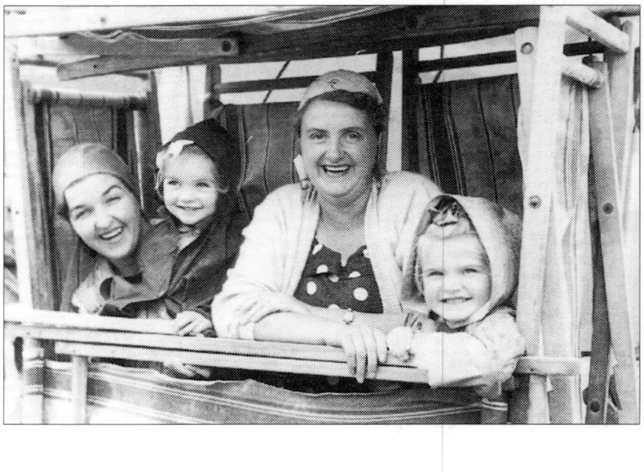

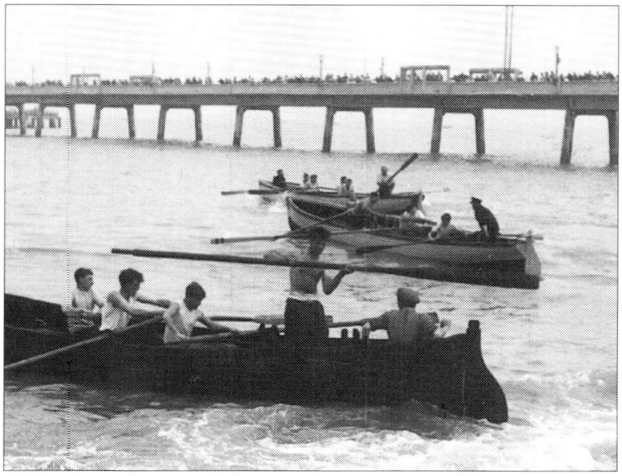

*The Deal 'galleys' were noted for their valour in going out in the severest storms to rescue seamen in the Downs. With time, motorboats took over from oars and sail, but after the war the Deal Regatta programme still included a Rescue Race. This was the start of the race in 1957. A flare was sent up from out at sea for 'help', and the race was launched from the beach to go out round the Bank Buoy and back. Now the last remaining galley is in the Deal Maritime Museum.* (Mrs W. Oram – River WI)

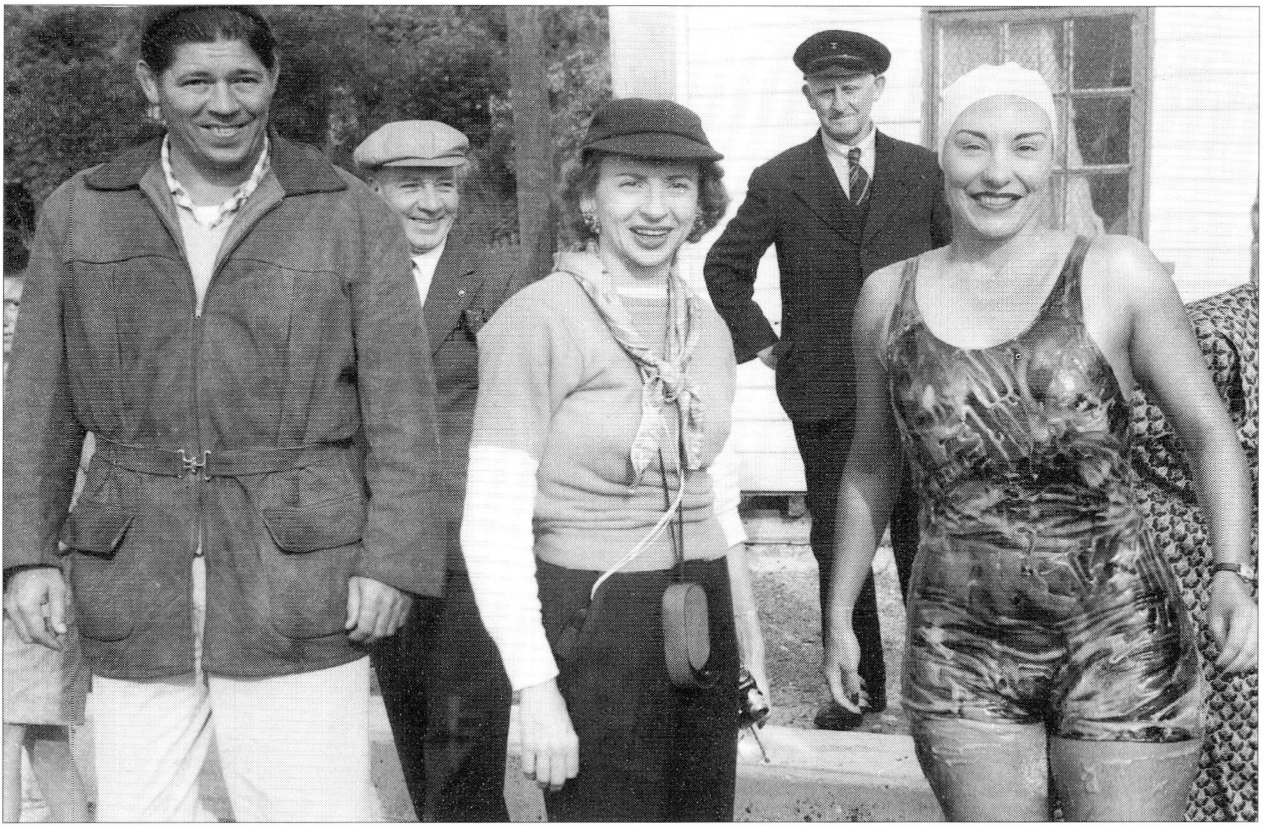

***Left*** *Wet weather has never put us off our enjoyment of a day on the beach. All this family needed at Ramsgate in July 1952 were a few deckchairs and a big smile.* (Jane Graham – Smeeth WI)

*Florence Chadwick, the American swimmer, all prepared to make what was to be the first two-way swim non-stop across the Channel, just before she set off from St Margaret's Bay on 2nd August 1953.* (Pamela Blaxland – Temple Ewell WI)

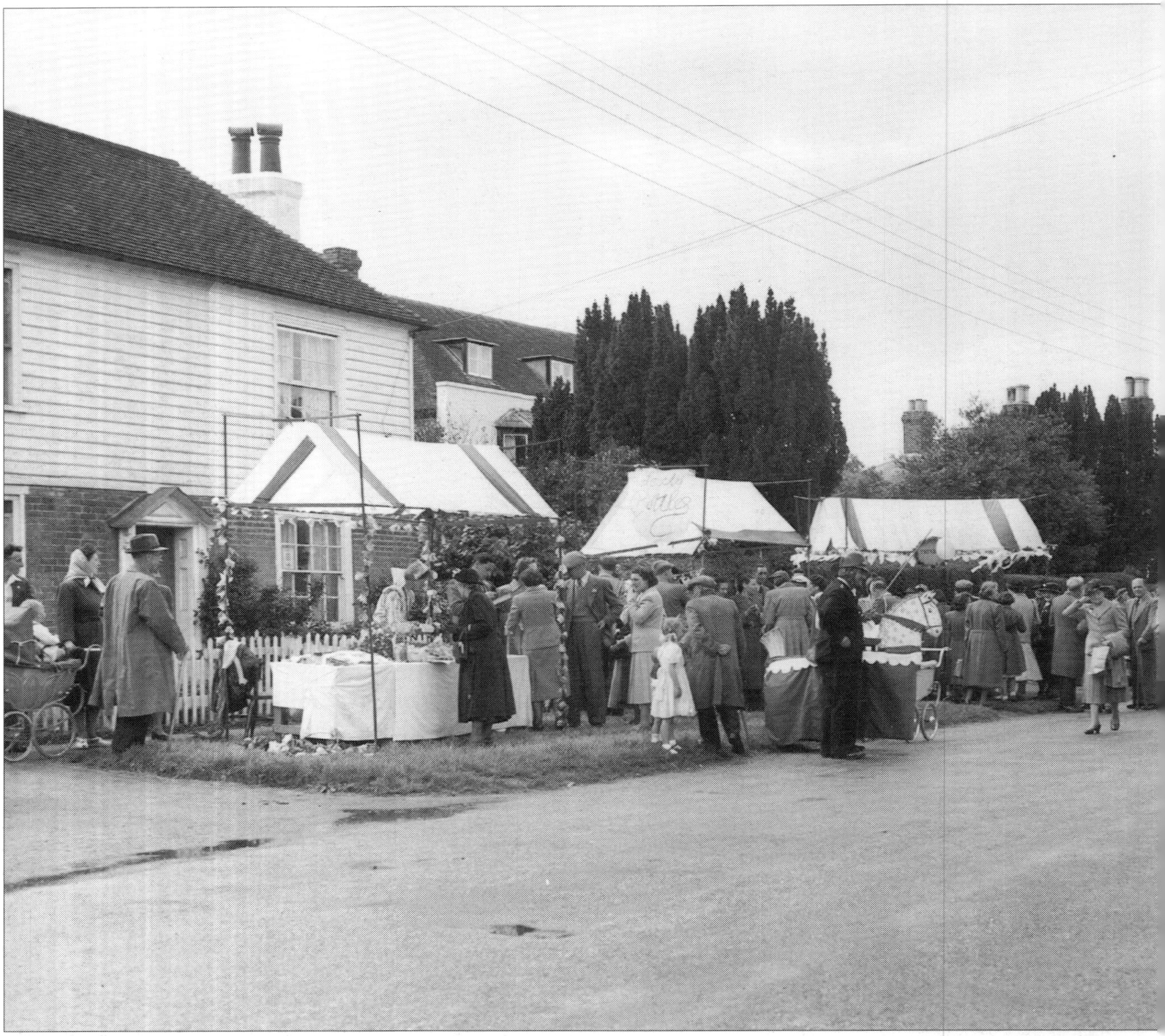

*A street fair in aid of charity was started in Appledore in 1958 and is still going strong – though increasing traffic through the village has forced it to move from the main street.*
(Mrs E. Knight – Appledore WI)

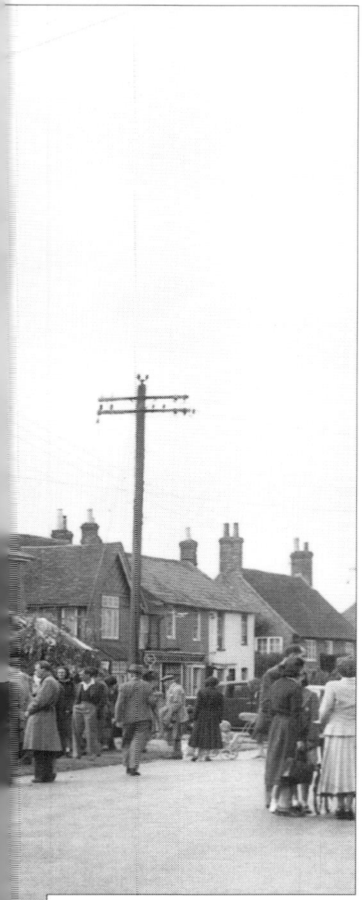

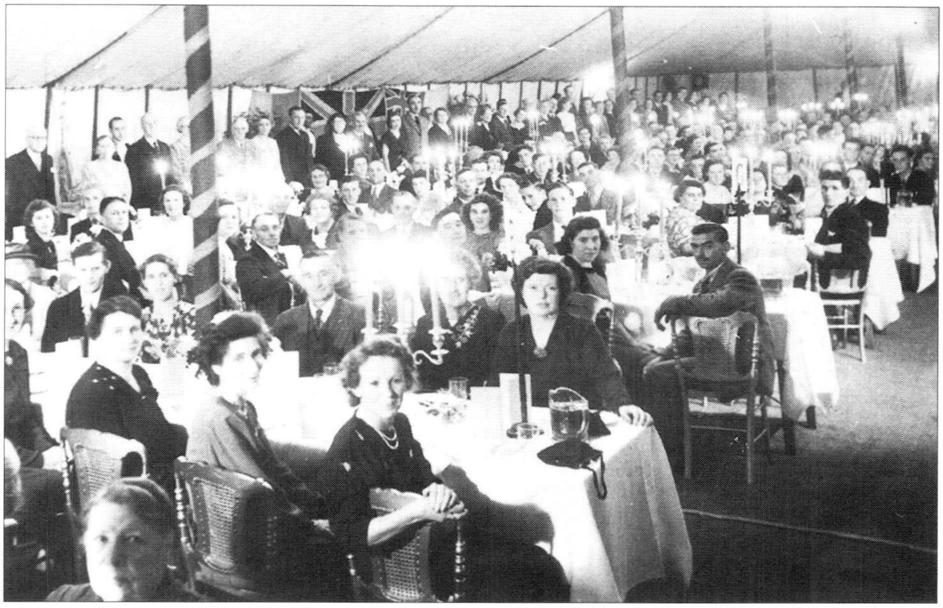

*A double celebration for estate workers – Harvest Home and Henry Rice's 21st birthday at Michaelmas, 1949, held in a marquee in the grounds of Dane Court. The 'big house' still affected the lives of many in East Kent and celebrations like this could draw together such diverse guests as Lord Northbourne, Lady Curzon, footman Alec Easter and gamekeeper Bert Hogpen.*
(Hollingsbee Collection – Tilmanstone WI)

*May Day celebrations at Brabourne school in 1958.*
(Brabourne WI)

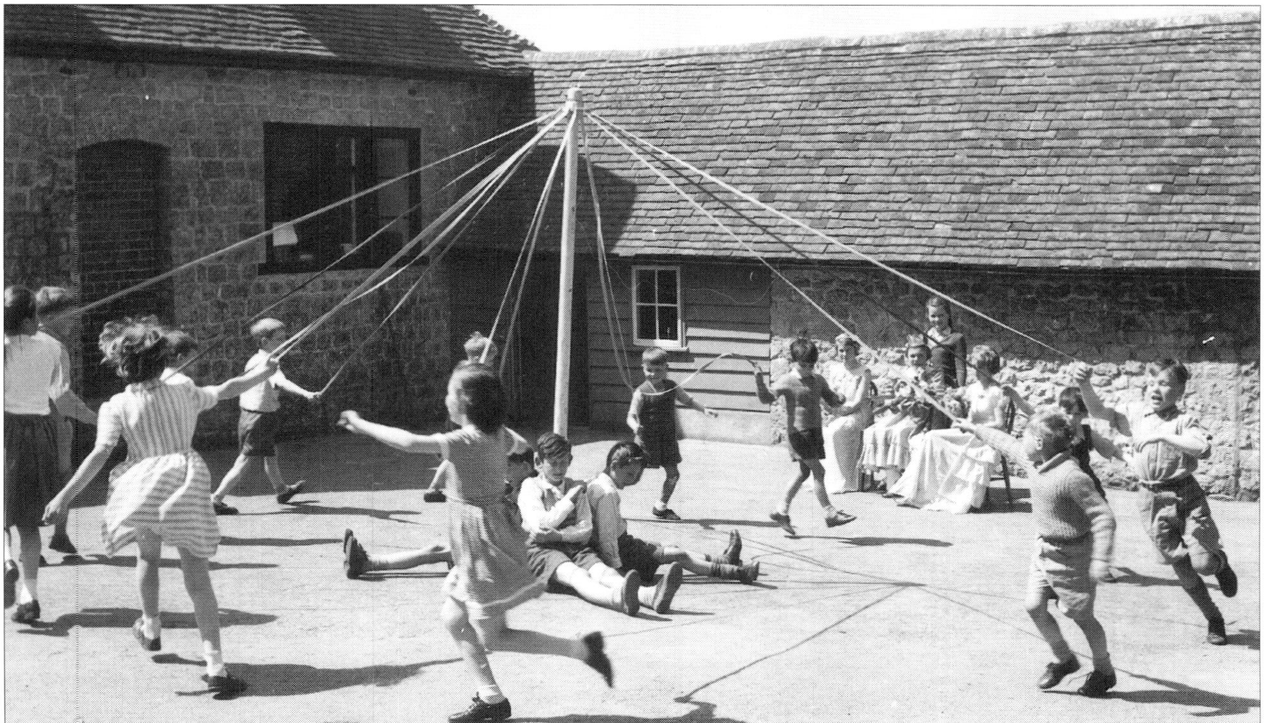

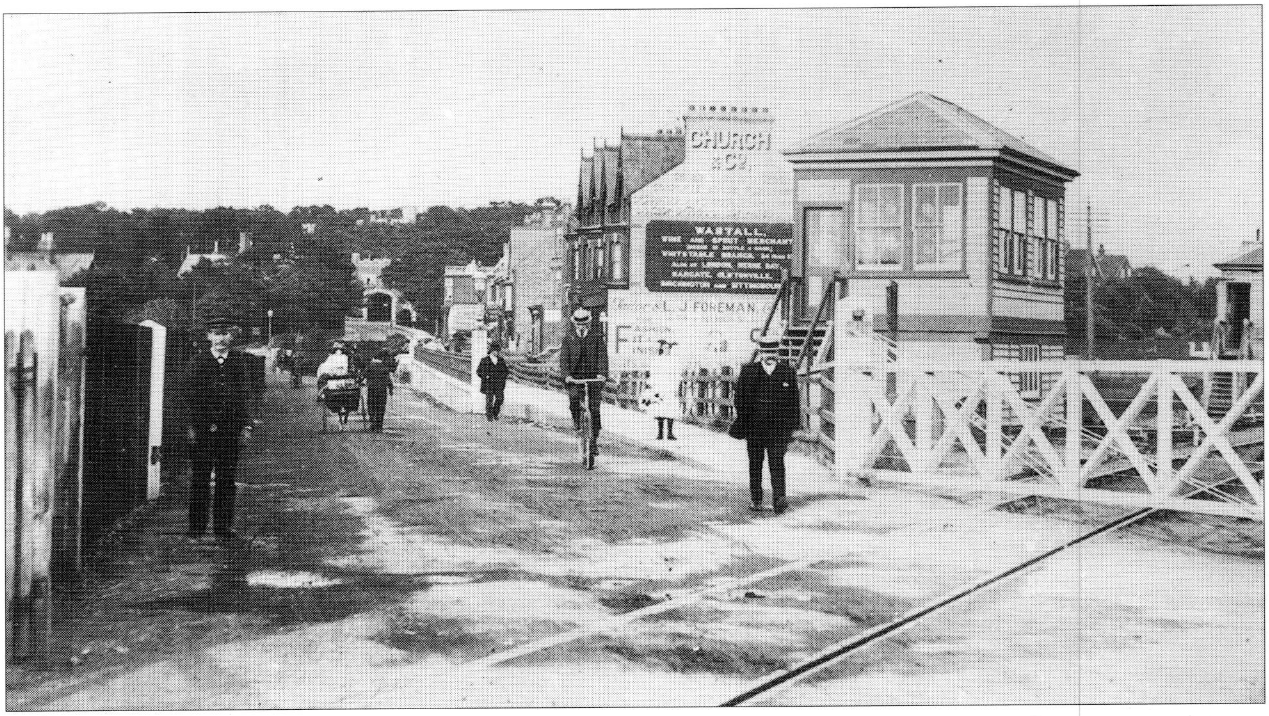


*The 'Crab and Winkle' line, running between Canterbury and Whitstable Harbour, was officially closed in 1952. The line opened on 3rd May 1830 and was the first in Britain to operate a passenger service, allowing people from Canterbury to take a breath of sea air at Whitstable and Tankerton. The photographs show a train at Whitstable station, and an earlier view of where the line crossed the road at Tankerton to enter the harbour. All this was eventually demolished; the Whitstable Youth and Sailing Club now stands where the signal box was, and a block of flats stands on the site of the station.*
(Betty Recton – Selling & District WI)

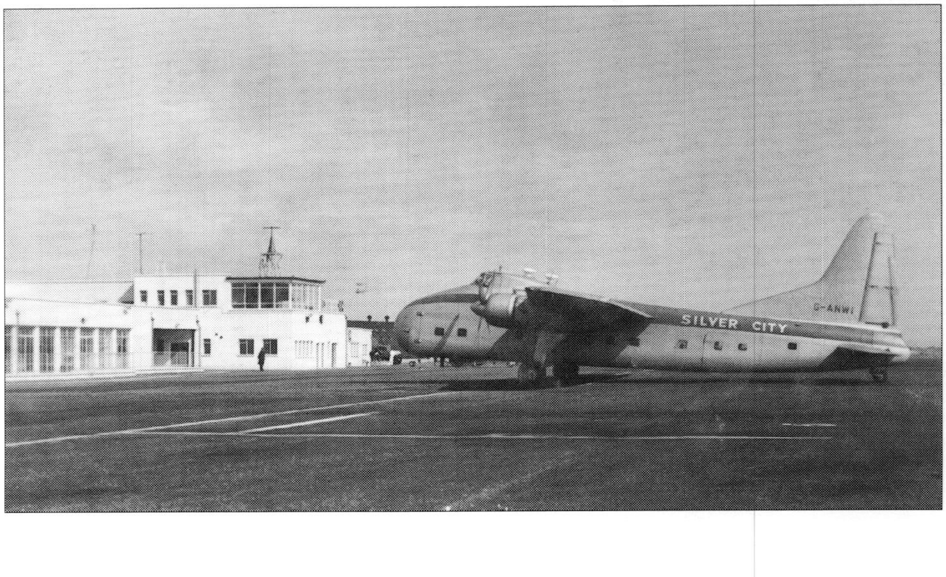


*A Silver City plane at Ferryfield Airport, Lydd in the 1950s. Silver City planes could carry two cars at a time – the passengers sat in front of the plane, which flew from Lydd to Le Touquet at about 2,000 ft above the sea all the way. In this relaxed era of air travel the Customs at Lydd are remembered as being informal and friendly.*
(Barbara Ware – Orlestone, Ham Street & Ruckinge WI)

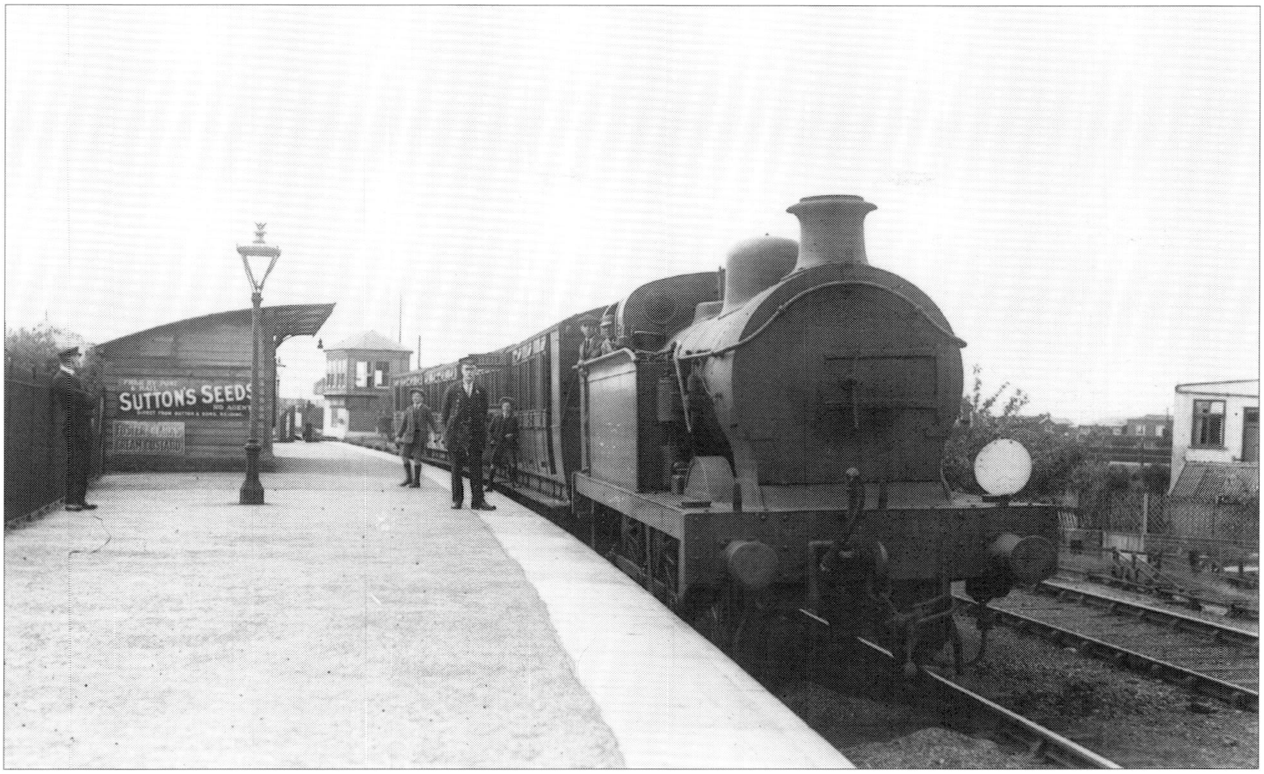


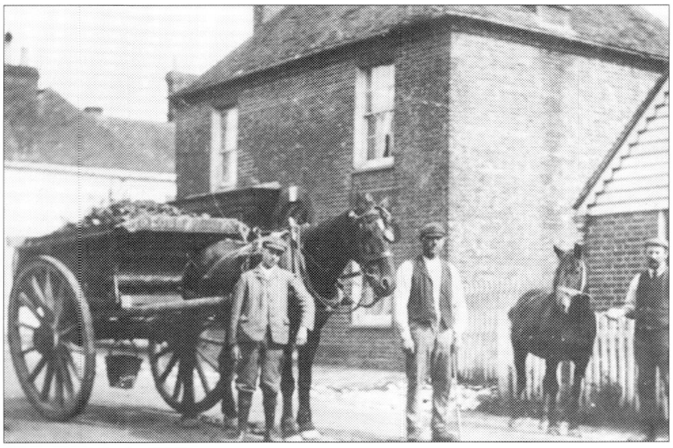

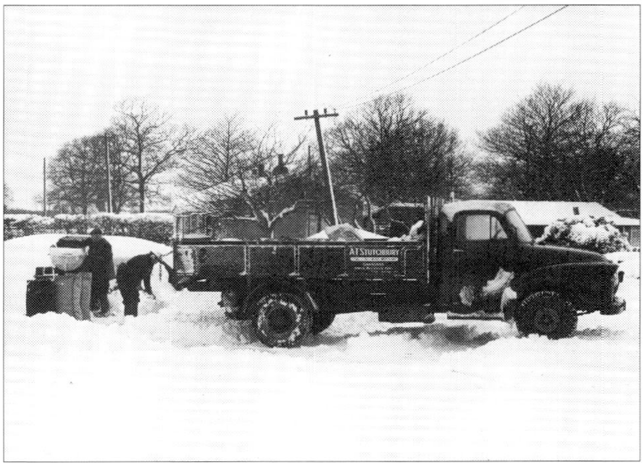

*THEN & NOW. An enduring local business which developed from woodcutting in the 1900s – the Cobb family delivering wood and coal in Ham Street in the early 1920s. The yard was taken over by Stutchbury in 1927, and the firm was still delivering wood and coal from the Ruckinge depot in the 1960s – whatever the weather – and, adding oil to their wares, continued into the 1990s.*
(Barbara Ware – Orlestone, Ruckinge & Ham Street WI)

# The Sixties and Seventies

## (1960 – 1979)

The 'Swinging Sixties' ushered in a new era of permissiveness and created a youth culture that expressed itself in dress and music. For a time, unfortunately, at the end of the 1950s and into the 1960s it was fashionable for Mods and Rockers to descend on East Kent coastal resorts to fight each other – Bank Holidays were particularly busy for local police forces.

In 1965 the University of Kent in Canterbury was granted its charter. Sixty years before, the child of a working family was unlikely to have had the opportunity to be educated to his or her full potential, but now every child had that right. The Open University, started in 1969, also encouraged older people to become students again and make the most of educational facilities.

Most homes now had labour-saving devices undreamed of a few decades before. Private telephones were commonplace, and in 1960 the first telephone exchanges in Kent were converted to Subscriber Trunk Dialling.

During the 1960s the WI continued to be at the forefront of social debate – in 1964 alone they called for restrictions on smoking in public places; routine cervical smear tests; dispensing by doctors in rural areas; and drew attention to the dangers of pollution from toxic chemicals in agriculture and of drugs and chemical hazards in food.

In 1962 the Dartford Tunnel was opened, and the Dover-Boulogne Hovercraft Seaspeed service was started. The enormous increase in car and lorry travel to the Continent was largely due to the size and number of 'Roll on, roll off' ferries operating at this time. Ten years later, the last Golden Arrow train ran direct from Victoria to Paris and a little of the romance went out of cross-Channel travel. Links with the Continent – so important to East Kent – were strengthened when in 1972 Britain joined the EEC, leading to massive changes in trading patterns. In 1971 decimal coinage had been introduced.

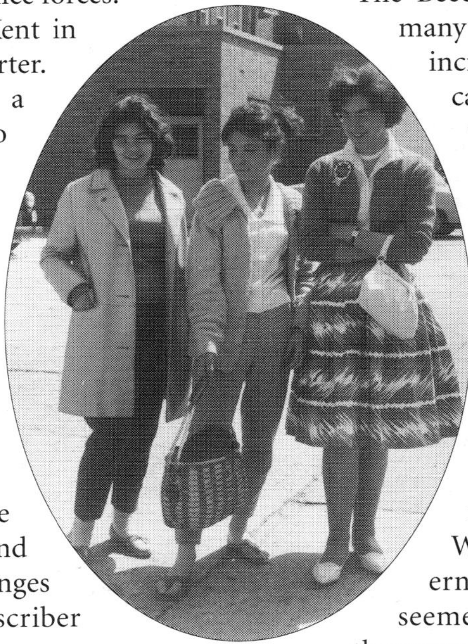

The 'Beeching Axe' had led to the closure of many rural rail services, and hence to an increasing dependence on the motor car. The ever growing housing need was met in part by the creation of housing estates, firstly on sites in towns made available by wartime bombing and slum clearance and later on green field sites. Supermarkets began to threaten the livelihood of the village shop.

The rapidly rising cost of living, and national strikes staged by first the dockers and then the miners, led to the 'Three Day Week' and the fall of the Heath government. Yet in a decade which seemed all conflict and disharmony, there was some evidence of reconciliation in at least one area of human relationships, when in 1970 the 800th anniversary of the martyrdom of Thomas à Becket was celebrated in part by a High Mass for 10,000 Roman Catholics in the precincts of Canterbury Cathedral.

In 1978 Queen Elizabeth The Queen Mother was installed as Lord Warden of the Cinque Ports, a post she holds to this day.

The age of majority was reduced in 1968 from 21 to 18. It was a time when anything seemed possible. In 1969 man walked on the moon for the first time, and Concorde made its first flight.

*In 1960, the 'teenager' had been invented and these girls at the start of the Swinging Sixties would have opportunities and freedoms their parents could never have imagined.* (Kath Carr – Smeeth WI)

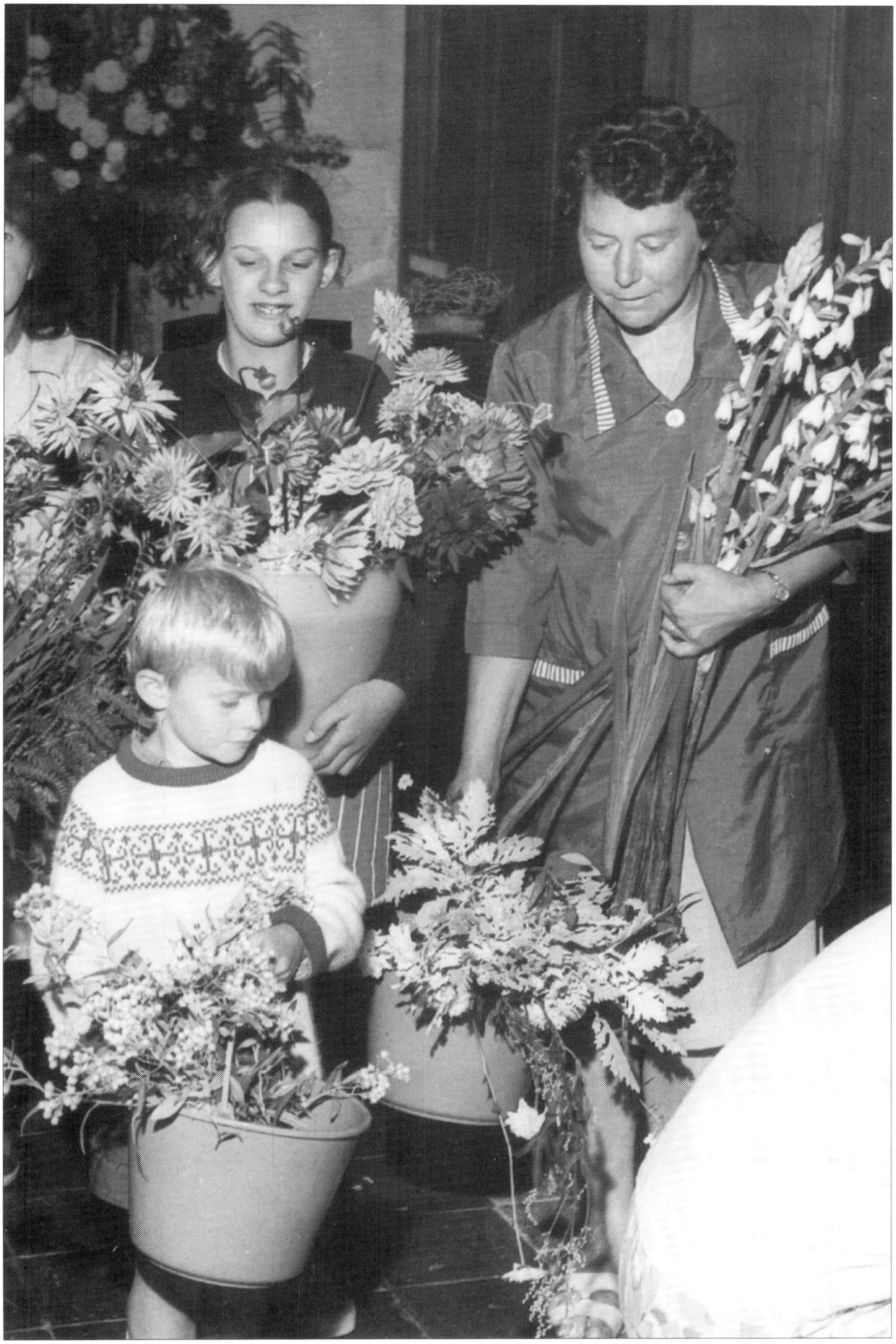

1960 – 1979

*The flower festival at Appledore church was started in 1960 and has been an annual event ever since. It is a busy time for the villagers and attracts visitors from far and wide.* (Mrs E. Knight – Appledore WI)

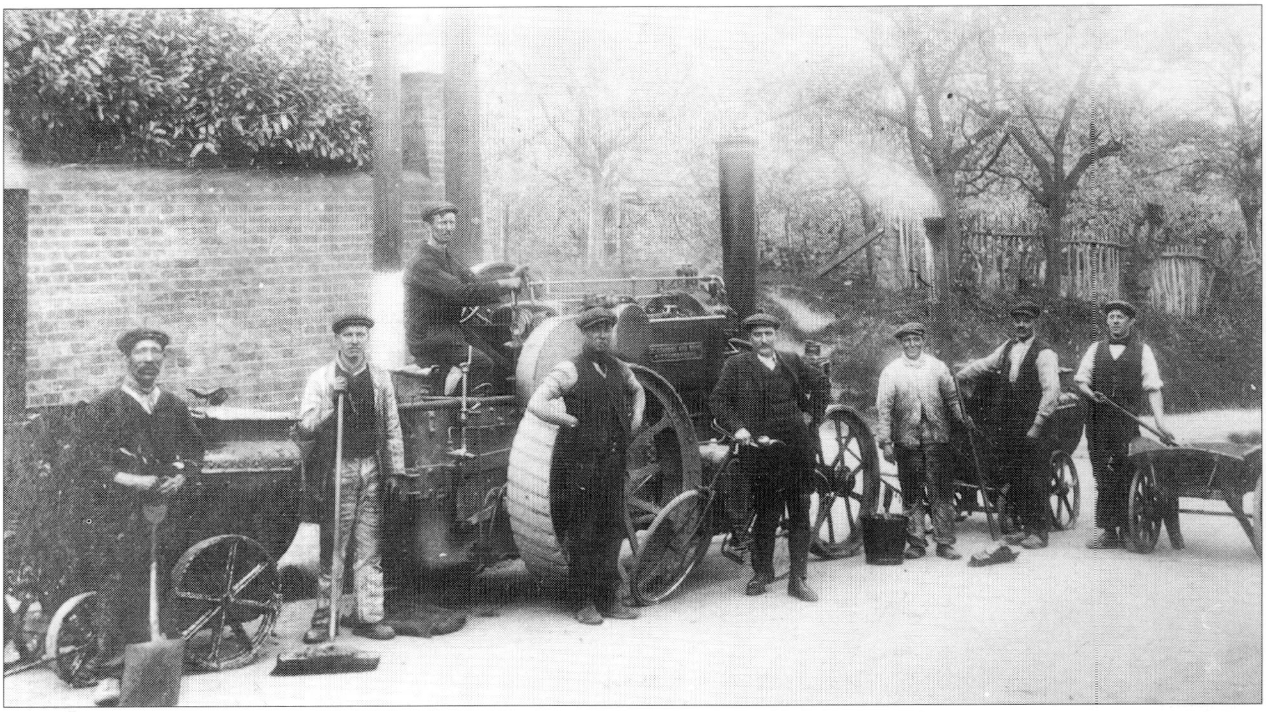

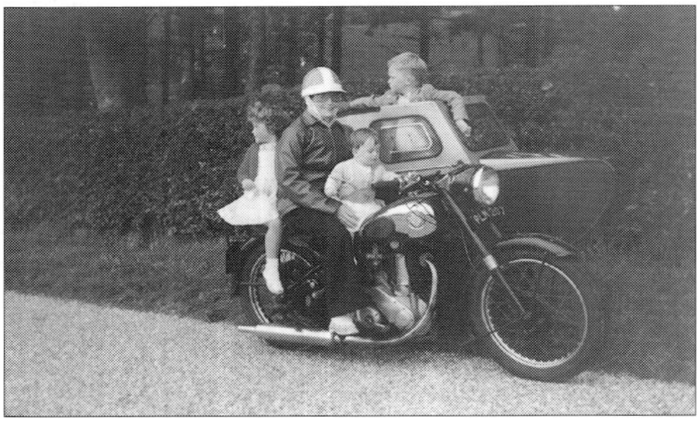

*THEN & NOW: The road gang, with Ovenden's steam engine, building the (now) A2 before the First World War, pictured at Keycote Hill, Sittingbourne, contrasts with the building of the M20 at Ashford in the mid 1970s.*
(Mrs D. Ovendon – Kennington WI & Mrs R. Bowles – Wye WI)

*A motorbike and sidecar was transport for the Williams family of two adults and three children in 1960.*
(Mary Williams – Kennington WI)

*The end of the war had not meant an ending to defence planning, as this Civil Defence exercise in Ashford in 1961 shows. All the food – enough for 30 firemen and women – was cooked on the contraption in the left of the picture, made out of a dustbin, various tins and lots of mud! Afterwards everything had to be returned as it was found.*
(Mary Williams – Kennington WI)

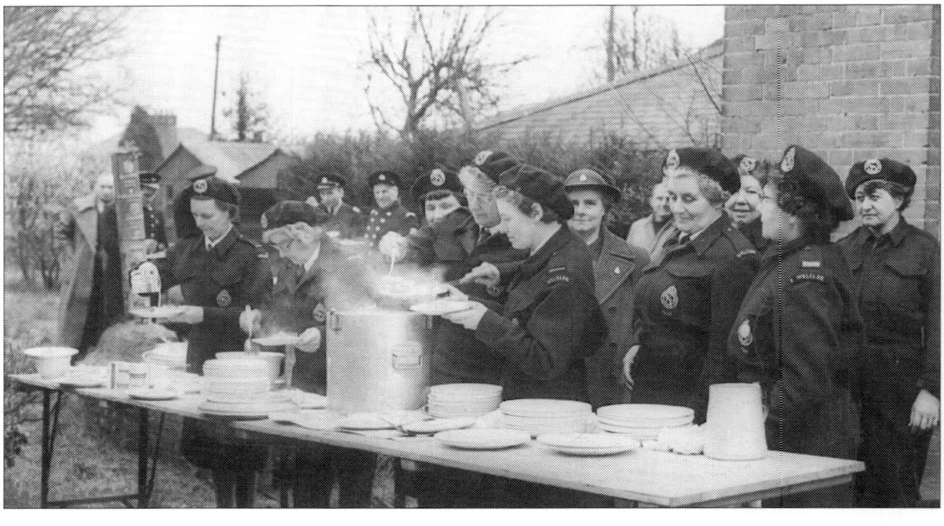

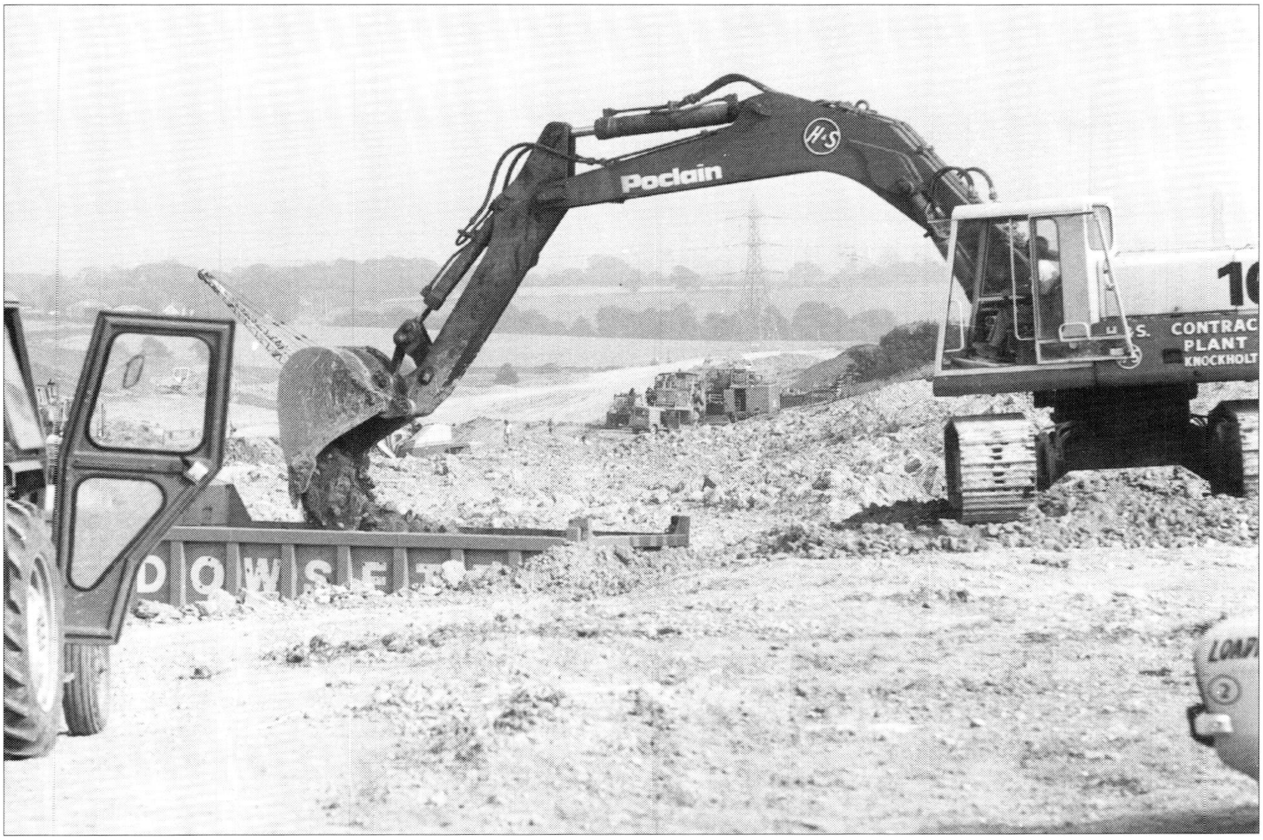


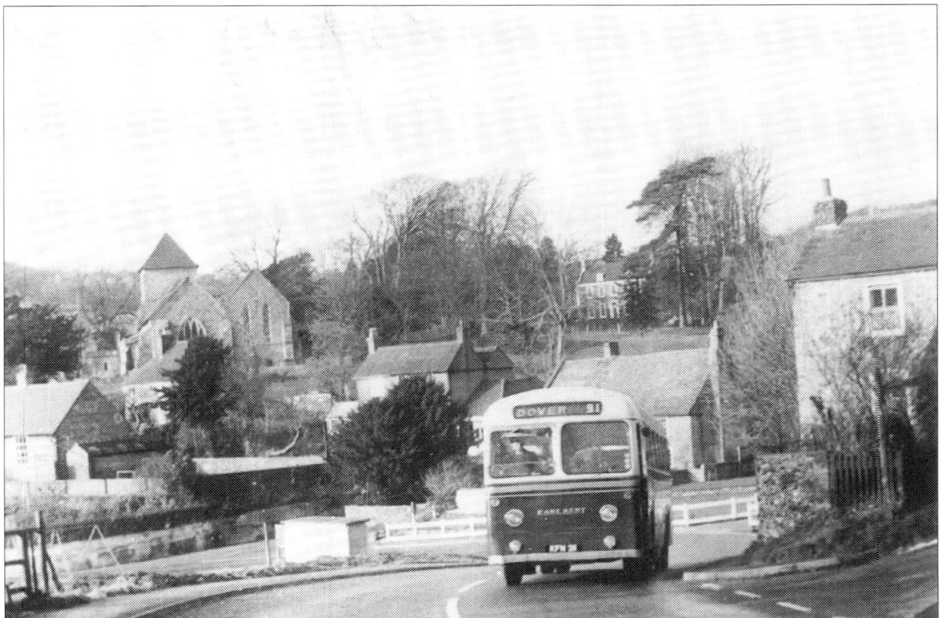


*A view of Alkham in the 1960s. Though car ownership was increasing at a rapid rate, the country buses were still a vital amenity for rural areas. (Susan Lees – Alkham WI)*

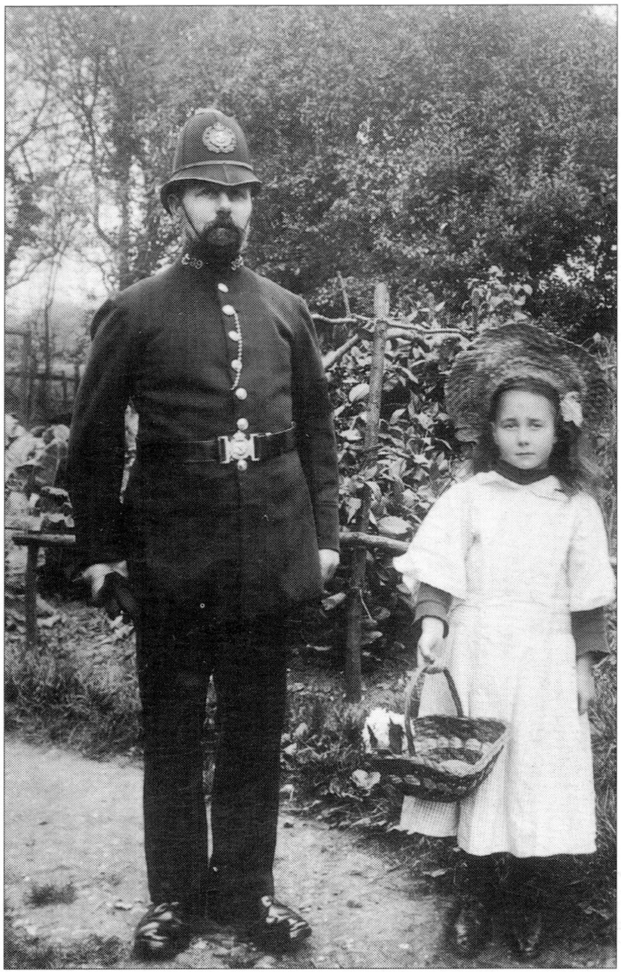

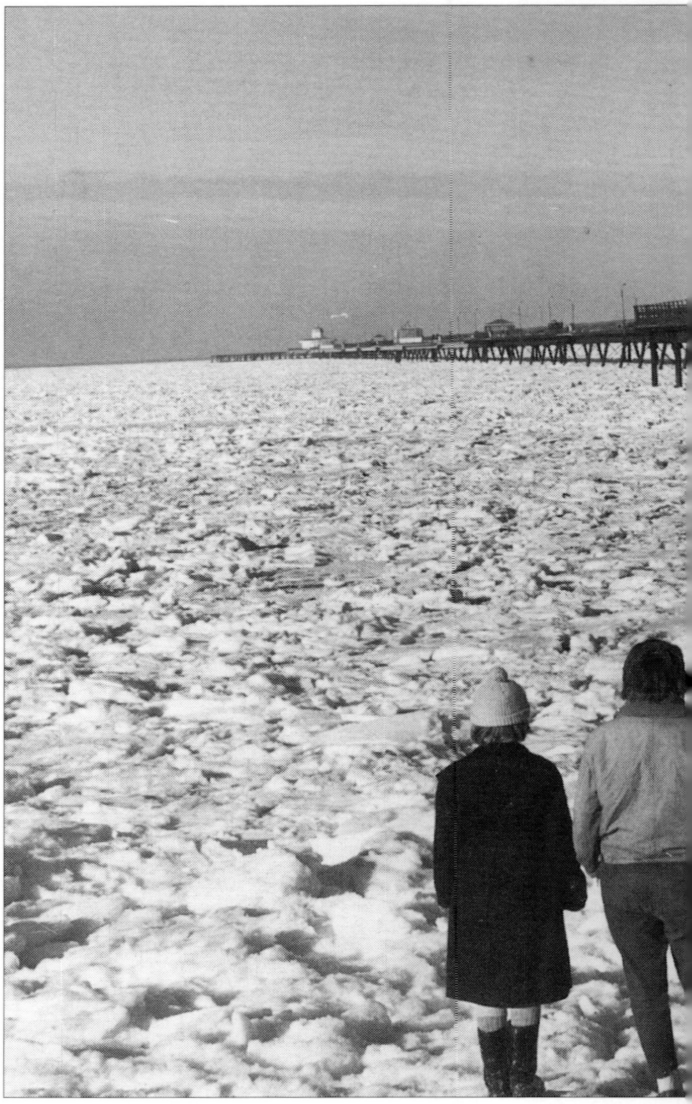

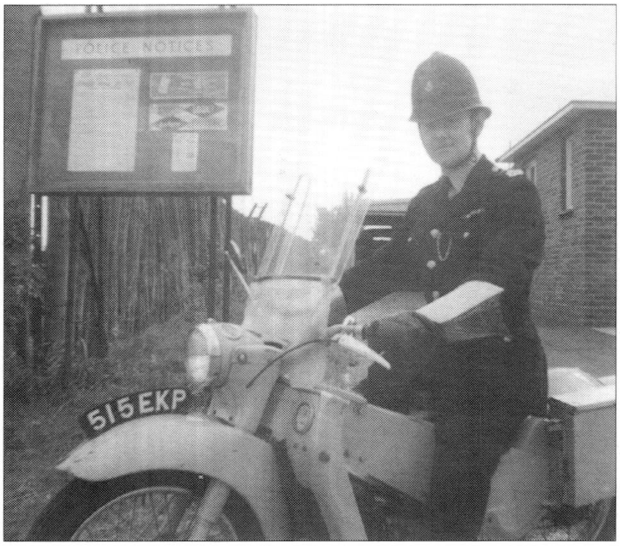


*THEN & NOW: PC Potter of Ham Street, the village policeman from 1906 to 1910, and PC Simpkins off on his beat in 1961. The latter was at Lower Stike on the Hooe Peninsular, a very busy area which included the traffic to and from the BP oil refinery on the Isle of Grain, as well as all the foreign seamen coming in off the oil tankers. Peter Simpkins, as with all ex-service policemen, had his medal ribbons sewn on to his tunic.*

(Barbara Ware – Orlestone, Ham Street & Ruckinge WI
& Mrs J. Simpkins – Swalecliffe with Chestfield WI)

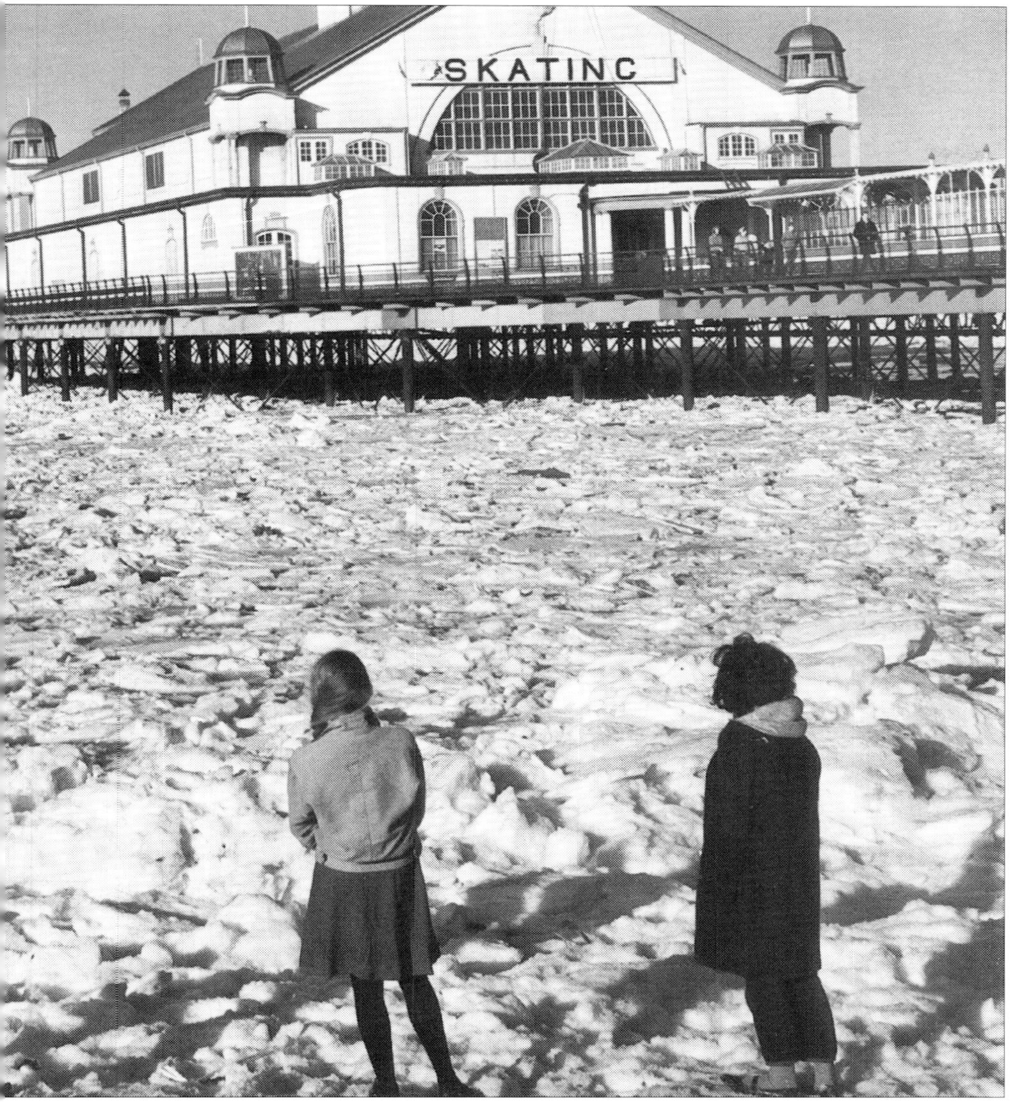


*The severe weather that began before Christmas 1962 and continued for several months into 1963, froze the sea at Herne Bay and other areas off the coast of East Kent.*
(Mrs V. Thompson – Goodnestone WI)

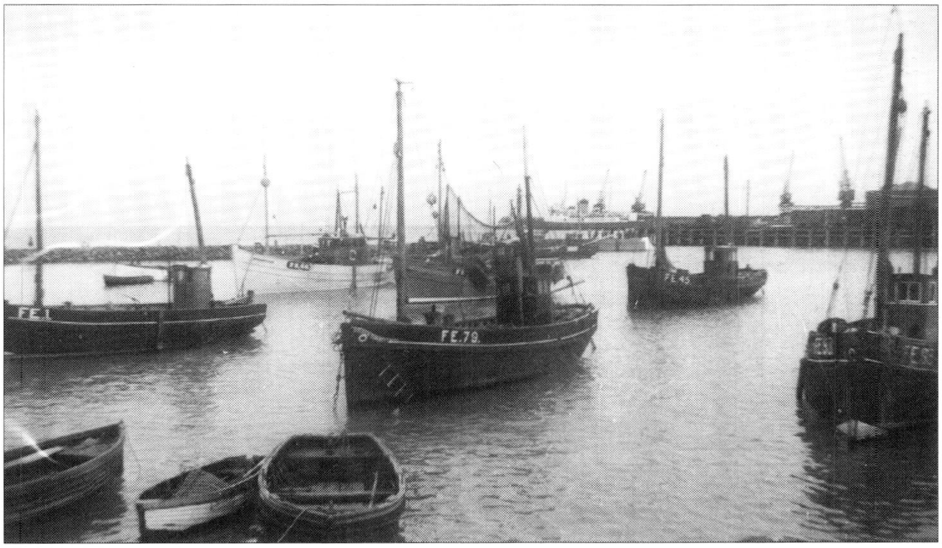

*Fishing continued to be an important part of the local economy – the fishing fleet in Folkestone harbour in 1960.*
(Priscilla Harper – Egerton WI)

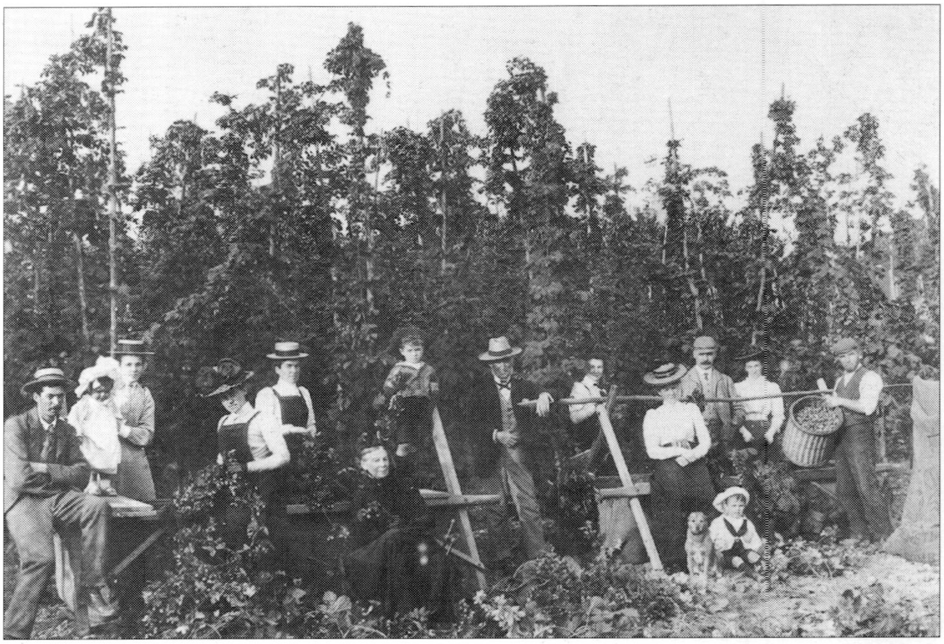

*THEN & NOW: Through the century, many local families spent several weeks each year in the hopfields of East Kent, earning extra cash for the winter months. It is remembered as a time of great comradeship as well as hard work.*
*The Bensted family at Street Farm, Ulcombe in 1902, showing the wood-framed hop bins with hessian pockets, the bushel basket for measuring, and the hop poke into which the hops were packed.*
(Jane Oliver – Boughton with Eastwell WI)

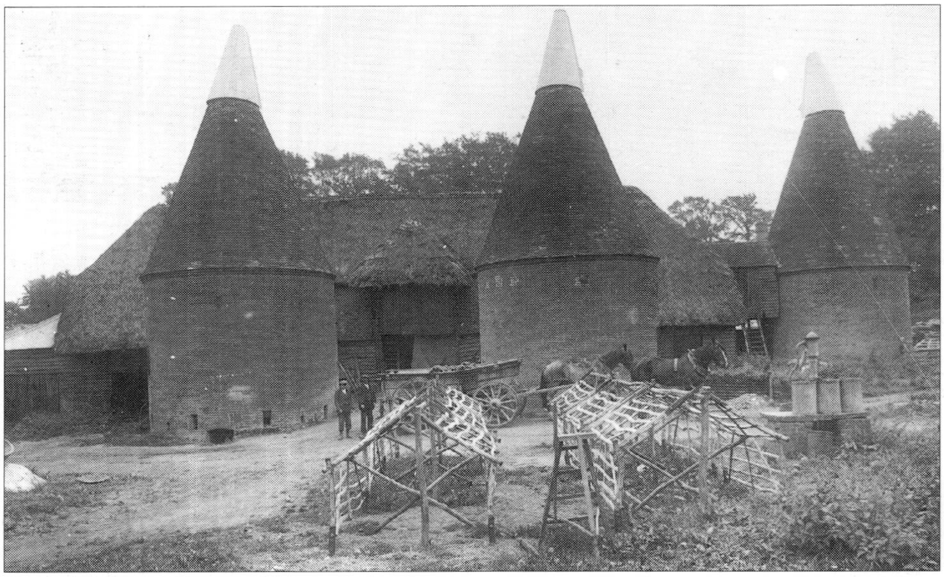

*The old oast at Owens Court Farm at Selling in the 1920s, part of the Sondes Estate and still a working hop farm today. The wooden hurdles in the foreground were called 'horses', the large pokes of green hops being laid out on them prior to going into the kilns for drying.*
(Mrs E. Higgs – Selling WI)

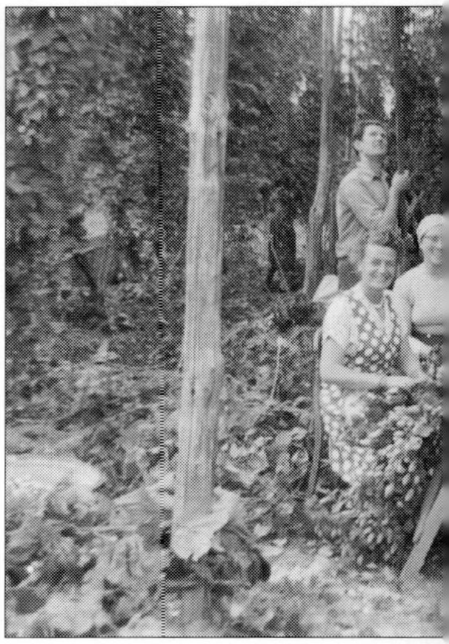

*Pickers at Wye College in the 1960s. Within a few more years hop-picking was revolutionised by the introduction of machines which required the complete vines to be brought to them for stripping.*
(Grace Thompsett – Kennington WI)

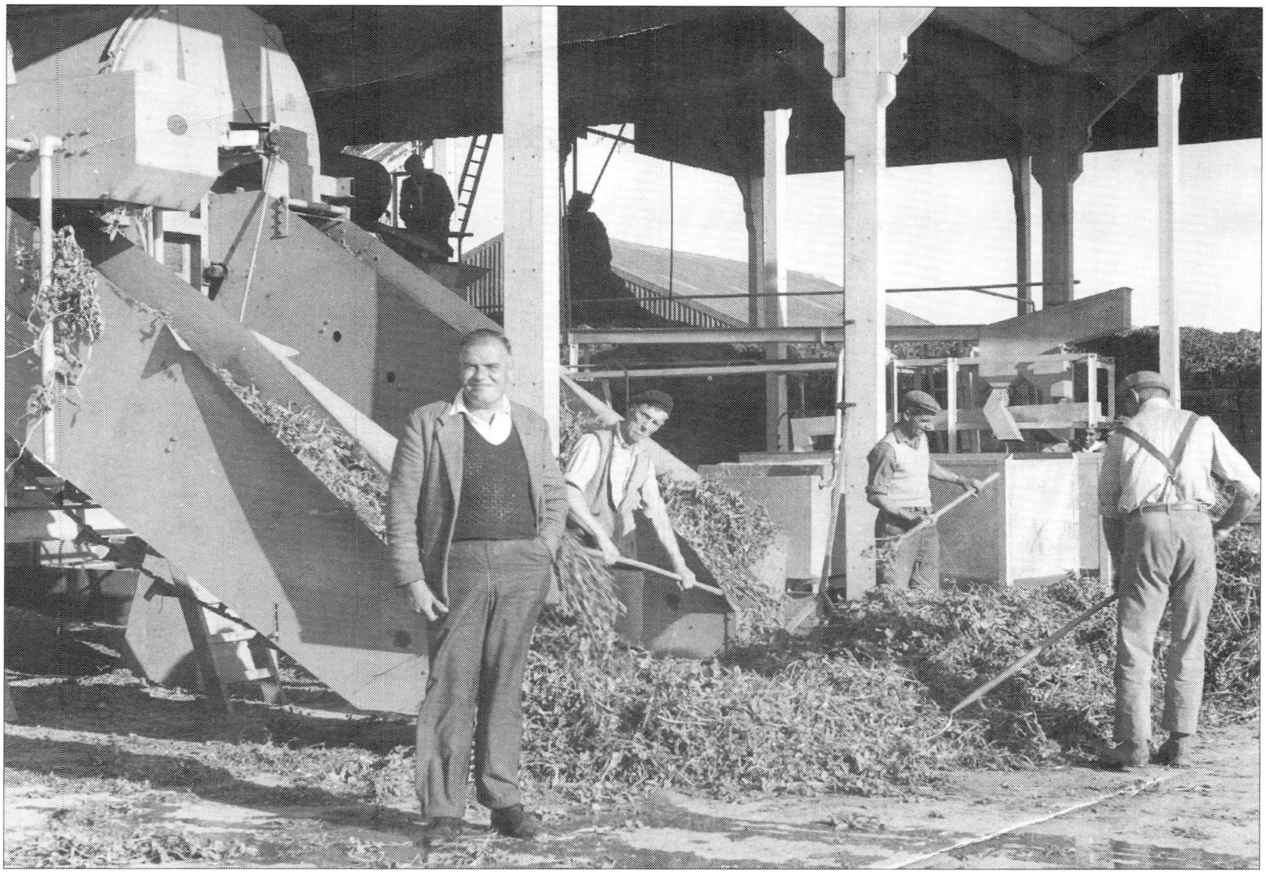

***Above*** *Pea vining in 1960 at Court Lodge Farm, Appledore. The peas have been cut and transported to the barn where Dennis Clifton's men load them onto a conveyor belt. The machine stripped the peas into bins. The work went on for 24 hours non-stop during harvest. 'Nowadays a machine goes into the fields and the whole is done in one go.'*
(Mrs E. Knight – Appledore WI)

***Below*** *The old manual telephone exchange in Tufton Street, Ashford in the early 1960s. Every Ashford subscriber had a direct line to this busy exchange, and when all the lines had been taken some residential subscribers had to share a service line. It closed in 1968 when the new automatic exchange opened in Regents Place.*
(Barbara Ruffle – Little Chart WI)

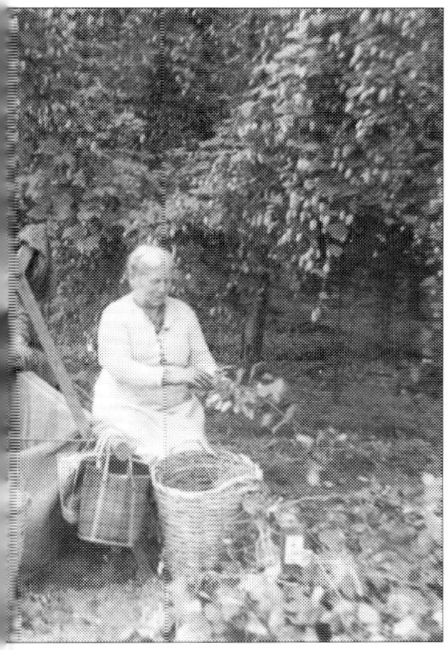

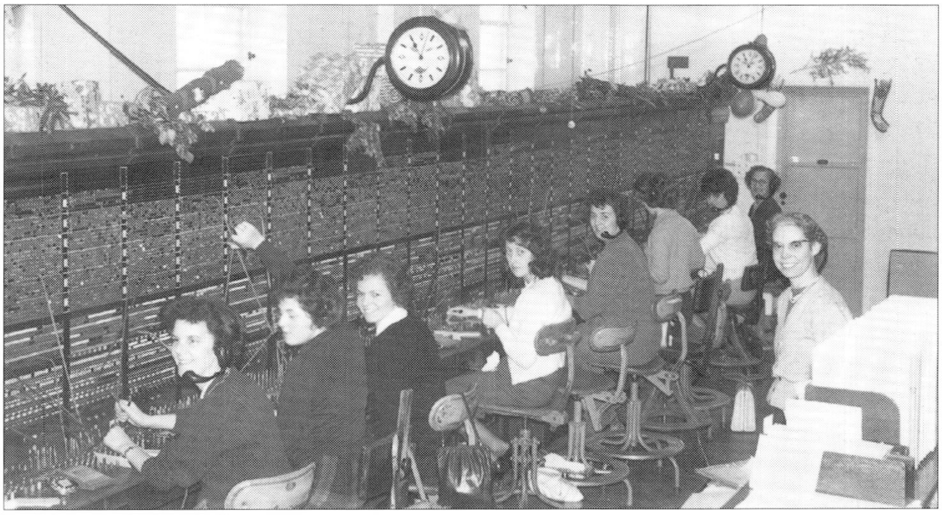

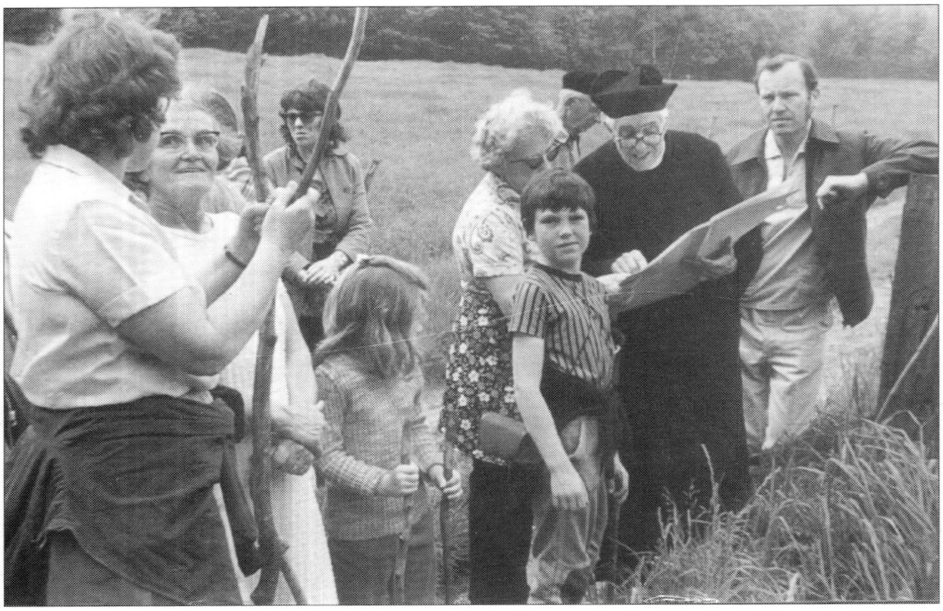

*Parishioners beating the bounds at Rogationtide in 1973, around Godmersham parish. Canon Brade -Birks was vicar of Godmersham for nearly 50 years, until 1977. He was also a lecturer on soil at Wye College, a world authority on millipedes, an acknowledged authority on local history and a successful mechanic at keeping his Norman motor bicycle running for his pastoral work.*
(Celia Armitage – Godmersham with Crundale WI)

***Below*** *Traditional activities have lost none of their appeal – the 2nd Birchington Brownies maypole dancing in Birchington's main street in the 1960s.*
(Elsie Foreman – Acol & District WI)

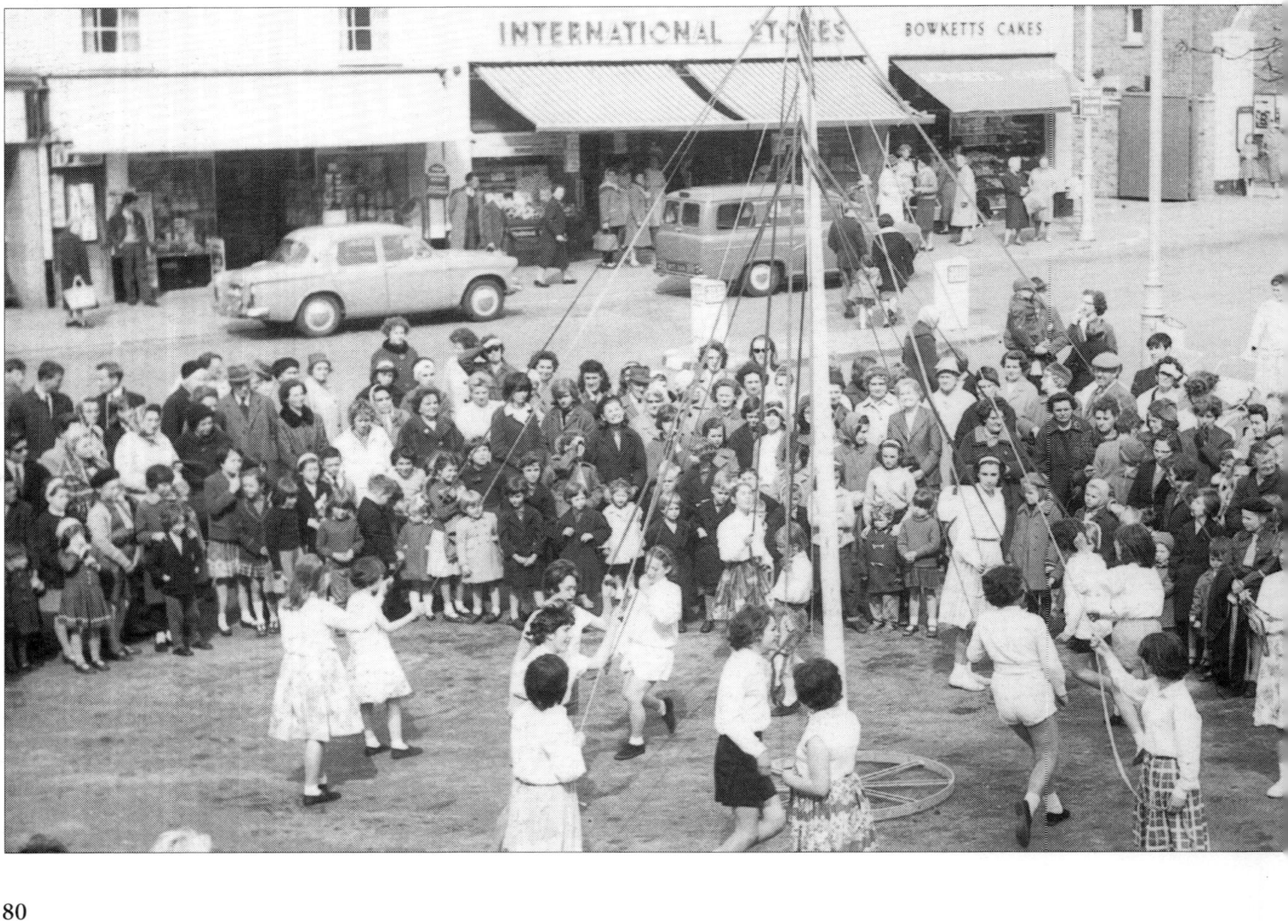

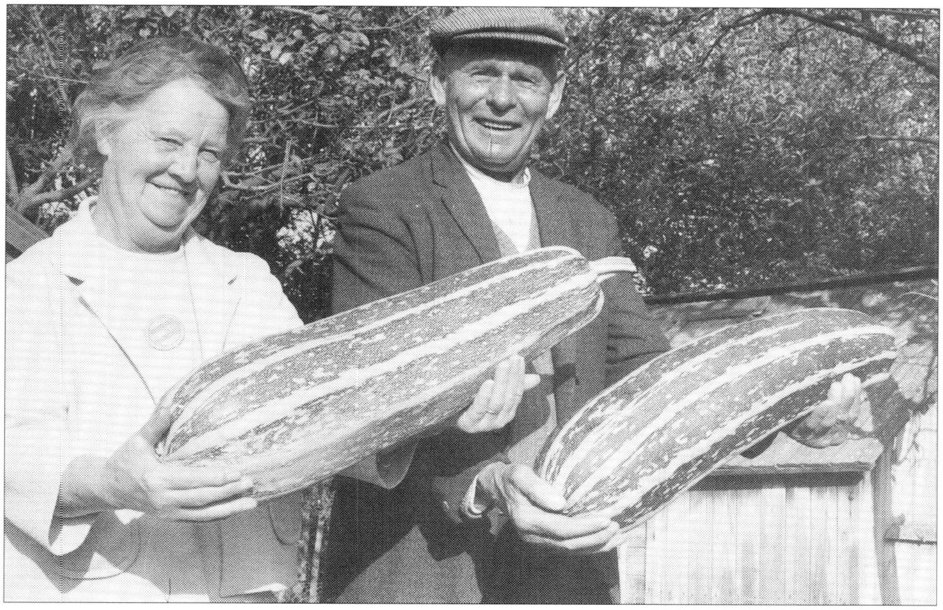

*Mr and Mrs Barham, founder members of the Acol Horticultural Society.*
(Elsie Foreman – Acol & District WI)

*In June 1977 the Queen's Silver Jubilee was celebrated in towns and villages all over East Kent. Egerton school held a party, and elsewhere there were street parties, sports, dances and fireworks.*
(Priscilla Harper – Egerton WI)

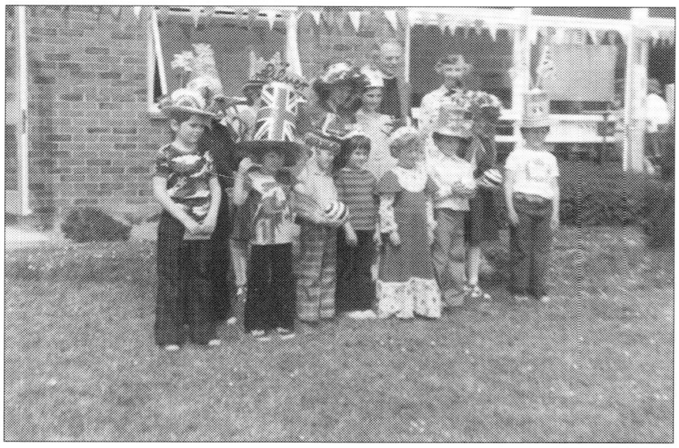

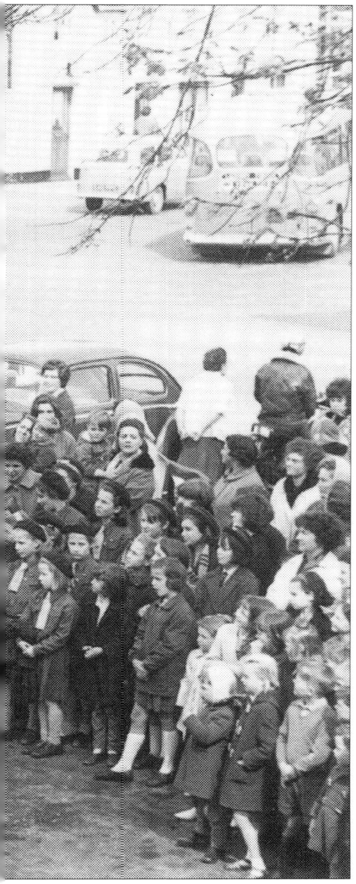

***Below** Sellindge village school Nativity play in 1976.*
(Mrs M. Yarnold – Sellindge WI)

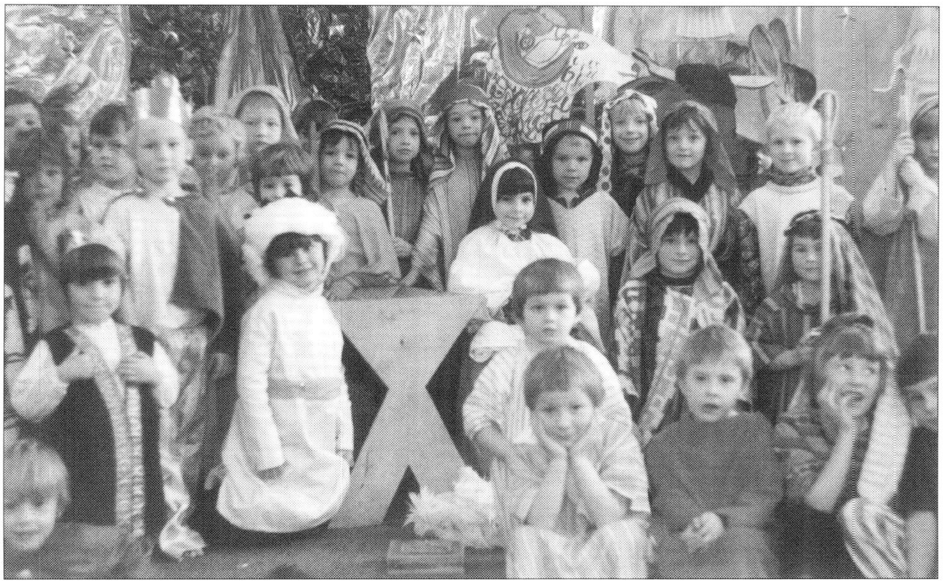

# THEN & NOW
# CHANNEL TUNNEL

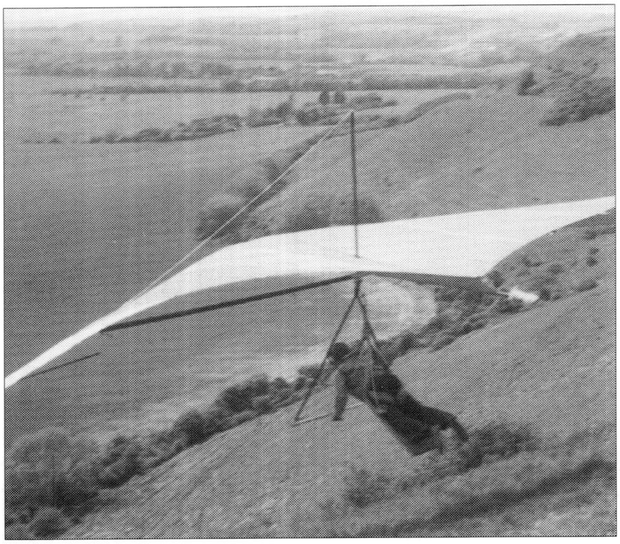

*The area chosen for the Terminal buildings, where the road and rail links meet the tunnel entrances, was an open site a mile and half inland and below the escarpment overlooking Cheriton and the villages of Newington and Peene. The hang gliders had to go elsewhere.* (Celia Armitage – Godmersham with Crundale WI)

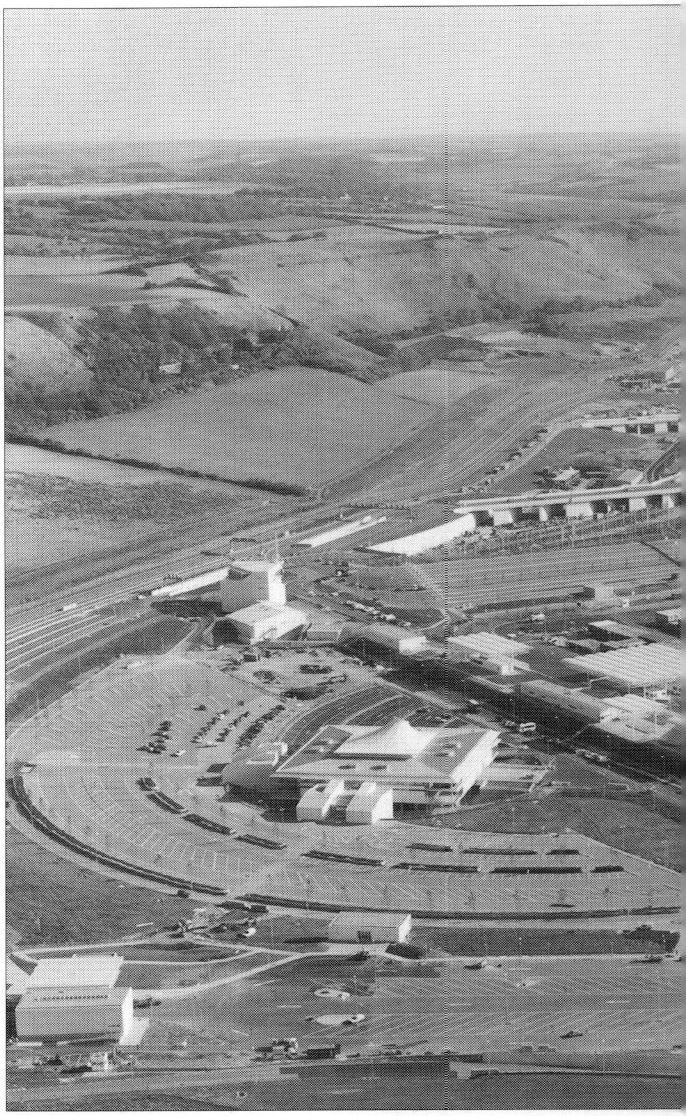

*The construction of the Tunnel required a platform close to sea level from which the boring machines could be serviced, the spoil from the borings disposed of and where the massive amounts of constructional materials brought by rail from the Isle of Grain could be stored. The Lower Shakespeare Cliff platform was steadily enlarged with the massive quantities of spoil from the tunnels and has now been renamed Samphire Hoe, landscaped and re-seeded to make a Public Amenity and Leisure Area.* (Mrs E. Spicer – Capel le Ferne WI)

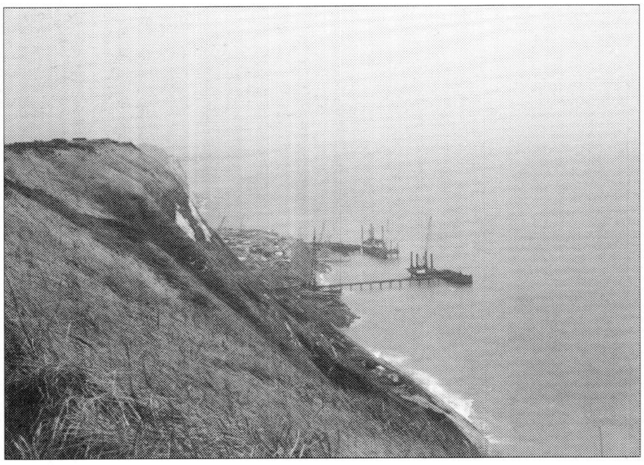

*During construction, an observation tower and exhibition centre were built and sightseeing tours of the area arranged. When the boring was finished, one of the big boring machines was displayed, marked 'For Sale, one careful owner'.* (Mrs J. Owen – Chartham WI)

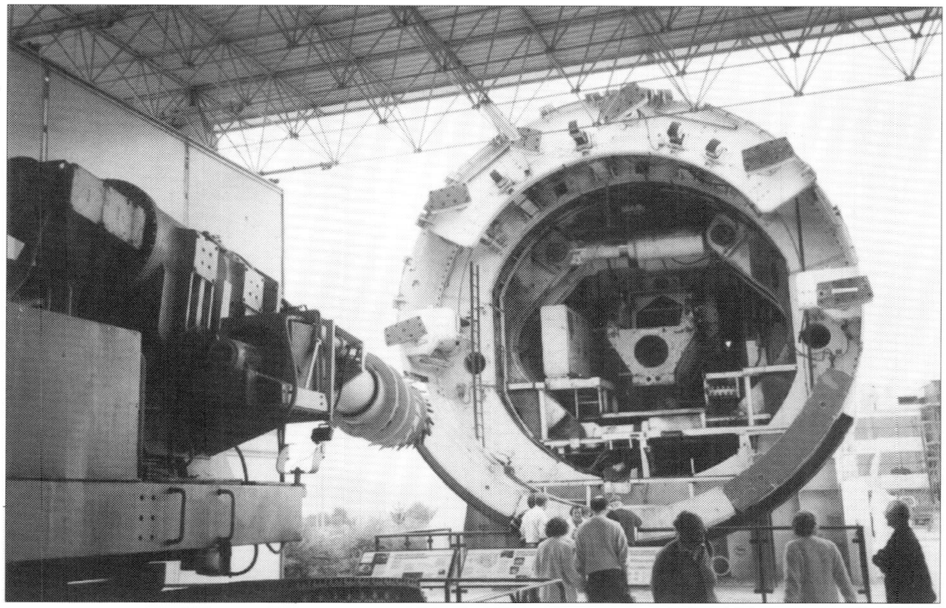

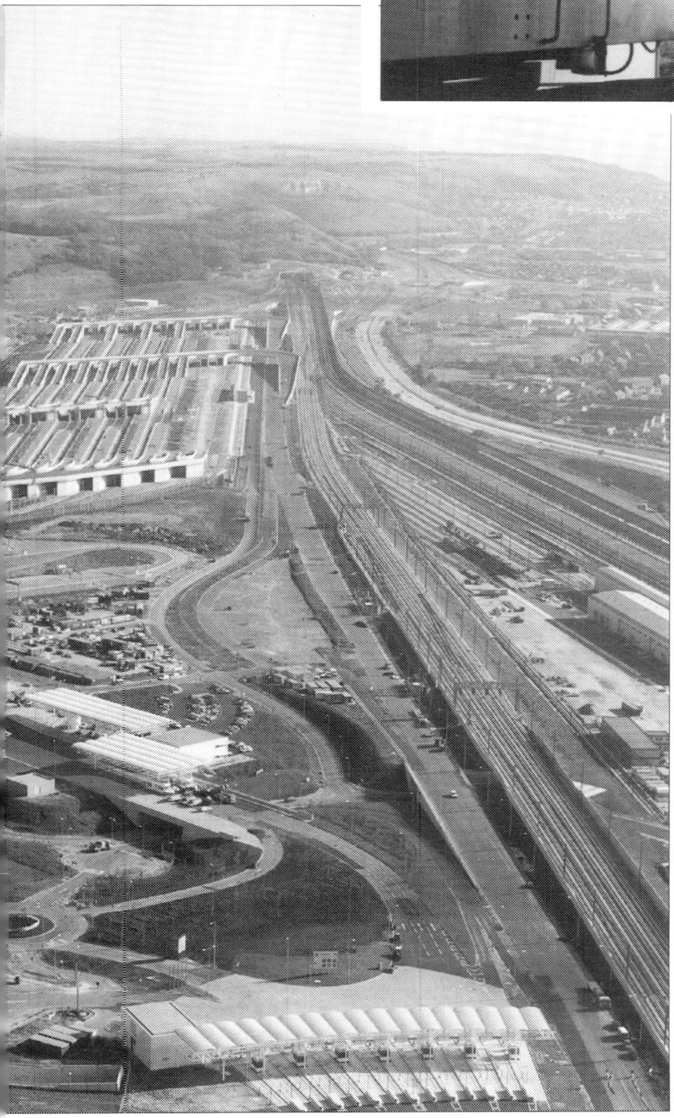

**Below** *The whole project required extensive new motorways stretching all the way from London to the site itself and beyond to Dover. The precise route of the new road, and later, the rail link which was also required, was everywhere fiercely contested.*
(Mrs M. Yarnold – Sellindge WI)

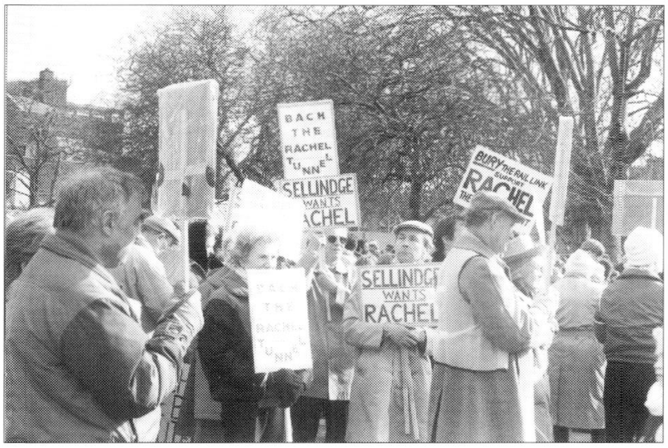


**Left** *The Cheriton Terminal nearing completion in October 1993. The pay booths are in the right foreground, while the Terminal building housing duty free shops, restaurants etc is the large square building middle left. Passports and Immigration booths are in the middle with the loading ramps beyond and the two portals of the Tunnel itself in the distance.* (Eurotunnel Press Office)

# MODERN TIMES

## (After 1980)

Since 1958, the number of goods vehicles licensed in the UK had increased threefold and their size doubled by the 1980s, while the number of private cars had increased to over 21 million. Concerns about pollution, noise and congestion have affected everyone in East Kent as elsewhere and substantial road building programmes have attempted to deal with the problem.

The building of the Channel Tunnel has dominated East Kent in these decades. In October 1986, before the contract for the building of the Tunnel had been awarded, the East Kent Federation of WIs arranged and hosted a conference in Canterbury attended by all the bidders for the contract and all the relevant authorities. This was effective in bringing to light all the concerns of the different organisations.

The whole project was regarded locally with hostility. Every village threatened by the many different schemes for the approach roads and railway links had its band of protesters. In the event the builders, Eurotunnel, showed themselves to be sensitive to local concerns and determined to cause as little disruption as possible. They sponsored events large and small in villages round about, and in the reclaimed land created from the spoil from the Tunnel they have left a Recreation and Amenity Area for future generations called Samphire Hoe. The contractors for the rail link have not, so far, been so successful in their public relations.

In May 1994 a festival was held at the Eurotunnel Exhibition Centre to mark the official opening of the Tunnel. On 6th May the Queen travelled by Eurostar from London while President Mitterand of France travelled from Paris. Their trains met nose to nose at the Calais terminal and later they both travelled in the royal Rolls-Royce by Le Shuttle back to Folkestone.

There has been a steady increase in awareness of the environment. Many households now conscientiously save their waste for recycling and try to reduce the amount of carbon fuels that they use. Stringent industrial regulations have gradually ensured that the environment is better protected, and the Coastguard now have a Marine Pollution Control Unit.

Farming life has changed almost beyond recognition since the 1900s. Many independent farmers have been forced to sell up to wealthier landowners who can employ contractors with very large machines to work the land. The cottages once lived in by the farm workers are often bought by people retiring to the countryside or commuters moving out of town. Many small farmers have had to find new ways of making their farms profitable and have turned their buildings to other uses, such as holiday lets or as bases for small rural industries.

The national coal strike of 1984–5, which was as bitterly conducted in Kent as anywhere, led to the final closure of all the Kent coalfields by 1987. Very high levels of unemployment resulted and it was a terrible blow to the close-knit mining communities.

In July 1981 the East Kent Federation of WIs presented a new bell to Canterbury Cathedral. It is named 'Mary', weighs 7 cwt 12 lbs, and has the musical note of D sharp. It is the only bell in the Canterbury peal to be donated by a women's organisation.

The following year Pope John Paul II visited Canterbury for an historic meeting between the Heads of the Church of England and the Roman Catholic Church. After driving through the streets of the city, crowded with well-wishers, they

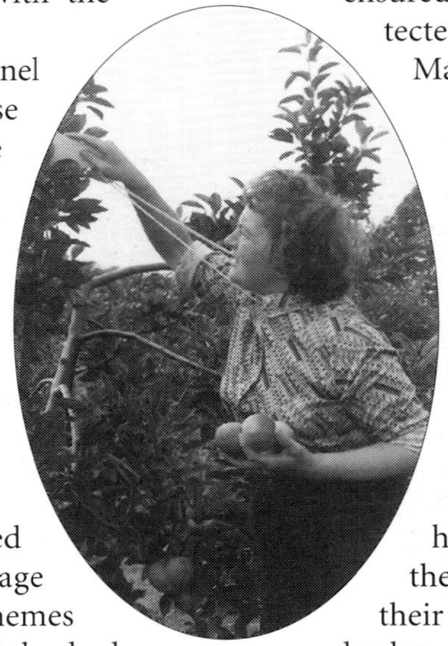

*Picking Discovery apples at Stonebridge Green Farm, Egerton in 1985. Note the measuring disc – on some farms apples are picked when they reach a certain size.* (Priscilla Harper – Egerton WI)

# After 1980

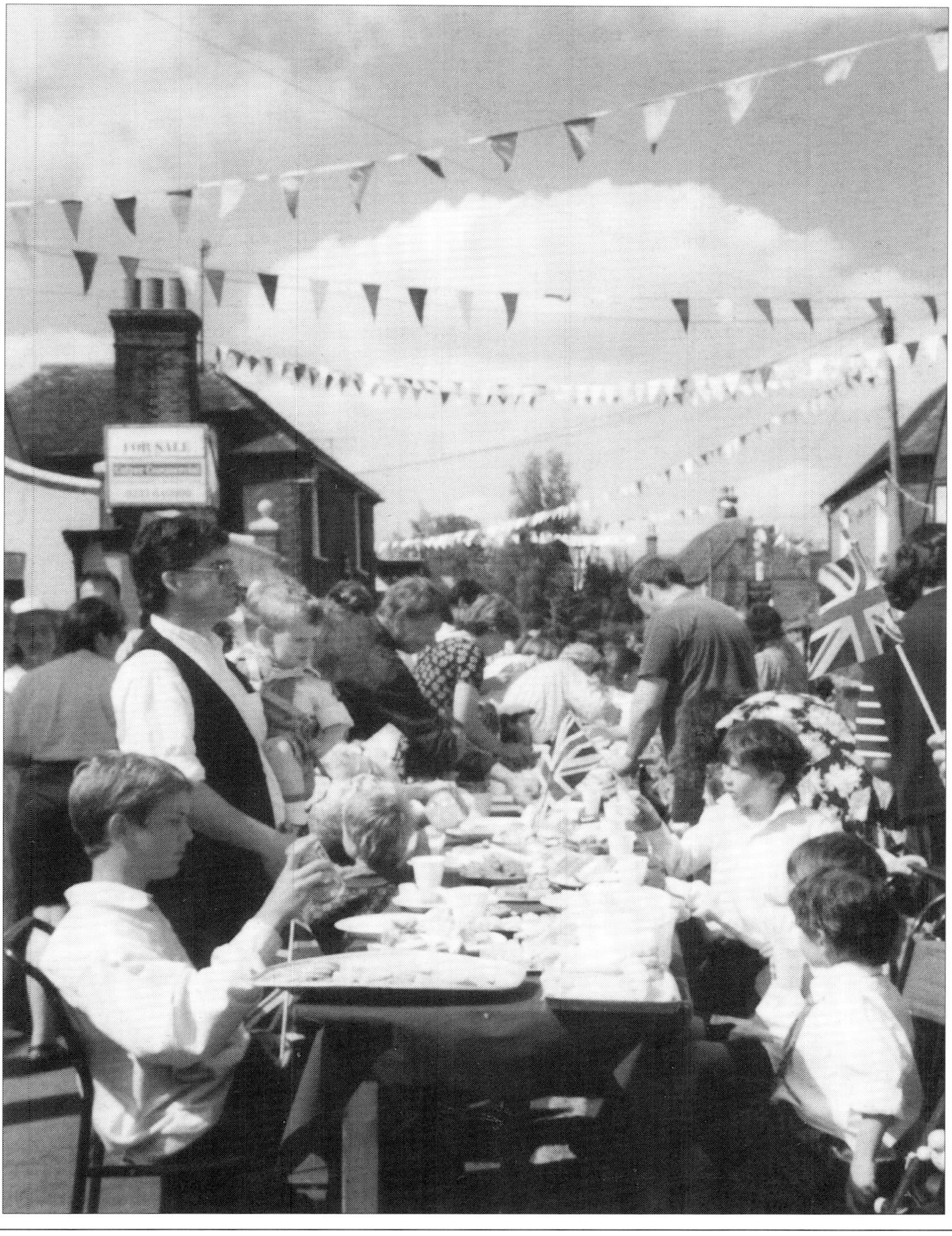


*The 50th anniversary of the Second World War was much in people's minds during the 1990s, perhaps especially in this county which suffered so much. A street party in Ham Street was one of those arranged to celebrate the 50th anniversary of VE Day in 1995.* (Barbara Ware – Orlestone, Ham Street & Ruckinge WI)

conducted jointly a televised service in the Cathedral.

In October 1987 a hurricane swept across southern England and thousands of trees were lost. All across East Kent electricity and telephone lines were brought down, railway lines blocked, roof tiles dislodged and house walls blown in. The damage was so widespread that a wartime spirit immediately took hold, neighbour helping neighbour. It was many months before all the houses were repaired and years before the fallen trees could all be removed. Local authorities were able to provide funds to help towards the replanting that followed.

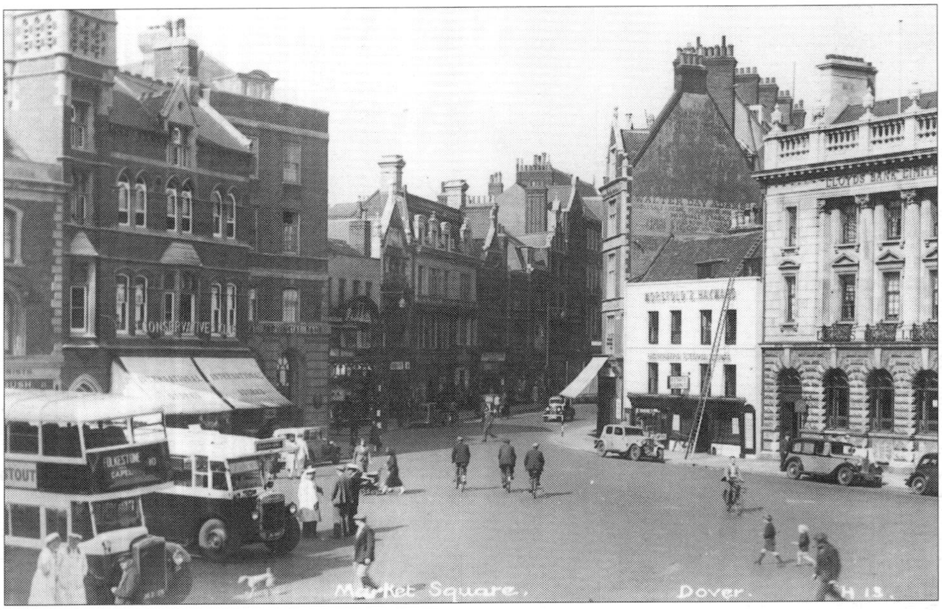


*THEN & NOW: Dover Market Square over the century. In 1900 it was bustling with market traders, trams, horses and pedestrians. By 1930 the trams had gone, replaced by modern bus services, and the motor car had not yet driven the bicycles and pedestrians off the road. Today a fountain adorns the square, now a pedestrian area.*
(Vera Fisher – Temple Ewell WI, Audrey Lowley – Whitfield WI, & Daphne Foster – Temple Ewell WI)

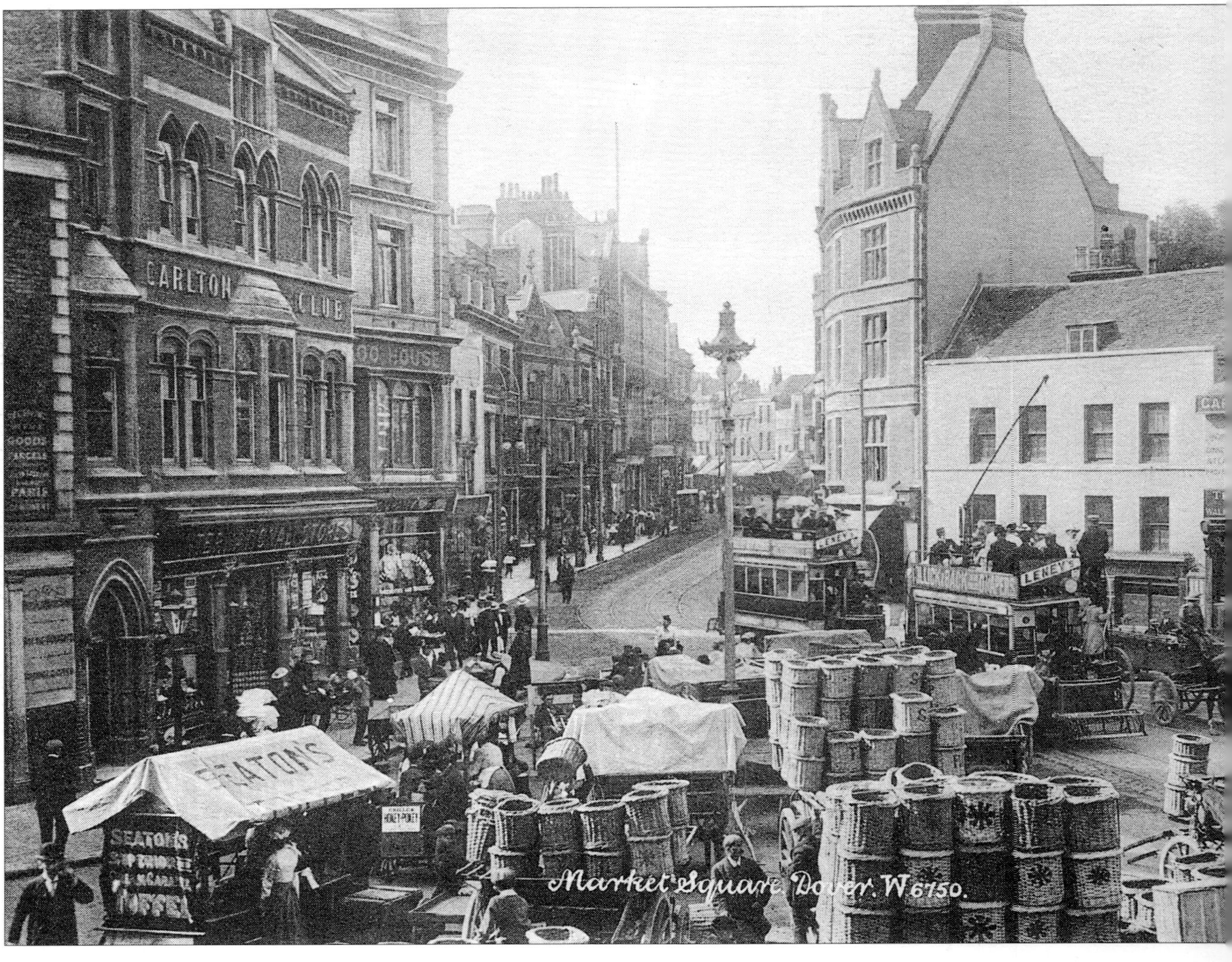

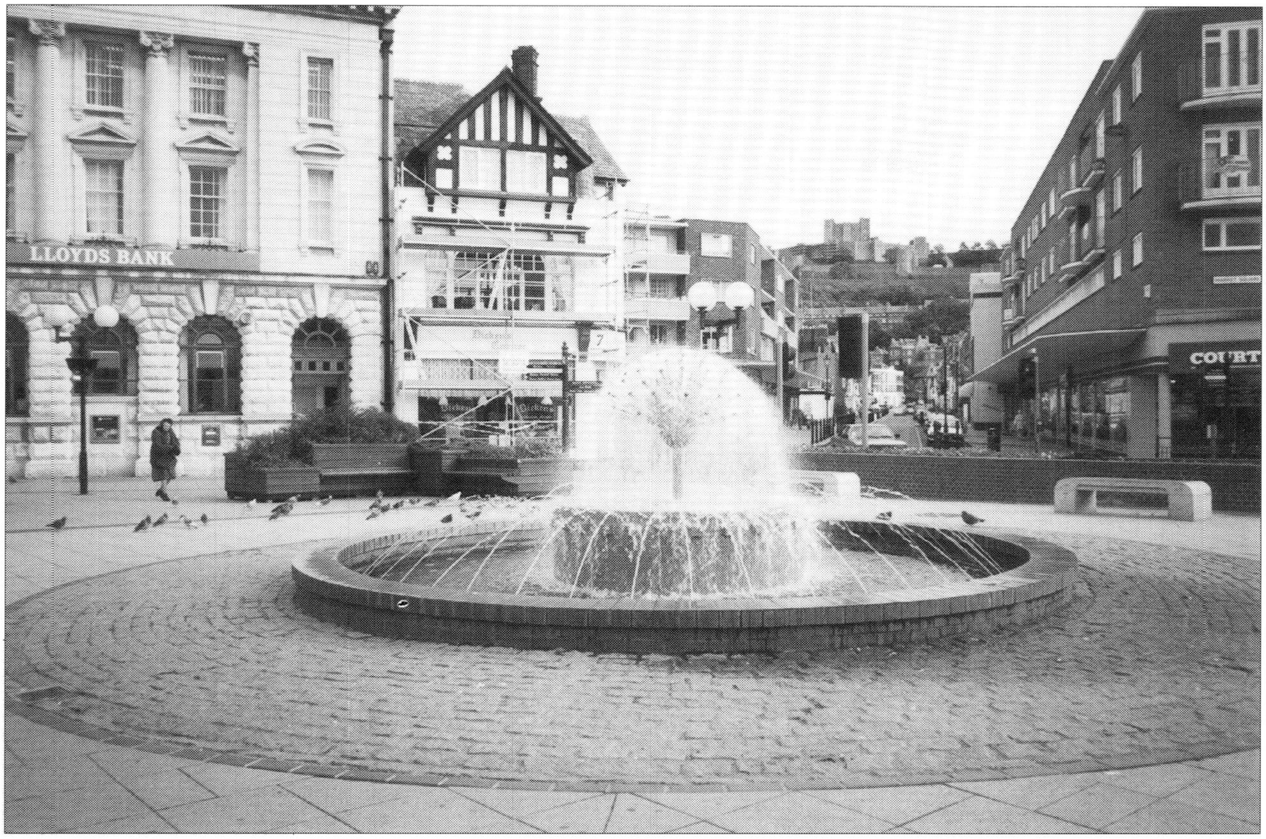


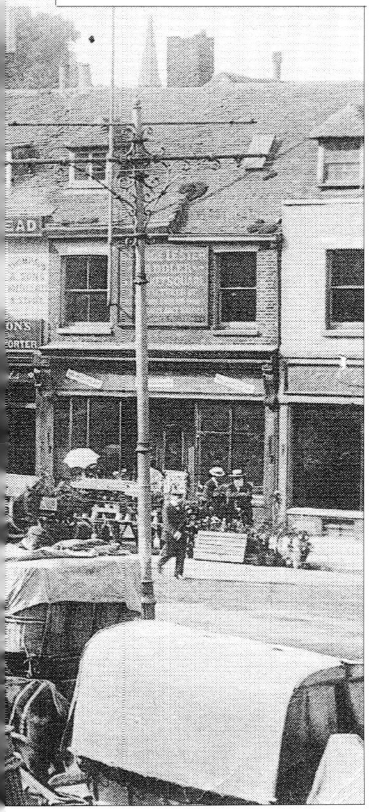

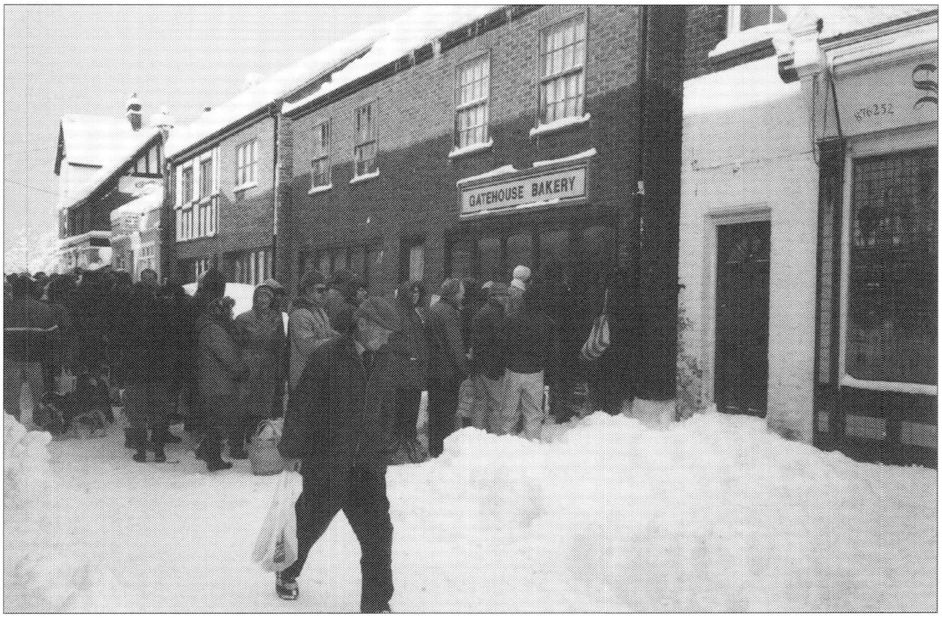


*After a heavy fall of snow in January 1987, Sheppey was cut off by road from the mainland. Minster residents had to queue for bread at the local bakery. The baker could only bake a limited amount at a time and some people stood in the cold for two hours.* (Mrs M. Ingleton – Abbey WI)

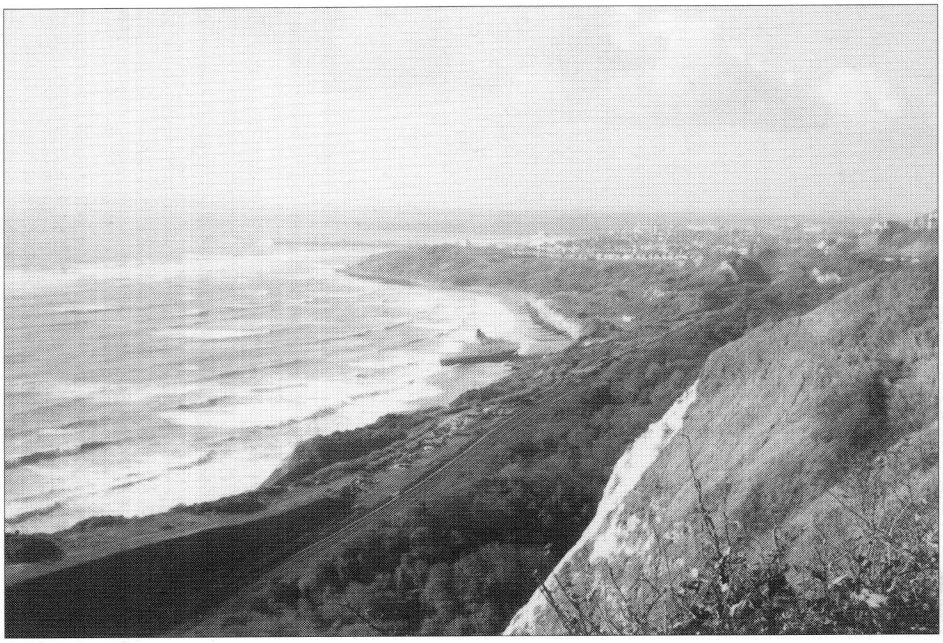

*All over southern England on the night of 15th/16th October 1987 trees were uprooted and buildings damaged by winds reaching hurricane force. The Stena Sealink ferry* Hengist *was blown onto the concrete apron of the Warren, Folkestone.*
(Isabel Brent – Capel le Ferne WI)

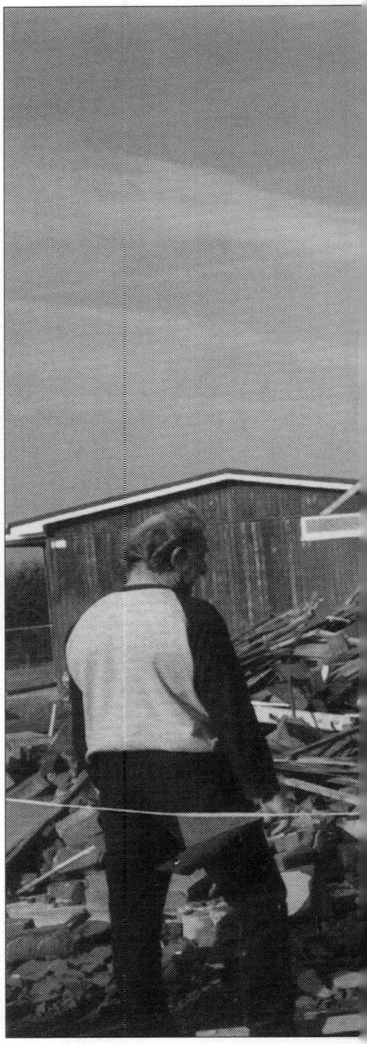

*All that was left of Wye small hall after the hurricane.*
(Pearl Worrell – Wye WI)

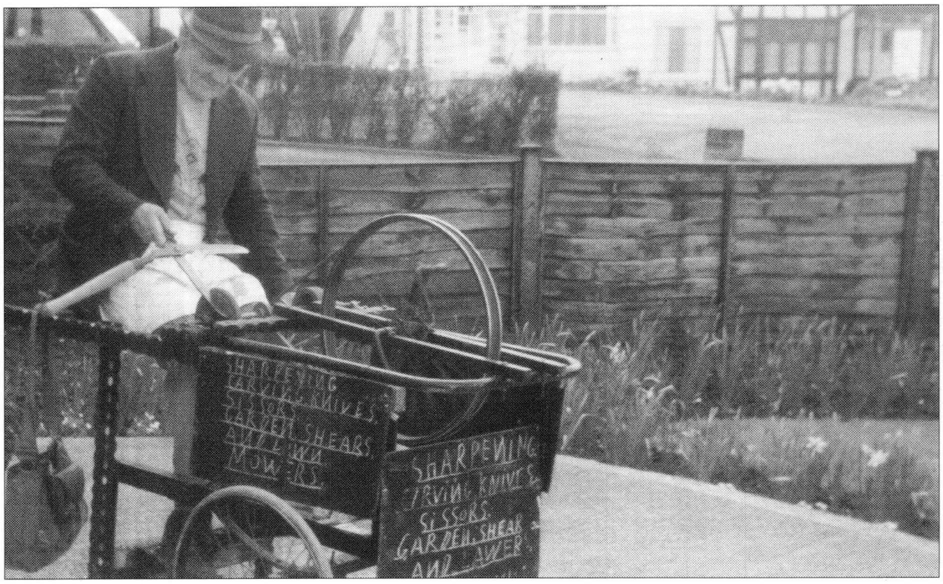


*A scene from the past in Bramley Avenue, Canterbury in 1985, when the knife sharpener came to call. Once a familiar sight on town streets, could he have been the last of his kind in the county?*
(Mrs M. Heatlie – Thanington Without WI)

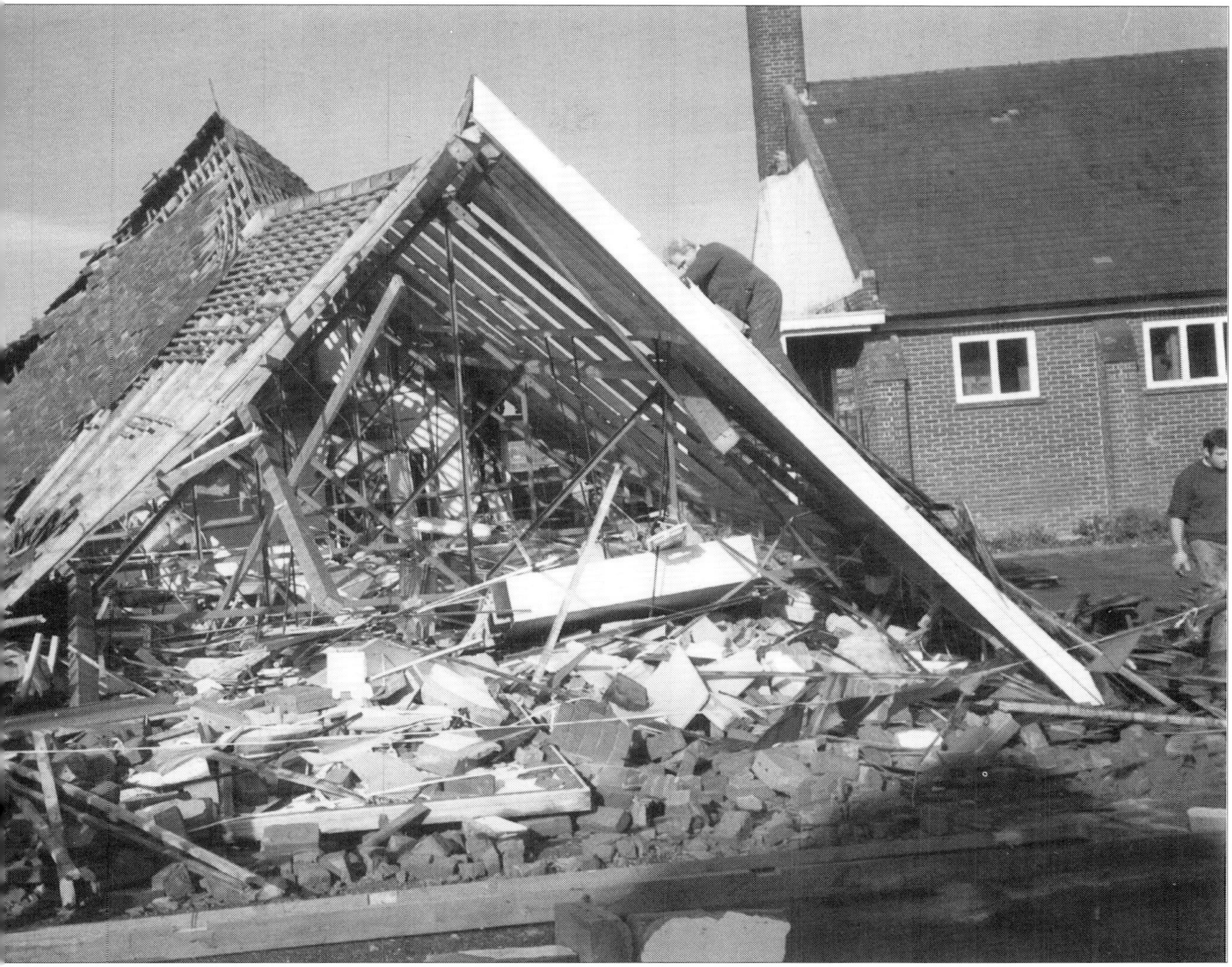

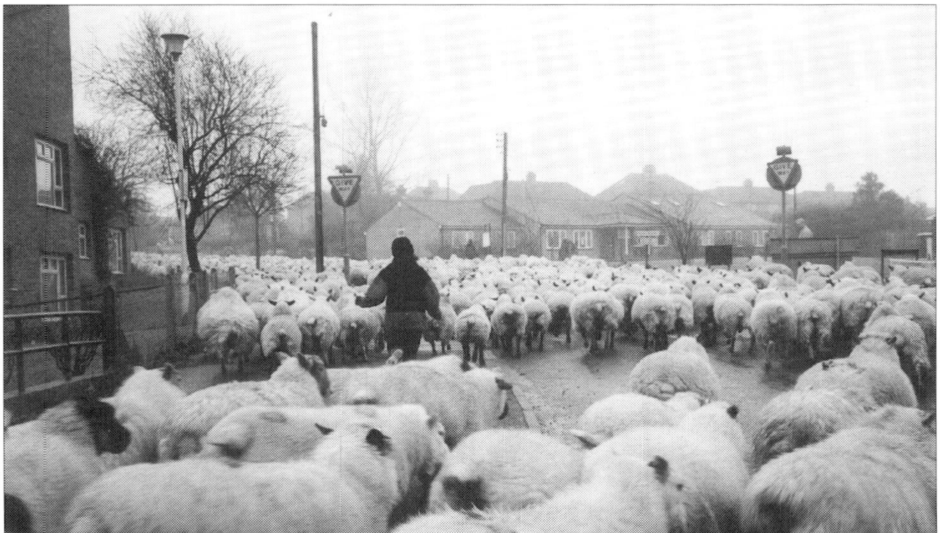

*Sheep are still herded along the roads around Ham Street and Ruckinge and the Romney Marsh. This picture was taken on New Year's morning 1996 when two men, two boys and two dogs took 500 sheep through Ham Street. Sheep Fairs ceased to be held in Ham Street only in 1965.*
(Barbara Ware – Orlestone, Ham Street & Ruckinge WI)

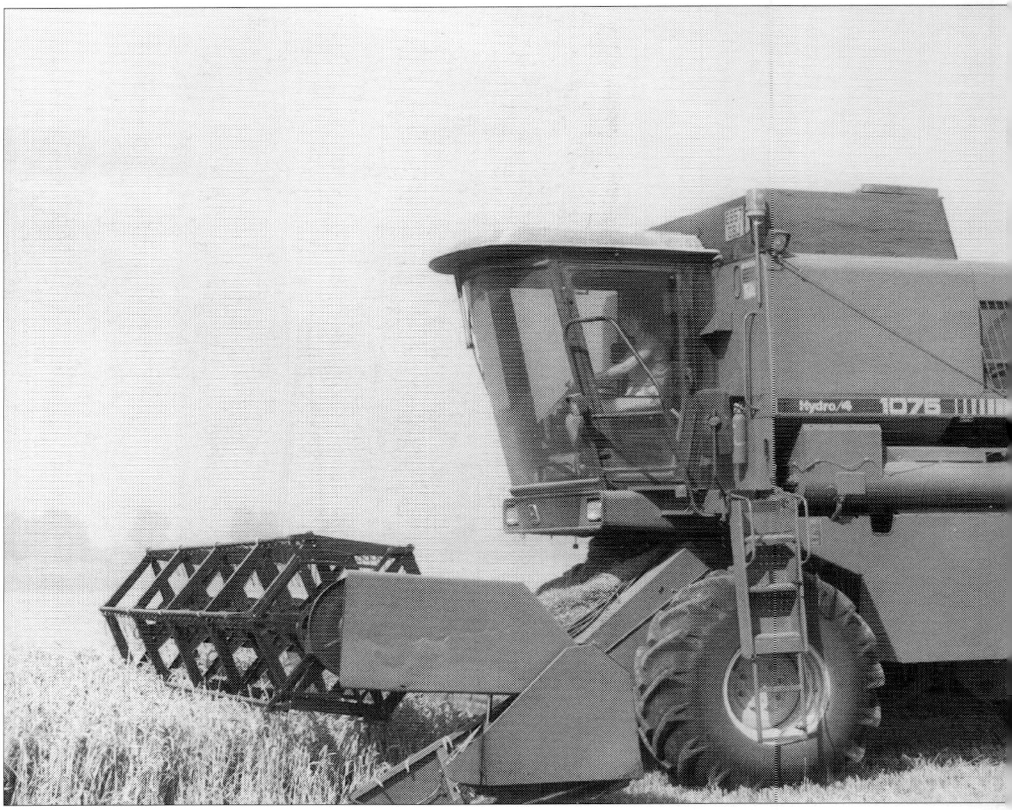


*Sharon Christmas driving a modern combine harvester in the 1990s at Woodchurch. With an agricultural and engineering degree, Mrs Christmas could show no greater contrast with countrywomen of the early years of the century.* (Sharon Christmas – Bethersden WI)

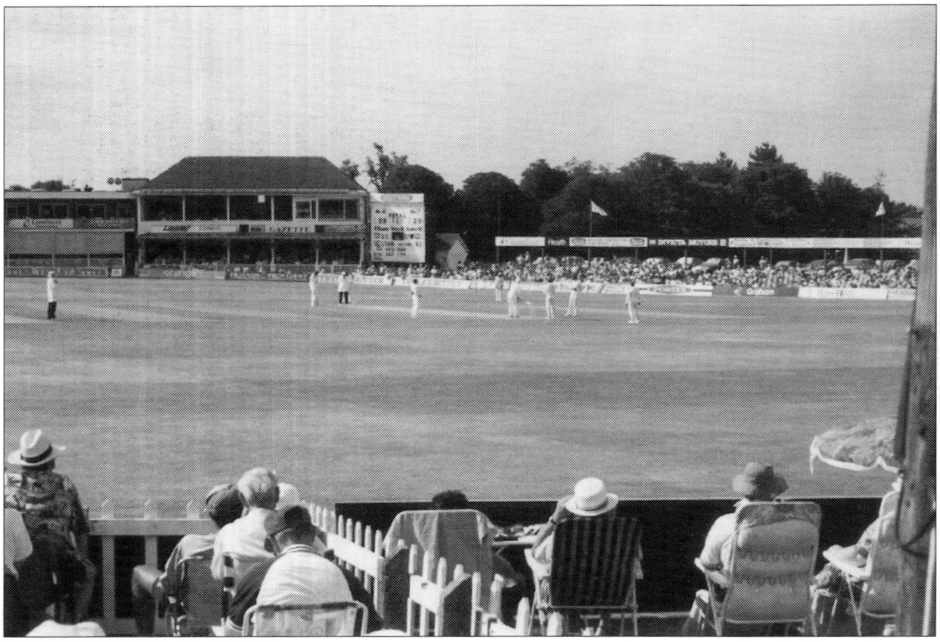

*County cricket played at the St Lawrence ground, Canterbury on 22nd July 1996, when Kent met Pakistan. The Kent County Cricket Club was founded in 1870, but the St Lawrence ground has been in use since at least 1847.* (Mrs J. Jordan – South Street WI)

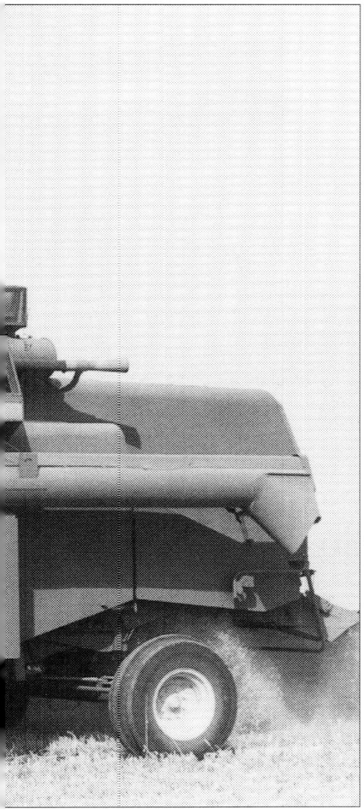

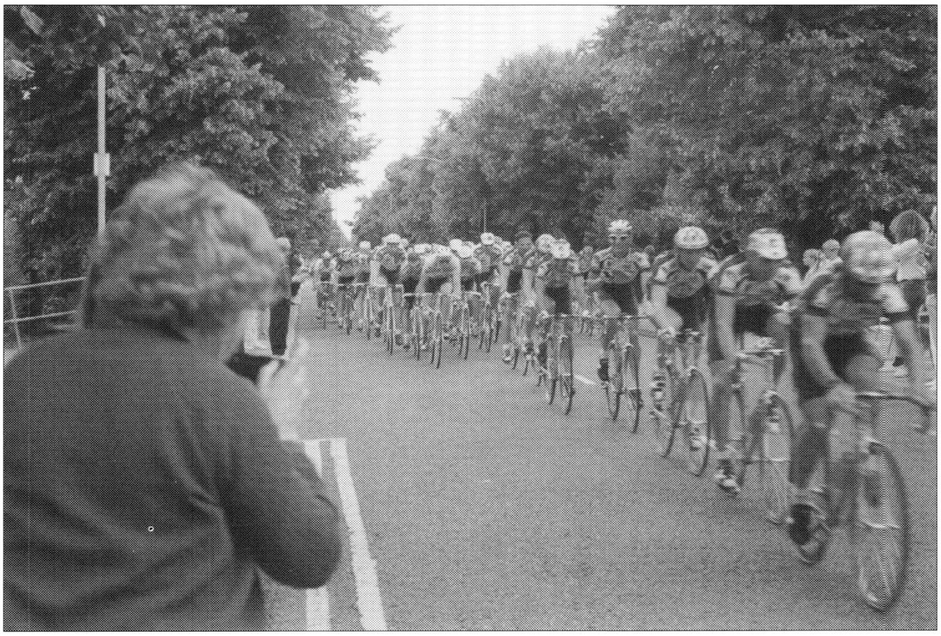

*The Tour de France, in Britain for the first time, passes through Kennington on 7th July 1994, epitomising the growing links with the Continent.*
(Mrs D. Ovenden – Kennington WI)

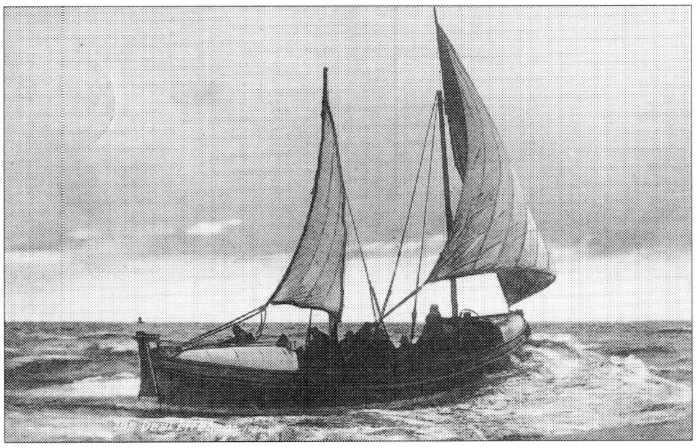

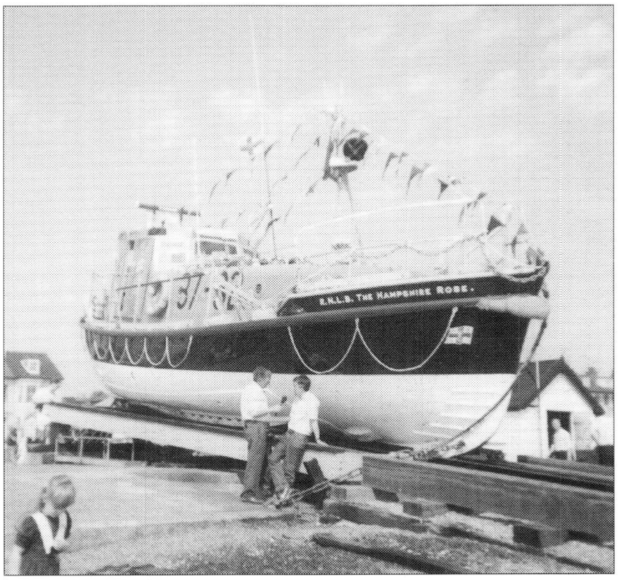

*THEN & NOW: Deal lifeboat before the First World War, in the days of sail, and the Walmer lifeboat, the* Hampshire Rose, *on its last day in service on Sunday 6th May 1990. It had been at Walmer since 1975. A new £45,000 inflatable craft now answers distress calls.*
(Mrs M. Court – St Martins WI)

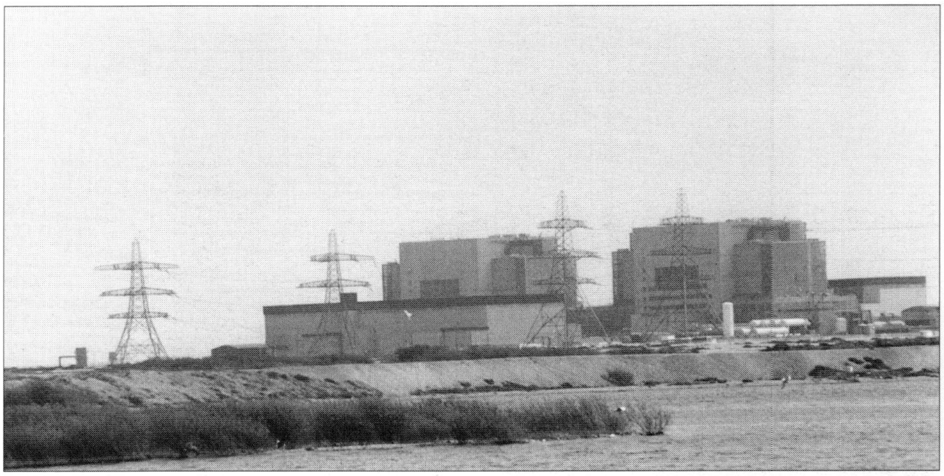

*Dungeness nuclear power station in 1993. The station opened on 21st September 1965 with the sixth Magnox reactor to be started in the country, followed in 1983 by the country's first advanced gas cooled reactor.*
(Margaret Down – Saltwood WI)

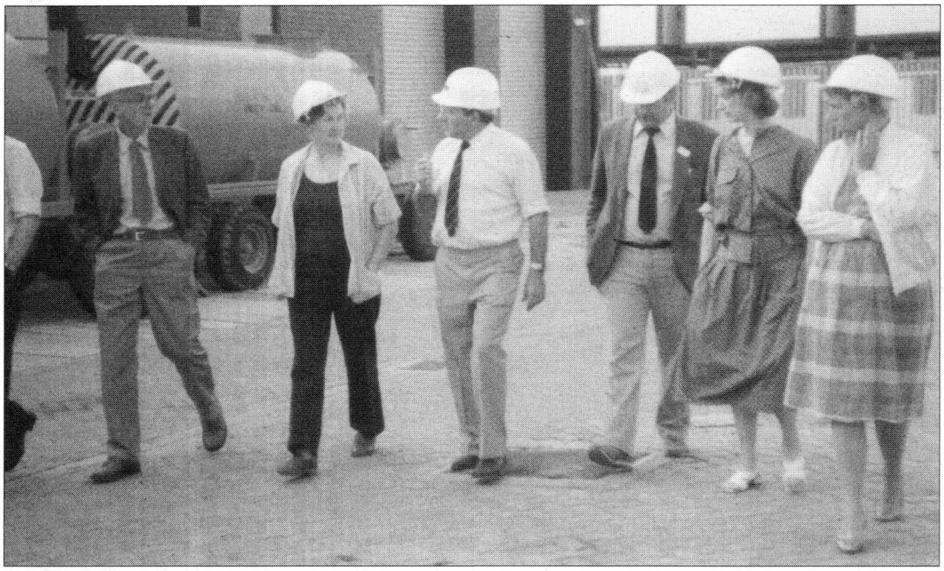

*Members of Sellindge Parish Council being shown round the converter station built outside the village in 1985 to share electricity with the Grid in France. There was much opposition to the plant at the time, many local people regarding it as a huge blot on the landscape.*
(Mrs M. Yarnold – Sellindge WI)

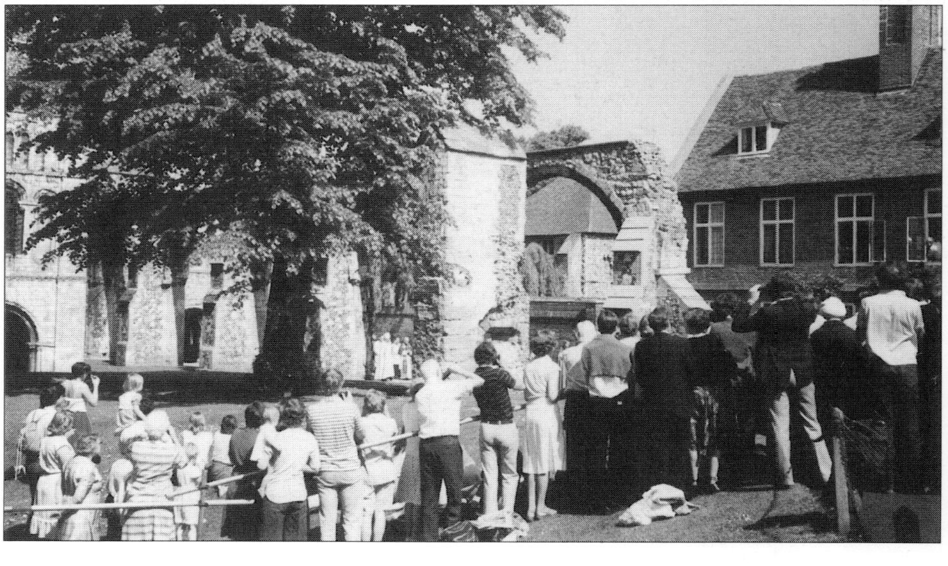

*Some of those who gathered outside Canterbury Cathedral in 1982 when Pope John Paul II met with Robert Runcie, Archbishop of Canterbury. All denominations were present at this historic meeting. One onlooker recalls the spontaneous way in which all those outside settled down on the grass to wait and, although it was only eleven o'clock in the morning, sat sharing food.*
(Mrs A. Mahoney – River WI)

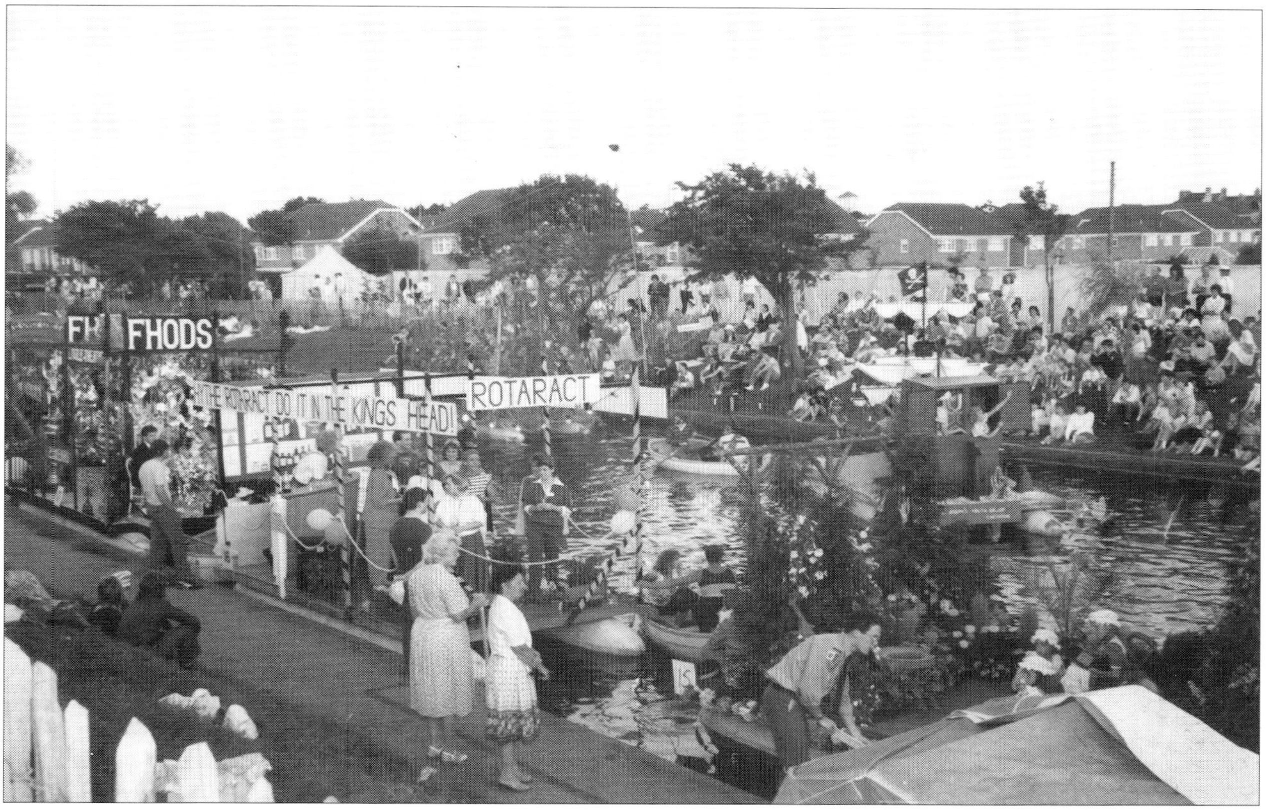


*A busy scene at the Hythe Venetian Fete in August 1989. The fete, started in 1860, takes place on the Royal Military Canal and was once part of Hythe Cricket Week, when national cricketing personalities and celebrities took part. From 1928 it became a separate attraction with decorated floating tableaux on the canal. Since 1956 it has been held every other year and thousands attend from all over the county.* (Mrs E. Spicer – Capel le Ferne WI)

***Below** Footpaths are being restored all over the county, and in 1989 Ron Lobeck, local TV weatherman, officially opened the Romney Marsh Village Footpath, linking communities on the Marsh.* (Frances Gillett – Lydd WI)

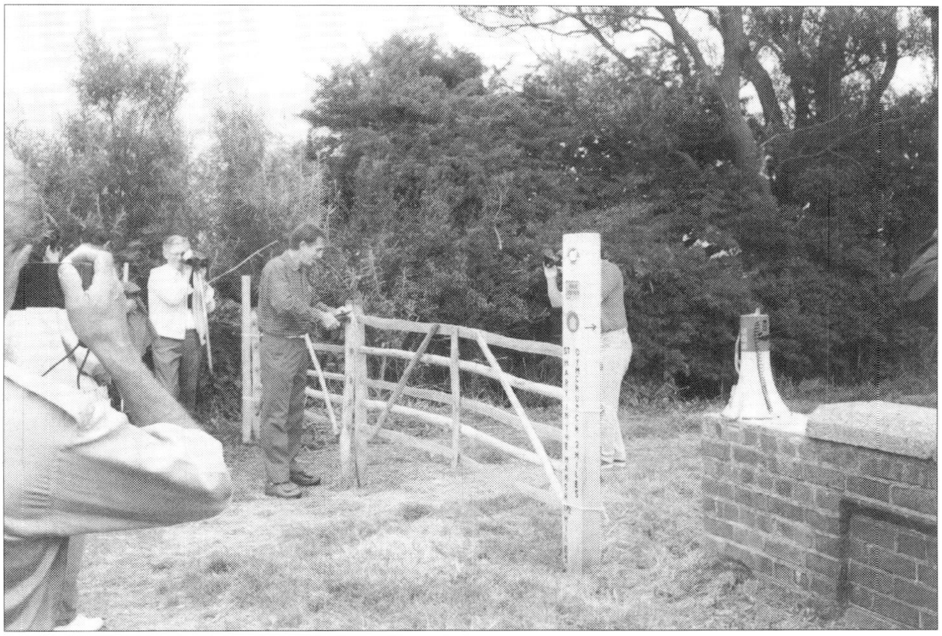

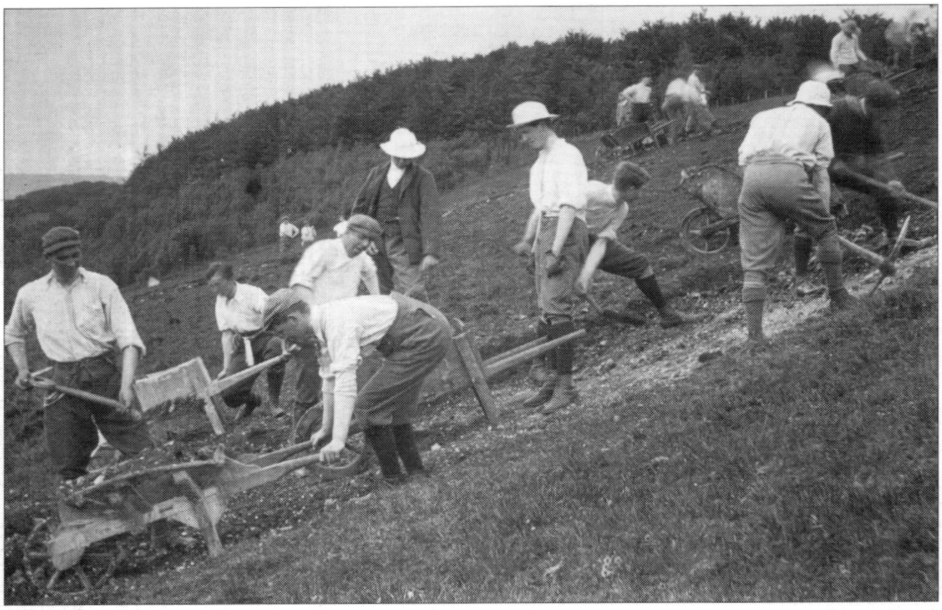

*The famous Wye Crown (opposite), carved in the chalk downs, underwent a programme of restoration from 1991 to 1994, to celebrate its 90th anniversary since it was first marked out by students at Wye College in 1902 (left). As part of the recent work, a total of 22 students carried up and built in 150 tons of flints, all on a slope of 1 in 3.*
(Mrs M. Snelson and Mrs R. Bowles, Wye WI)

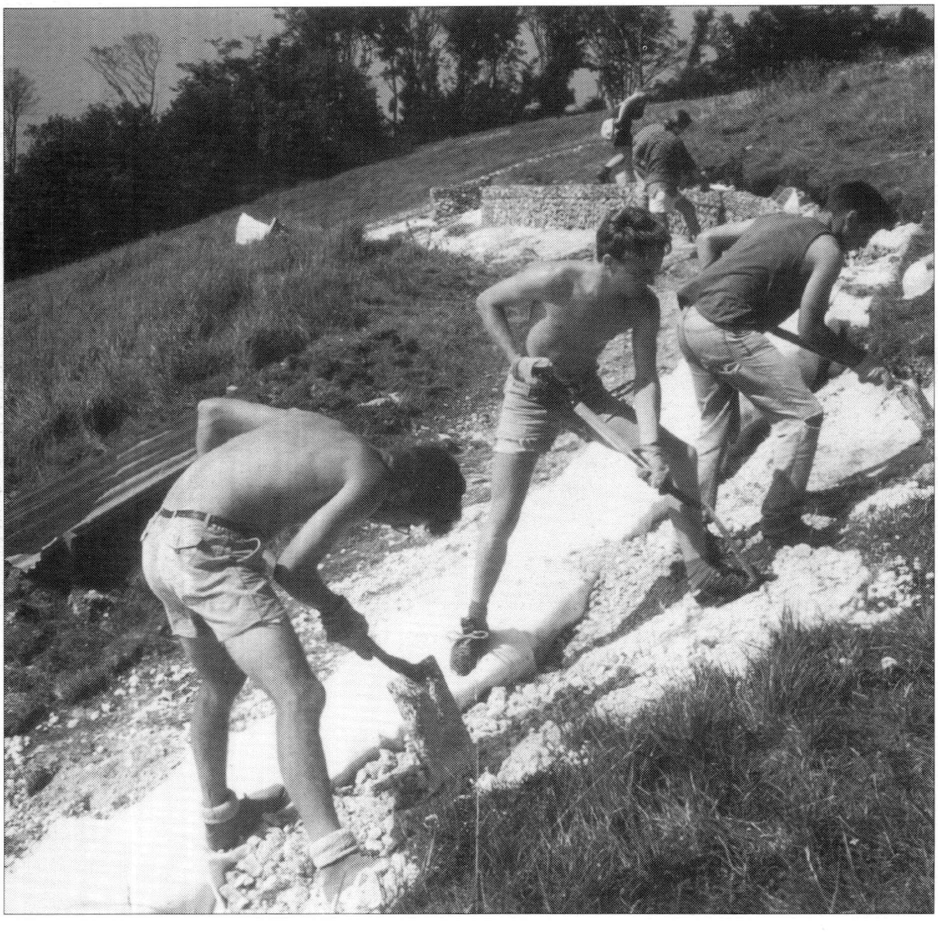

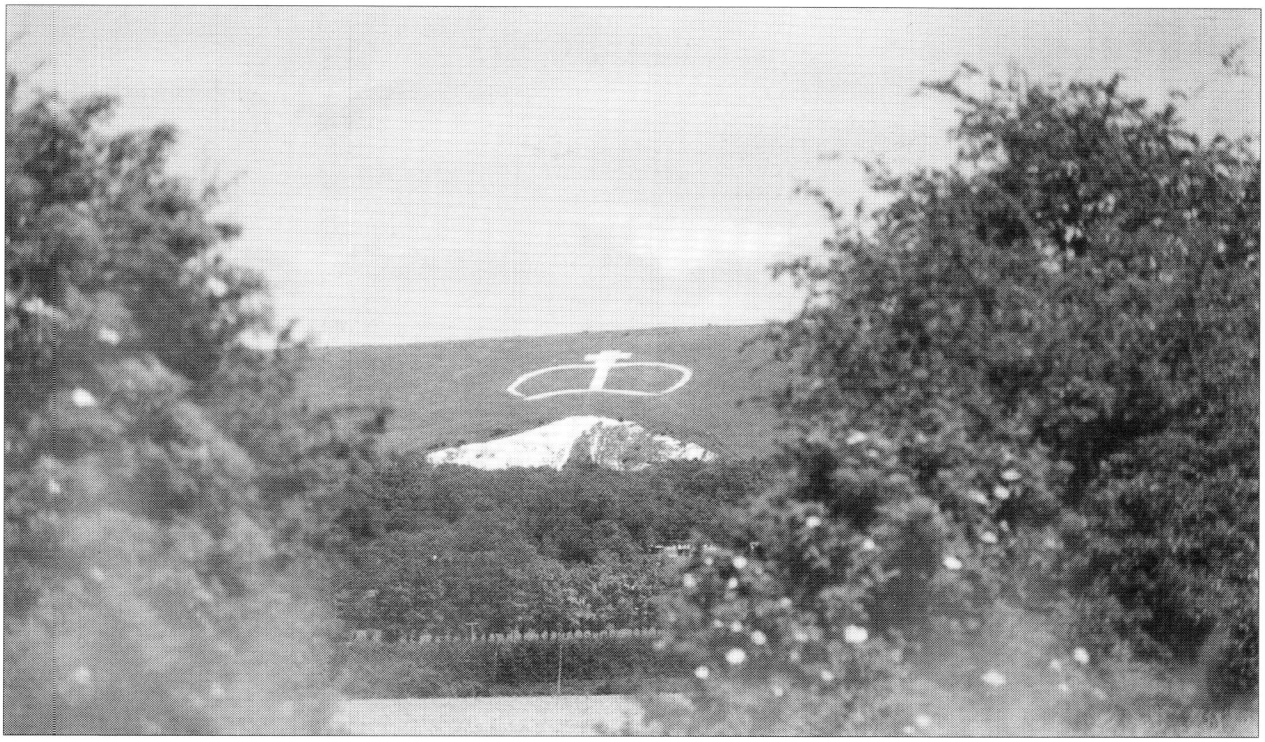

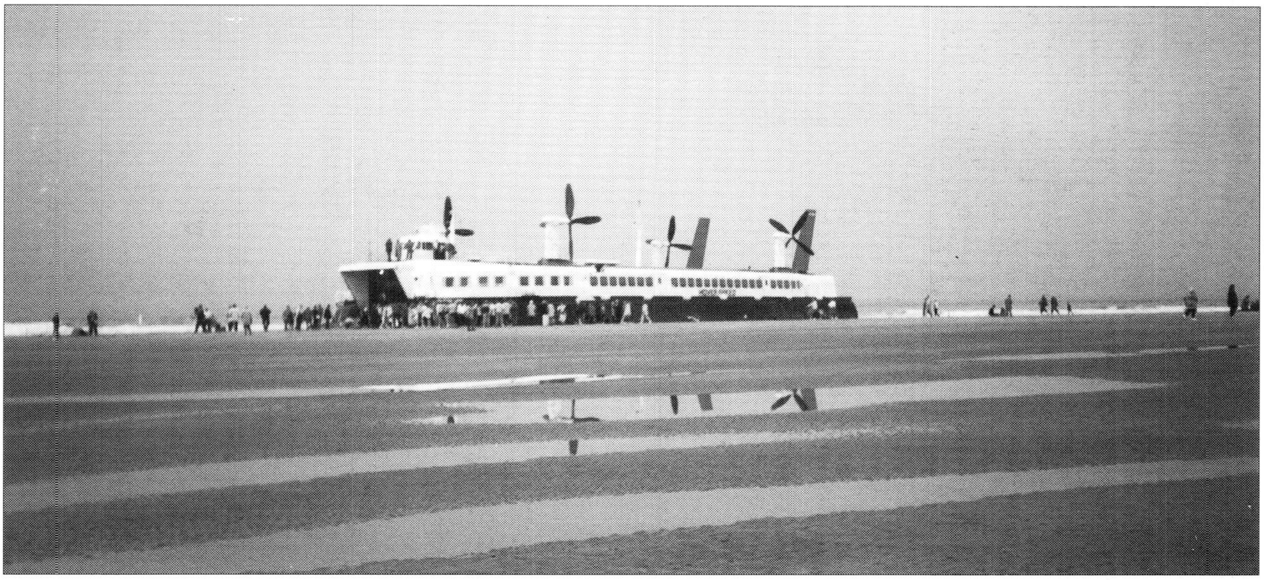

*Accessible only by Hovercraft during very low spring tides (three or four times a year) the Goodwin Sands are 3½ miles off the Deal coast. In 1994, and for the three succeeding years, the WI have chartered a Hovercraft and taken some 1,000 members and their families there for sports, barbecues and sponsored walks and races, raising money for the Julie Rose Sports Stadium and for Denman College.*
(Doreen Clark – Kingswood with Ringwould WI)

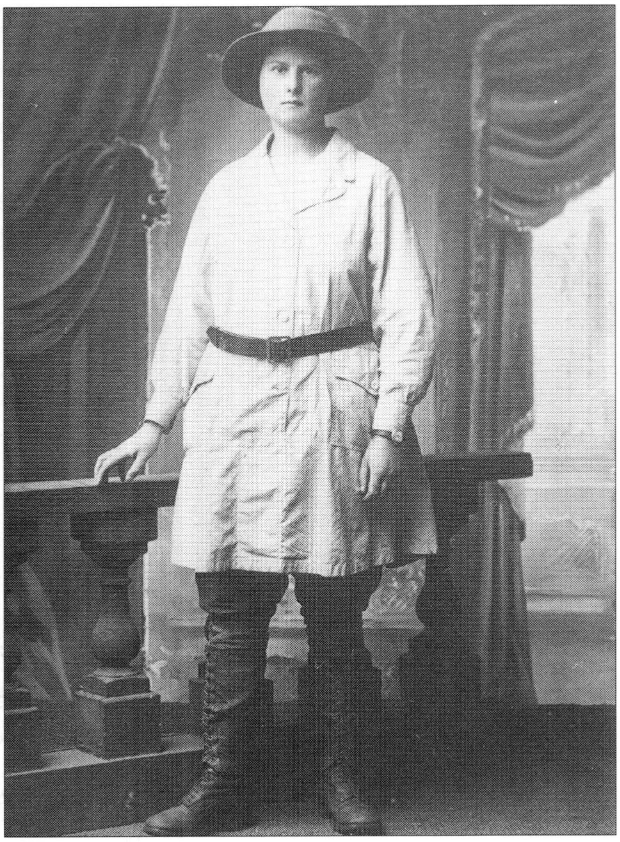

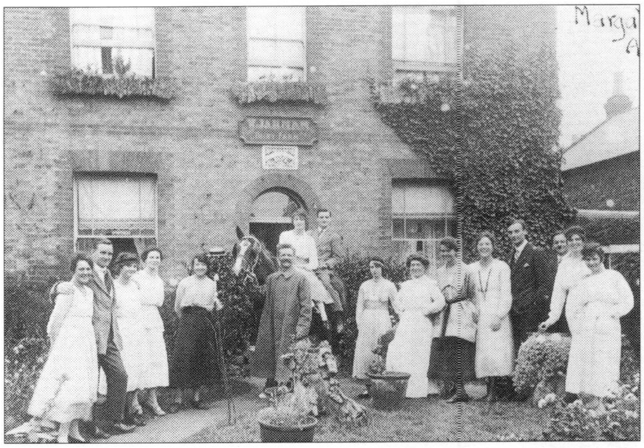

*A remarkable lady whose life has spanned the century. Mrs Gertrude Jarman of Margate, 101 years of age in June 1997, remembers as a young girl riding on the very first motorised omnibus in London. In 1916 she was working as a wartime land girl and a Red Cross nurse. When she was 22 she married into the family who owned and ran the Jarman Dairy of Margate, shown above with the family and dairy workers in the early years of the century. Her own family comprises nine children, 28 grandchildren, 50 great grandchildren and ten great great grandchildren. For her 100th birthday she went for a trip through the Channel Tunnel and on a flight on Concorde from the Kent International Airport at Manston.* (Mrs R. Back – Cliftonville WI)

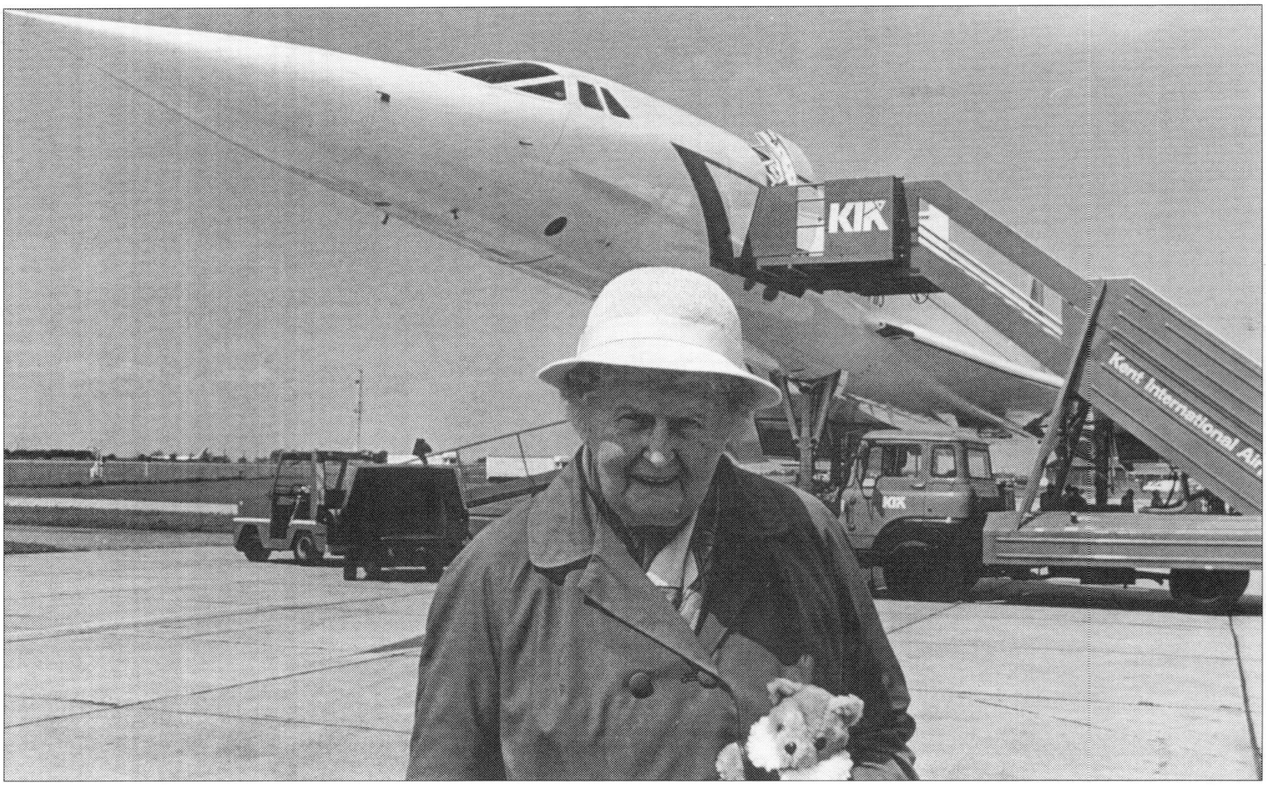